Speaking  Minds

A Guide to Public Speaking for Canadians

Second Edition

SANDIE BARNARD

Centennial College

Prentice Hall Canada Inc.
Scarborough, Ontario

Canadian Cataloguing in Publication Data

Barnard, Sandie, 1946–
    Speaking our minds

2nd ed.
Includes index.
ISBN 0-13-241605-0

1. Public Speaking. 2. Oratory. I. Title.

PN4121.B355 1996 808.5'1 C95-933103-4

© 1989, 1996 Prentice-Hall Canada Inc., Scarborough, Ontario
Pearson Education Canada

Prentice-Hall, Inc., Englewood Cliffs, New Jersey
Prentice-Hall International (UK) Limited, London
Prentice-Hall of Australia, Pty. Limited, Sydney
Prentice-Hall Hispanoamericana, S.A., Mexico City
Prentice-Hall of India Private Limited, New Delhi
Prentice-Hall of Japan, Inc., Tokyo
Simon & Schuster Asia Private Limited, Singapore
Editora Prentice-Hall do Brasil, Ltda., Rio de Janeiro

ISBN 0-13-241605-0

Acquisitions Editor: Rebecca Bersagel
Production Editor: Kelly Dickson
Copy Editor: Dianne Broad
Editorial Assistant: Shoshana Goldberg
Production Coordinator: Sharon Houston
Cover and Interior Design: Julia Hall
Page Layout: Gail Ferreira Ng-A-Kien

30 31 32 DPC 09 08 07

Printed in Canada
Every reasonable effort has been made to obtain permissions for all articles and data used in this
edition. If errors or omissions have occurred, they will be corrected in future editions provided
written notification has been received by the publisher.

We welcome readers' comments, which can be sent by e-mail to
    collegeinfo_pubcanada@prenhall.com

For Sheila, D, Donna, Kay, and Val
with thanks,

and my students
with admiration for their
outrageous and unremitting
perception, honesty, and
compassion.

C O N T E N T S

CHAPTER 1   **Jump In: Getting Started   1**

CHAPTER 2   **Watch Closely Now: The Demonstration
                24**

CHAPTER 3   **Think It Over: The Informative
                Speech   60**

CHAPTER 4   **Thinking On Your Feet: Impromptus and Interviews   108**

CHAPTER 5   **You've Got a Friend: The Social Speech   145**

CHAPTER 6   **Keeping Bored Out of the Boardroom:
                     Presentations and Meetings   188**

CHAPTER 7   **There Comes a Time: The Persuasive
                     Speech   233**

CHAPTER 8   **Flying On Your Own: Last Words of
                     Advice   274**

PREFACE

Eight years ago when I first wrote this book, I knew that speaking was both an essential and undervalued skill. Few people realize the energy required to make the spark of connection that occurs in a truly good speech. I wanted to share the skills, the enthusiasm, and the power that speaking brings.

Today speaking is even more essential. I remember a lawyer in Vancouver who was hired as a policy analyst for the forestry branch of a government agency. Of course she was hired for her legal skills; then she was told she was presenting to an audience of 300 the following week. It was just assumed that she could speak in public. This happens all the time. Former students who are civil engineers, managers of hotels and hostelling groups, health services professionals, business people, hospitality workers, lawyers—tell me how often they use the skills outlined in this book. With two days or even two hours to prepare, they have found help—practical and personal—in these pages.

I also believe that we have the power to make change in our society by speaking up—whenever we speak against injustice and for fairness and compassion, we make a difference. Never undervalue the importance of having your voice heard in the world.

Speaking Our Minds deals equally with design and delivery: the basic organizational skills required to refine an idea or thesis and organize research and proof; and the techniques of speaking to and with an audience. The title reminds us that speaking is indeed the result of thought; it is not an automatic response. Before we speak, we need to think, to examine our purpose, and to organize our ideas. We need to consider how best to reach our audience and bring them to an awareness of our position. We also need to speak from the heart—to be brave enough to speak the truth, and trust that our conviction will help us reach our audience.

Do we need a special text for Canadians? That was often the first question I was asked by the people interviewed in this book. Yes we do. Our history, our manners, our boldness, our sense of responsibility, and our humour are special. This text provides Canadian examples, references, and anecdotes to make the learning more immediate.

In over 20 years of teaching this subject, I have been continually impressed by the honesty and integrity of students. Despite their initial terror, they have found the courage to speak. What students need is a clear, step-by-step approach. That's what this text provides. Beginners should start giving speeches early in the semester or workshop so that they may have as many speaking opportunities as possible during the course. To that end, I have ensured that although each chapter builds on the previous one, the first chapter has enough information to enable a person to start making short speeches immediately. The result is a complete course, with each new chapter adding techniques and refinements to the bare structure outlined in Chapter 1. Many instructors, of course, like to proceed in their own way, so the text also offers flexibility. It is possible to use the Table of Contents to design a course that is suitable to individual needs and methods.

Confidence is another key to developing good speakers. A positive group atmosphere is essential for a good class or workshop experience. As anyone who has recently spoken to a group can attest, you feel yourself on the line when you give a speech. The exercises, quizzes and games encourage practice through social exchange and debate—all within a supportive learning environment.

Public speaking is no longer the domain of the boom-and-holler type of orator. The sound and the atmosphere of many classrooms have changed. Softer voices, different philosophies, accents and rhythms are present. Each one has a place. Use microphones and good sound systems rather than calling out, "Speak louder—we can't hear you."

This book is enriched by interviews with and speeches by outstanding speakers. Their generosity in making time for the interviews and the thoroughness with which they answered my questions made the preparation of this text especially exciting. After all, why should students rely solely on the advice of their instructors? I set out to discover if people whose life's work involves speaking use similar techniques and have the same concerns as we in the classrooms. The forthrightness of the interviews reinforces the lessons of the chapters; they provide practical back-up for the theory. All the interviews were taped and transcribed; they have the rhythm and feeling of talking with the person concerned.

The speeches are also transcriptions and have the flow of spoken English. When I started this book I never anticipated how few speeches by contemporary Canadians we have on record. Their remarks are part of our history, and I hope that others will begin to share the task of taping and preserving them.

Knowing how easy it is to forget simple things, especially under pressure, I have included the checklists. A group of experienced speakers and facilitators provided input. The results are sometimes serious, often humourous, and always helpful.

Speaking well is worth the work and the risk involved. When you use your voice to make a difference in your work or community, you will know more of your own strength and brilliance. This book, together with thoughtful teachers and supportive classroom experiences, can inspire and guide new speakers. I recommend it to you and hope you know the passion and excitement of speaking your mind and heart.

ACKNOWLEDGEMENTS

This is a thank-you speech I am happy to make; I am truly grateful for the outstanding generosity of many people. Roberta Bondar, June Callwood, Edward L. Greenspan Q.C., Rick Hansen, Rose Anne Hart, Kahn-Tineta Horn, Waneek Horn-Miller, Dave Nichol, Svend Robinson, Gloria Steinem, and David Suzuki graciously permitted their interviews and speeches to be used. I am also indebted to the musicians who allowed their work to appear in the text and to my students who provided speeches, ideas, exercises, and inspiration.

The spark for this edition came from my editor Marjorie Munroe. Her persistent enthusiasm, coupled with the courteous thoroughness of Kelly Dickson saw it to completion. Paul Mason's cartoons still delight me.

My colleagues at Centennial College helped me many times: John Redfern, Wendy Struthers and Margaret van Dijk generously shared their inventiveness. Lori Martin, a former student and fine journalist, taught me by example how to interview. In earlier years my mother, Marie Boddam, heard all my speeches hundreds of times and Valerie Austin coached me in computers and courage.

I would especially like to thank Jack David and David Kent who advised and encouraged me throughout the long process of writing the first edition of this book. Jan Boyle, Cathy TeKamp and Gary Boydell provided encouragement for the second edition. Their passion for learning, teaching, writing, and publishing has been exciting to share. Sheila Goulet, my best and most loyal audience, originally contributed the material on logic and continues to show a belief in the subject and an unflagging interest in every word.

To others who affirmed my belief in the importance of speaking for social justice—Linda Galen, Karen Wheeler, Peg Archibald—I offer my sincere appreciation. To Kathryn Hindle who sees the worth of my fiery nature—thank you for so much. I am heartened by the example of all who speak out for the world and for the rights they hold dear. Last of all, my thanks to Annie who helped me the first time round, Shag who guards me now, Wilf who reviewed each new page, and Kodiak who hatched the chapters.

Jump In:
Getting Started

TIPS FOR SPEAKERS

1. The determination to speak your mind will give you the courage to do well.

2. Channel nervous energy to work for you.

3. The audience is your safety net. In a learning situation, you need each other.

4. Talk to your audience—have a conversation with them.

5. Make real eye contact; feel the energy that flows between you and your audience.

Why take the trouble to speak up?

Because you care, because it matters to you as a human being. You have to stand up and fight for the things you believe in.

(David Suzuki)

◑ SPEAKING OUR MINDS: A CANADIAN TRADITION

Audacity is not usually associated with the Canadian temperament, yet we have a long history of speaking out when conscience requires it. From William Lyon Mackenzie's battles against the suffocating grip of the Family Compact in 1837, to David Suzuki's championing of the earth's resources, people of integrity have spoken out. Often, they have done so at great cost to themselves. Nellie McClung, famous as a dauntless, controversial speaker, left her family to tour the country on behalf of women's rights, legal reform, and factory safety legislation. Waneek Horn-Miller talks about the physical and emotional scars she bears from the time she spent behind the barricades at Oka fighting for native rights.

Horn-Miller, Mackenzie, McClung, Suzuki—all demonstrate a belief in standing up for their convictions, in speaking with reason and compassion.

What compels ordinary citizens to speak out? A former student of mine lives in a small town that was trying to fight a proposed chemical dump. Outside of oral presentations in high school, she had never spoken publicly; however, she decided it was time:

I knew that if I didn't speak up for own town, something I loved very much would be lost. I think the need gave me courage.

Never throw away an opportunity to speak. When you talk to people, you can affect their lives. You may not think you're doing it, but a brief remark can give someone a new idea, advice they need that very day, the courage to go on. Speaking is extraordinarily important.

The next time you need courage to speak out, remember that it's part of our tradition:

I speak very calmly...I say what I mean and say it with force. I am a warrior and a woman.

(WANEEK HORN-MILLER)

Not one word do I retract; I offer no apology!

(WILLIAM LYON MACKENZIE)

For the first time I knew I had the power of speech. I saw faces brighten, eyes glisten, and felt the atmosphere crackle with a new power.

(NELLIE MCCLUNG)

Why else do we live if we don't struggle for things that matter to us?

(DAVID SUZUKI)

◑ EXPERT ADVICE: THE REAL STUFF

Whom would you ask for advice on speaking? Speakers, of course. To prepare this book, I interviewed outstanding speakers from all parts of the country. In the interviews that conclude the chapters, people such as June Callwood, Eddie Greenspan, and Svend Robinson share their struggles for preparation and delivery. Yet, they are not the only people who know how to prepare and speak under pressure. Over the years, my students have made suggestions that I have incorporated in this text. Here, then, is the real stuff, expert advice from professionals, and my own list of rules for good speeches, arrived at after making and hearing thousands of them.

Advice from the experts

A good speech must entertain. It is pointless to make an important point in a boring fashion because it may be lost. It has to be made in an entertaining and dramatic way.

(EDDIE GREENSPAN, LAWYER)

I prepare by giving a lot of hard thought to the audience, what experience they've got, and where they're at. I don't want to patronize people with information they already have.... What would be useful to them....for you to talk about.

(JUNE CALLWOOD, JOURNALIST, COMMUNITY ACTIVIST)

People should be nervous; if you're not scared to death before you give that speech, chances are it's going to be a bomb. Don't be afraid of fear. Use it to your advantage. All of that fear gets the adrenalin going and you use it.

(DAVE NICHOL, FORMER PRESIDENT OF LOBLAW INTERNATIONAL MERCHANTS)

Don't adjust your underwear in public!

(GAIL HEASLIP, COMMUNICATIONS CONSULTANT)

They [academics] tend to talk down to people and use jargon to cover up their inadequacies. That's total crap. Anybody who can't speak in very simple language is trying to cover something up.

(DAVID SUZUKI, ENVIRONMENTALIST, BROADCASTER)

I always use slides; I like talking to people as though we're watching home movies....You have to look at the audience as you speak, because if they're not looking at you, you might as well walk away, turn the slides off.

(ROBERTA BONDAR, ASTRONAUT, PHYSICIAN)

If you fail to use any part of yourself out of shame or fear, then the theft of self-esteem has begun. You have suffered the suppression of part of yourself. So, if you don't speak your thoughts, if you don't use your voice, your self-esteem is affected.

(GLORIA STEINEM, WRITER, FOUNDER OF MS. MAGAZINE)

There is nothing *more devastating than speaking to people who just aren't with you. To bring them around, you have to connect with them at a personal level....talk about real people, real issues—concepts they can relate to in terms of their own lives.*

(SVEND ROBINSON, POLITICIAN, ADVOCATE)

Making an analogy is vitally important to making your ideas understood. It helps people know precisely what you mean; for instance a cabby told Justice Berger of the U.S. Supreme Court: "Putting people in prison is like putting clothes in the wash without any soap. The clothes get wet but no dirt comes out."

(EDDIE GREENSPAN)

Speak directly from the pit of your stomach because that's where you get your wisdom and guidance. It goes to your head, then it comes out through your mouth. When you do that, it will come out right.

(KAHN-TINETA HORN, MOHAWK ELDER AND ACTIVIST)

Don't read to people! Don't stand up in front of four people or 400 and read to them. It's insulting. Have notes—don't get lost but whatever you do—don't read to me! I know how to read. Talk to me.

(JOHN DE SHANO, PRESIDENT, LEVI STRAUSS, CANADA)

I write in note form, sometimes full sentences, on folded pieces of white paper. Never any longer than five sides of notes. Just one word will sometimes remind me of a story. I take care with the opening and with the end.

(JUNE CALLWOOD)

So much depends on the crowd and the atmosphere. You have to be organized...but you also have to leave room to react spontaneously.

(RICK HANSEN)

I try to talk with emotion, to get excited, and to get others excited. Most people are afraid of dying during their speech. And most people are afraid to let emo-

tion enter into it. So they hang onto that script, they read it—I mean, they shouldn't have chairs, they should have beds for the audience.
  (DAVID NICHOL)

Keep the level of enthusiasm up throughout the whole speech—there's somebody out there who is as interested in minute fifteen of your speech as in minute one.
  (ROBERTA BONDAR)

Suggestions for the Best Speech Possible

Value It

1. Never miss an opportunity.
2. Explore the topic as if it were a gold mine: sift through all the possibilities until you find the really valuable material.
3. Know your audience. What do you have to offer them?
4. Research. Research. Research. Know the topic well and get excited about it.

Plan It

5. Stop researching and plan.
6. Get your thesis down to one simple, clear-cut statement. Apply the One-Sentence Shower Test.
7. Hammer out an overview—a three-part proof that makes the direction of your speech clear to you and your audience.
8. *Test* the thesis and overview. Can you state them clearly? If you are still wallowing in mushy generalities, go back to Step 2 and get a new angle.
9. Add colour—stories and examples that speak to the heart *and* mind.
10. Make clear *notes* in point form.

Do It

11. Practise, by yourself at first. Then persuade your friends and family to listen. Experiment with various tones and gestures. Know your speech and enjoy it.
12. Listen to your speech. Do you like it? Do you sound like yourself?
13. Get psyched up. A healthy amount of nervousness gets the adrenalin flowing.
14. Arrive on time and take a private moment to calm yourself. Mingle with the audience to get a feel for the group and the occasion.
15. Pause…
16. Make eye contact and—
17. *Go for it!* Connect with your audience. Give it everything you've got.

"Stop trying to sound like the speakers you admire. Sound like yourself—your voice has never been heard before."

(Vicki P. McConnell)

◑ SPEAKING FROM THE HEART
Conviction

The first rule of public speaking is to have something to say. Believe in what you're saying—speak from the heart. If your commitment to a subject is strong, that energy and enthusiasm show in your delivery. Even nervous speakers can move their listeners when it is apparent that the importance of their message has given them the courage to speak.

Language

Have you heard the story about two students talking about a visiting lecturer?

"Wow! That was an incredible speech!"
"Yeah, it was so significant."
"What statistics! What proofs!"
"Yeah!—did you understand it?"
"No—did you?"

David Suzuki, in the interview that concludes this chapter, says "anyone who can't speak in very simple language is trying to cover something up." Find your own words, your own examples. Avoid glib generalities, and find specifics that interest and excite you. Using the example of Alvin Law, a talented and practical thalidomide survivor, has far more impact than a vague discussion of the government's responsibility in the introduction of new drugs.

When you practise, listen for your own voice, your own words.

Voice

Put your hand over your heart. Can you get your voice to come from that spot in your body? If you do the breathing exercises in Chapter Five, you will sound warm, convincing, and in control. Basically your voice is **the barometer of your self-confidence**. If the sound is coming from high inside your head, you *sound* (and probably *are*) nervous. You've stopped breathing.

If the sound is coming from your chest, near your heart, you are breathing well. You are in control and sound confident. It is a voice that encourages trust. In most situations, speak from the heart.

If you need to be very even, very sincere, breathe even deeper, and get the air to come from your diaphragm. In times of great stress, this tone can change the mood.

Getting Ready

You're ready to start. In this chapter you will find sections on dealing with nervous energy, the importance of a good audience, the basic design of a speech, coaching yourself to success, and finally, the directions for your first solos—the mini-speeches.

◑ NERVOUS ENERGY

"I fall to pieces." Patsy Cline worried about falling to pieces but she didn't. Neither will you. Most beginners are afraid of the big three; they are sure they will panic, puke, or perspire. Some people blush; the rosy colour (always a bright red on fair-skinned people) starts at the neck level and rises steadily, like a gas gauge. I was once so nervous that my stomach knotted into balls of fire and I had to lie down in an empty cloakroom. I prayed the pain would go away in time for me to make the after-dinner speech. A famous publisher is convinced that his throat is dry whenever he has to speak because all the water in his body has gone to his hands and armpits. The best way to handle the nervousness is to **jump in**.

Nervous energy is useful. Actors call it getting up for a performance: athletes need to be on the edge for a big meet. Speakers need that same high—the rush of adrenalin that gives them extra drive. In this chapter, you'll learn to channel it.

Exercise: Truth and Consequences

Take a piece of paper and jot down

a) *three* things you hope to gain from the course;
b) *three* things you dread about it.

The instructor gathers all the papers and reads them aloud, mentioning no names.

Let's look at the results of this exercise. Some of the most common fears are

"blanking out";
"making a fool of myself in front of others";
"shaking and turning red in the face";
"boring people, putting them to sleep";
"my voice shaking and stopping";
"not knowing what to say."

Once you've read your list, you'll know that most people share the same fears, and we are going to deal with those immediately:

"Years of actually getting up in front of audiences have taught me only three lessons:

1) you don't die;

2) there's no right way to speak, only *your* way; and

3) it's worth it."

(Gloria Steinem)

You will *not* blank out in the first exercises because they are short and on a specific topic.

You are *not* going to make a fool of yourself. You are going to look like someone who is trying very hard, and everyone's sympathy will be with you.

If you shake, no one will notice unless you try to turn over a scrap of paper.

If you turn red in the face, you will have the class's sympathy, and they'll be pulling for you.

You will *not* bore people. They are all in the same boat and know that if they are to succeed, you must as well.

Your voice *may* shake but that is natural. This is a class for people to learn, and shaking is allowed within the class.

The things that you want from the course will vary. Some will want to get a few laughs; others will want to learn how to organize the present material in a way that is convincing or even thought-provoking. Some need organizational skills and others want to work on their voice. As long as you follow the lessons, everything is possible.

◑ YOUR SAFETY NET: THE AUDIENCE

Once you get to the front of the room, you will have to look at the people in front of you, and that is when you realize everyone *matters*. Are they judgmental? Bored? Are they helping you? In a learning situation, it is everyone's responsibility to help. Everyone is noticed.

If you are sitting in the audience, you may think it is like being in high school. No one notices if you read a newspaper, eat your lunch, turn around to borrow a pencil, or change your shoelaces. However, as soon as you are up front you will see that *everyone* matters. As a member of the audience in a public-speaking group, it is your job to help one another. You require a good audience to help you through your speeches, so you had better learn to listen well and help others. This is teamwork.

Exercise: The Slouch Versus the Real Listener

One member of the class goes to the front of the room. Everyone else then adopts typical postures of a bored or hostile group: slouching, tilting their chairs back, chewing gum, talking, filing their nails, yawning, glaring at the speaker, and mentally directing hideous insults his or her way. Exaggerate your pose as much as you can. Then, on a signal, sit up, lean slightly forward, make genuine eye contact, smile, and look forward to what the speaker has to say.

a) What sort of message did your postures convey?
b) How much can an audience affect a speaker?

The following diagram of energy exchange shows you the importance of the audience and the enormous impact it can have on the speaker. By applying yourself, by being attentive, you can improve the quality of the speech you are hearing.

Eye Contact: Fake or Real?

Have you ever fallen asleep in class and had your elbow slip off the desk? Have you gazed aimlessly in front of you while you planned your shopping list, reviewed your finances, or resolved never to procrastinate again? We all know what fake eye contact is. Slouch back and gaze aimlessly at the wall in front of you; your eyes are open but glazed over. You are totally lost to the situation. This is fake eye contact and it happens when people are bored or uninterested. Although it is commonly seen in classrooms, it is unnerving for speakers.

Simply by knowing this, you can correct it. Sit up and look at the speaker, really look. Genuine eye contact will help that person; it gives her or him a sense that the audience is supportive and interested in the content of the speech. Practise real eye contact. It works.

Energy Level

Speakers and listeners *share* energy. Whatever energy a speaker generates reaches the audience and they, in turn, contribute excitement and strength to the event.

Energy Cycle

Speakers and listeners *share* energy. Whatever energy a speaker generates reaches the audience and they, in turn, contribute excitement and strength to the event.

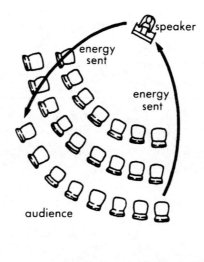

Exercise: See Me, Hear Me: Real Eye Contact

Two or three people go to the front of the group, one at a time. As each attempts to talk about the importance of sleep (or money, food, etc.), the rest of the class engages in fake eye contact. On a signal, give real eye contact. What's the difference?

What Happens If No One Listens?

Why is so much emphasis placed on you as a listener? Suppose the first volunteer from your group goes forward to make a speech and you give that person the same look you would give an instructor lecturing on the "The Effects of the White Pine Weevil on the Canadian Lumbering Industry" or "The Use of the First-Person Narrative in Anglo-Saxon Poetry." That person will be finished before he or she starts. You are necessary: speakers need the support of their listeners.

◑ BEGINNING, MIDDLE, AND END: LISTENING FOR INFORMATION

If you know how a speech is organized, you'll know when to listen and when to relax. The old formula for an essay or a speech holds true:

- Tell them what you are going to say;
- Say it;
- Tell them what you've said.

Generally, this follows the plan you've already learned elsewhere as introduction, body, and conclusion. We will now look briefly at the organization of a speech (the topic is covered in detail in Chapter Two).

Some people use elaborate outlines with headings and subheadings. Others prefer to work with scraps of paper and old envelopes. Organization does not need to be elaborate to be effective, but clear organization is vital. The introduction should have a brilliant grabber that seizes the audience's attention and leads them to your thesis—the main argument or point of your speech. It includes an overview of your three to five main supporting statements. This flows to the body of your speech in which you give the main arguments in the order you listed them. Then, in the conclusion, you clearly summarize your points and drive them home with a zinger, which leaves your audience convinced of your argument and admiring your technique. The plan looks like this:

I Introduction (Beginning)	a) Grabber: a hook to seize audience attention b) Thesis: a precise statement of your main idea or argument c) Overview: an outline of your major supporting points
II Body (Middle)	Main Point One *plus supporting statements* Main Point Two *plus supporting statements* Main Point Three *plus supporting statements*
III Conclusion (End)	a) Reference to Thesis b) Review of Main Points (if necessary) c) Strong finish

Good listeners zero in on the thesis and the main points of the overview; then they can relax. The speaker, if he or she is good, will give those main points in order; listen to each one. Make notes of the thesis and supporting arguments. Write down any examples that appeal to you or that may be useful, and wait for the conclusion. A good speaker will reinforce his or her argument. If both speaker and audience know and make use of a similar structuring principle, everyone *should* know what is happening and arrive at the same conclusion.

Active and Encouraging Listening

Real or active listening involves more than hearing. We hear many things; we listen to few. We may hear but not understand. We may hear but reject. We may hear and forget. What's the reason for not listening effectively? Is there a vocabulary difficulty, or can you not hear properly? If you are not familiar with a specialized term like RRSP, you may not be interested. Perhaps an accent stands in the way. If an Australian says what sounds like "clear the table, we need spice," he doesn't mean cinnamon or nutmeg: he needs space.

Can you teach yourself to listen well and get involved so that you learn from the speech and encourage the speaker? Here are some well-known strategies:

1. **Prepare yourself mentally**. Set yourself up for the chance to hear another person's opinion, to learn a technique, to receive helpful information, or to enjoy yourself.

2. **Get past blockades**. A person's clothing may not be your idea of fashionable, mannerisms may get in the way, or an introduction may be trite or exaggerated. Your willingness to listen should overcome these obstacles.

3. **Adopt a listening posture**. Lean forward slightly, sit up straight, and look directly at the speaker. Make real eye contact and try to show with your own expressions that you are actively involved in the speech. You are both putting yourself in the right frame of mind and helping the speaker.

4. **Attune your ears**. What happens when a speaker has a soft voice? Often, people call out "speak louder" or "we can't hear you." Listeners need to practise attuning themselves to different voices; if you give your full attention to others, you will hear them. People don't need to speak louder; we need to listen better, to concentrate on making a connection. Obviously there may be problems in larger auditoriums, but we should make an effort to hear since softer voices and different accents are part of our world.

5. **Withhold judgment**. If someone is going to speak on "The Use of Laser Beam Technology in Optical Surgery," do you expect to be bored? Remember, it is the mark of an intelligent person to want to stretch his or her intellectual capacity, and to give new ideas a chance. What if a speaker is going to talk on unions, and your family has always adopted an anti-union attitude? This is the hardest part: to listen and to reserve judgment until you have heard that speaker.

6. **Anticipate main points and reflect on the ideas**. Follow the speech and make mental comments.

7. **Take notes**. Speeches are an entertaining way of learning new material. Take notes; they will help you remember. You can make files on the speeches you have heard: if you date the notes and write down the speaker's name correctly, you may be able to use those speeches as part of primary research for essays or projects. If you know how the speech is structured, then taking notes is not complicated, but rather a simple matter of thesis, overview, main points, and conclusion.

8. **Listen to the tone of the speaker for the real meaning**. Remember, a speaker uses more than words—he or she also uses tone and gesture to convey the message.

The Speaker's Responsibility to be Heard

Automotive-technology students identified three things for a speaker to consider:

1. Are shop noises interfering with your talk?

2. Does your listener trust you? Can you use diagrams, models, or old parts to explain what must be done?
3. Does your listener understand you? Are you using terms that your client doesn't know? If you don't share a common language, yelling won't help. Again, use diagrams and parts to help in the demonstration. Talk calmly. Don't put others down and don't put yourself down.

◑ SPEAKING AND SKIING: COACHING YOURSELF TO SUCCESS

Good speakers are like good skiers: they make it look easy. They also know about the hours of practice, the rush of excitement, and the need for good coaching. Coaching for speakers? Of course. Whenever I ski down a hill, I can hear my instructor's voice: "Crouch, relax." It took me years to get it right but one day it finally happened and I flew down the hill.

How can you coach yourself in speaking? Some people talk to themselves before they start; others write cues on their note cards:

pause

count to 3

eye contact

breathe

relax

To achieve the technique and maintain it, you need to practise. Designing a good speech is half your job; delivering it well is the other. Some people worry so much about their speeches, they end up without enough time to rehearse, and try to read disorganized notes. Why should the audience have to listen to a speaker who didn't care enough to practise? When you read over your notes, your mind interprets words that were meant to be read. The same words sound very different when they are spoken. **Practise your speech and listen to yourself.**

This book offers you more than 17 specific speaking opportunities; that's more times before an audience than most people experience in five years. As you follow the exercises, remember that technique, coaching, and practice are all part of your training. After 17 practice runs, you'll be great!

TAMING THE JITTERS

Channel your nervous energy by

1. Knowing your material well.
2. Practising at home—out loud.
3. Having a friend in the audience for support.
4. Speaking on something you know well.
5. Pampering yourself. Will a new shirt or haircut make you feel better? How about a cup of cappuccino or some herbal tea?
6. Breathing deeply before you start (In-2-3-4; Out-2-3-4). This helps calm your nerves, and lowers your voice almost an octave. It's reassuring to sound in control. (For breathing exercises, see Chapter Five.)
7. Putting your notes on the podium. Never hold them in your hand; the shaking will give you away.
8. Holding on to something if you need to— the edge of the podium, a tissue in your pocket, a lucky stone in your hand.
9. Knowing that your nervousness is not only normal, it's an ally.
10. Remembering the advice of Nellie McClung, writer, reformer, and politician: the surest cure for nervousness is to have something important to say, and concentrate on getting it across.

SPEECH ASSIGNMENT: JUMP IN

You are ready now; the audience is geared up and should be aware of positive listening strategies. You can channel your nervous energy to your advantage. Try one of these mini-speeches:

1. Two-Minute Exercises

With one or two days to prepare, develop a two-minute speech on either

a) A great Canadian: this person can be a well-known public figure, a person in history, a family member, or someone you admire;

b) An introduction of yourself using a line drawing depicting your secret talent or special interests (e.g., a picture of a ballet dancer, a water skier, a musical instrument).

You may use brief notes. Limit yourself to four words or phrases.

2. Desert Island Semi-Impromptu

Your instructor announces that he or she has won a million dollars and is sending each of you on a special trip to a desert island. You have no idea of what the island will be like but your instructor promises you creature comforts: food, water, various facilities. What is the one thing you will take with you? Avoid something all-inclusive such as your wallet or knapsack. You have 15 minutes to leave the room to find the one essential thing, and develop a mini-talk on its importance and the three reasons you chose it. You may use brief notes. Limit yourself to four words or phrases.

3. Alternative Semi-Impromptu: The Perfect Gift

Instead of finding the one necessity to take to a desert island, use your time to find a gift for the Prime Minister of Canada that would make your political concerns obvious. Outline why your gift would be effective.

Good luck with your first real speech.

DELIVERY TECHNIQUES TO REMEMBER

1. When you reach the podium, pause, count to three mentally.
2. Make eye contact. At the very least look once to the left, once to the right, and once to the centre back.
3. Pause at the end before you leave the podium. Stop, count to three, make eye contact and then leave. This helps you look more like a speaker and less like a sprinter.

INTERVIEW

David Suzuki
Environmentalist, Professor, Broadcaster

Dr. David Takayoshi Suzuki is a world-renowned geneticist, a television and radio show host, and a university professor. He speaks unceasingly for the things in which he believes, and the combination of his integrity, scientific ability, and personal warmth makes him a popular speaker worldwide. As host of *The Nature of Things with David Suzuki* on CBC television, he makes Canadians more aware of science and its moral implications.

Q
How do you make a speech interesting for such diverse audiences?

A
I think of an audience in terms of my father. He was a labourer and I pitch my speeches to him. When I taught I found I had a talent for translating esoteric material into terms that everyone could understand and get excited about.

One of the problems we have today is that people think if you don't have an education, you can't understand what's being discussed. In my shows, we assume that the audience, anybody, can understand the material.

Q
Do we use jargon too much?

A
Academics tend to talk down to people and use jargon to cover up their inadequacies. That's total

crap. Anybody who can't speak in very simple language is trying to cover something up.

Q
Have you heard a good speech lately?

A
The greatest speaker I've heard recently is George Wald at Harvard. He gave a lecture on the Origin of Life and it was so wonderful that I could have wept with enjoyment. It's a great subject and he used good visual images. He shared his personal philosophy and made it seem he was talking to you personally.

Q
What speech are you proudest of?

A
In a subtle way my speeches evolve and change from week to week; they are constantly undergoing a process of growth. Really, I'm fondest of the latest one.

Q
As Canadians, how could we improve our skills as speakers?

A
Discourse is not part of our culture; we have no love of give and take, of really debating. When I was young, I used to go to dinner at my girlfriend's house, and her father loved to debate and argue. I enjoyed it and got right into it.

I also think that television is an alienating medium in terms of conversation. There's an emotional response to pictures but very little thinking involved.

Q
You give generously of yourself to so many issues. Why do you take the time to speak about difficult issues (e.g., South Moresby Island, protecting the environment, preservation of a distinct Canadian culture)?

A
Why take the trouble to speak up? Because you care, because it matters to you as a human being. You have to stand up and fight for the things you believe in. Why else do we live if we don't struggle for things that matter to us?

David Suzuki
Speech: The Good Old Days

As part of Patrick Watson's Struggle for Democracy *series, outstanding Canadians, including David Suzuki, commented on their perspectives of this country.*

You know, I hear a lot of people who say they wish we could go back to the good old days when people were more honest, and society was a better place to live. I think there's another way of looking at it. I think Canada has changed immensely in the past few decades but it is a much richer, more vibrant, and, I think, a far more preferable society today.

When my parents grew up in the '20s and '30s, it was inconceivable that someone with slant eyes like mine or skin colour like mine could ever be an entertainer, or be on television in prime time. The notion that Canadians would look to people like Adrienne Clarkson or myself, or that British Columbia would have a premier, Dave Barrett, who is Jewish, or that P.E.I. would have a premier of Lebanese background, or that we would have a black lieutenant-governor in Ontario—those ideas are very recent, and, I think, a reflection of the extent to which Canada is a much greater multi-ethnic society. And, I think, a richer and a far better one.

The good old days really exist in people's heads; the good old days are now.

OUTLINE OF A TWO-MINUTE SPEECH

Name: _____

Date of Speech: _____

Purpose Statement: _____

INTRODUCTION

Grabber:

Thesis:

Overview:

BODY

Supporting Argument #1

Supporting Argument #2

Supporting Argument #3

CONCLUSION

Reference to purpose (thesis):

Summary of main steps:

Zinger:

SELF-EVALUATION FORM

This form is to help you evaluate your own speech. It can be kept private or shared with your instructor or peers.

Type of Speech: _____

Name: _____

Title: _____

Date: _____

DELIVERY

Physical Presence

Did I make eye contact with others?

Was my posture natural and appropriate?

Was I aware of my facial expressions and hand gestures?

Were there any distracting mannerisms that I was aware of?

Did I feel good?

Could I feel an energy exchange with my audience?

VOCAL DELIVERY

Was my voice under control?

Did I sound confident?

Was I aware of breathing calmly?

How was my enunciation?

Did I manage to avoid um's and ah's?

Did I sound interested/excited/committed?

How did my voice sound to me?

DESIGN AND CONTENT

How well did the introduction and conclusion work?

Did the framework unify my speech?

Was there a natural progression from point to point?

Did my notes keep me on track? Did I use them?

Did the audience seem to understand the organization of my speech?

Was the information clear?

What was the energy level of the conclusion?

What would I change the next time?

What worked very well?

OVERALL EFFECTIVENESS

Did I connect with this audience?

Did I achieve my purpose?

What do I remember most about making the speech?

What unexpected or unforeseen things happened?

What am I most pleased about?

OTHER COMMENTS

Grade: _____

PEER EVALUATION FORM

Peer evaluation should be done in a constructive and supportive fashion. The speaker may choose people to do assessments or they may be assigned alphabetically. Some groups maintain the same speaker/assessor teams for the entire course; others change for each speech. The instructor may wish to see this evaluation before the speaker receives it.

Type of Speech: _____

Speaker: _____

Title: _____

Assessor: _____

Date: _____

DELIVERY

Physical Presence

Did the speaker maintain eye contact?

Did she or he establish a rapport with the audience?

Were gestures natural and effective?

VOCAL DELIVERY

Did the speaker sound convincing/spontaneous/excited?

Was his or her voice clear and loud enough?

How did you respond to the speaker's mood?

DESIGN AND CONTENT

Did the introduction interest you?

Did the overview give you an indication of the main proofs?

Did the speech flow easily and logically from one point to another?

Was the conclusion strong and memorable?

Did the conclusion reinforce the thesis and main points?

What was the thesis of the speech?

Were you moved by it?

What was the most outstanding part of the speech?

What changes do you recommend?

What parts should the speaker definitely keep?

OTHER COMMENTS

Grade: _____

EVALUATION FORM

Type of Speech: _____

Name: _____

Title: _____

Length of Speech: _____

Date: _____

Legend: S=Superior   E=Effective   NW=Needs Work

DELIVERY

Physical Presence

Eye Contact

Rapport with Audience

Posture

Gestures

Use of Notes

Appropriate Use of Audio-Visual

Support Material

VOCAL DELIVERY

Naturalness/Spontaneity/Enthusiasm

Clarity

Variety (Tone, Pitch, Pace)

Volume

Absence of Verbal Tics (um, ah, okay, like)

Sense of Control and Calm

DESIGN AND CONTENT

Use of Framework for Introduction and Conclusion

Clear Thesis and Overview

Coherence/Use of Transitions

Strong Finish

Language

Word Choice

Impact on Audience

Grammar

OVERALL EFFECTIVENESS

Treatment of Topic

Intelligent Awareness of Audience

Achievement of Purpose

Impact on/Connection with Audience

OTHER COMMENTS

Grade: _____

CHAPTER

Watch Closely Now: The Demonstration

Every speech is different—different environment, different people. You have to come from the heart...make them feel they're the most important people in your day, in your life, at that time.

(Rick Hansen)

TIPS FOR SPEAKERS

1. Brainstorm for ideas, for a topic that you are interested in or feel strongly about.

2. Trust yourself: off-beat ideas may lead you to exciting topics.

3. Audience analysis is essential for every speech. Learn as much as you can about the audience: their background, attitudes, knowledge of the topic.

4. Mapping your Success. With a Three-Part Plan, everyone will know where your speech is headed.

5. A good thesis should pass the "One-Sentence Shower Test."

6. Prepare a Seven-Day countdown and stick to it.

7. Practise your delivery. Believe in yourself and why you are speaking.

W A R M - U P S

Confirm or Deny—Spot the Lie

Divide into groups of three or four. One volunteer in each group makes three statements, one of which is false. Each of the other group members can quiz the speaker for 30 seconds to determine the truth of each statement. At the end of the questioning, each person votes on which statement is not true. This exercise can be spread over several classes, ensuring that everyone has a chance to attempt to outwit their classmates.

This chapter has two functions:

1. To demonstrate how to organize and prepare a speech;
2. To outline the techniques involved in delivering a competent demonstration.

Like every good demonstration, the section on organizing a speech has a natural progression:

1. How to find a topic;
2. How to build a speech;
3. Zeroing in on a thesis;
4. Matching your speech and your audience;
5. Putting you and your audience at ease.

If you follow the steps, your speeches will be well constructed. The process starts with a three-part plan—the nuts and bolts of speech preparation.

How to throw a cream pie

How to change a tire

How to organize a speech

◑ THE PLAN THAT WORKS

Why do you need a plan? You've just spent 14 hours researching bats. You've been to the Ministry of Natural Resources, the library, the museum, and the local pest-control office. You know everything about bats: how to remove them from old buildings, plans for bat houses, how the brown bat reproduces, the mythology of bats, the use of bat droppings for fertilizer. You are brimming with bat lore and bat stories.

Indeed, you know so much about bats that you could talk for hours, and *that's where the danger lies*. What do you hope to accomplish? Will people be able to follow you? How should you organize the material?

"I feel a recipe is only a theme, which an intelligent cook can play each time with a variation."

(Madame Jehane Benoit)

Organize In Threes

The three parts of the plan you use are simple.

Introduction: Grab the audience's attention and tell them what you're going to tell them;

Body: Tell them;

Conclusion: Tell them what you've told them and leave them with a powerful finish.

Not only does your speech have three main sections—introduction, body, and conclusion—but you should also arrange your main arguments, reasons, steps, or challenges, in *three* clear sections. Why three sections? The human brain cannot absorb and *remember* more; the audience does not have written backup. Although your speech is well researched, dynamic, and logical, the audience is listening, not reading. They need very precise statements of your argument, your reasons, and your summary.

If you prepare a speech on how to catch and release a bat without harming it in 13 easy steps, no one will be able to remember more than four steps. By the time you get to the crucial step 10, no one will retain the information.

Organize in threes: stoplights have three colours: baseball has three outs. Three is a magic number in western society—use it as an organizing principle.

In an expanded form, the plan looks like this.

The Three-Part Plan That Always Works

I. Introduction

The introduction itself has three parts.
a) *Grabber*.
   Why should anyone listen to you? The grabber answers that question. It captures the attention of the audience and makes them *want* to listen to you.
b) *Thesis*: Why are you speaking? The thesis is a clear and precise statement of the point you wish to make, the explanation you have to offer, the argument you seek to present.
c) *Overview*.
   Where is the speech going? The overview is a preview of the three main points you will use to support the thesis.

II. Body	Present the main supporting arguments outlined in the overview *in the order you gave them.* Supporting Argument #1 plus back-up examples Supporting Argument #2 plus back-up examples Supporting Argument #3 plus back-up examples Remember, pare down your reas⟨⟩ points. **Throw out your weak ideas.**
III. Conclusion	The conclusion also has three m⟨⟩ a) It rounds out the speech and ad⟨⟩ pletion; b) It reinforces the thesis, and revie⟨⟩ (if necessary); c) It jolts the audience with a stron⟨⟩ appropriate, it urges them to a⟨⟩ sion should be so dynamic that everyone remembers it.

Handwritten note:
speech

Intro - Grabber - antedote
— Thesis - main point
— overview

body — #1
#2 arguements
#3

conclusion — reiterate.
-strong final statement

The following outline of a demonstration speech shows how to apply the three-part plan.

Sample Speech: The South Magnetawan Bat Brigade

Purpose: After hearing my speech, the audience will know how to remove a bat from a house without injuring it.

I. Introduction	a) *Grabber.* A personal story: "Imagine waking up at night to the flutter of a bat's wings as it swoops just above your face." b) *Thesis.* How to remove the bat from the room without hurting it or frightening yourself. c) *Overview.* Three main sections: a) equipment b) capture c) release

	Equipment
	• bat hat with wide brim for protection
	• bright flashlight
	• sieve and sturdy cardboard
	Capture
	• forcing yourself to get up off the floor
II. Body	• finding the bat
	• putting the sieve over the bat and the cardboard behind to make a cage
	Release:
	• carrying the sieve cage gently to a door
	• releasing the bat with a single swooping motion to avoid hurting its wings
	• shutting the door quickly to avoid re-entry.
III. Conclusion	• Refer to purpose and the main steps—equipment, capture, and release.
	• Clincher:
	"This humane way of getting rid of bats really works. The only problem is that bats have excellent memories and may live for 20 years. Sooner or later, they'll remember the entrance and visit you again."

This, then, is the framework of a speech. By using this simple and dependable outline, you will be able to build your argument, no matter how complex, and know that the structure is sound. You will not get bogged down in detail, and your audience will be able to understand and follow you.

Once you understand the process, the next step is to find a topic.

◑ THE SECRET OF FINDING A TOPIC

Mental agility, emotional calm, and steely discipline are what you need to find a topic, narrow it down, and hammer out a thesis that will work.

There are three scenarios in getting a speech topic:

1.   Your instructor tells you what the topic is;
2.   You are given a wide-open assignment—make a speech on anything;
3.   The double flip: start with a given topic, and, using free association, arrive at an offbeat but workable topic.

Scenario One: Your Instructor Sets the Topic

Your first assignment is a brief speech on "Successful Management Strategies," "How to Help the Homeless," "The Best Children's Book on the Market," or "Resource Management." What is your first reaction to these topics? Do you like any of them? Do any of them mean anything to you?

First Steps

1. What does the instructor mean? Are there limits?
2. Clear up any difficulties of vocabulary. What is meant by "management strategy"? How old is a child? If your instructor sets a limit, you have to follow it. If she does not, you can take an open approach to the whole topic. Of course, your instructor is going to deal with the most obvious questions: how long does the speech have to be? when do you have to speak? Remember, if you have questions at this point, either ask them in class or go right to your instructor.

Scenario Two: The Wide-Open Topic

Make a three-minute speech "on anything that you find interesting," or "anything you think is of significant interest to your class." If you get a wide-open assignment, STOP, and remember what I am going to say.

Do not try to find your final topic immediately. Students worry unnecessarily when they insist that the perfect topic spring complete into their minds. If that perfect topic, complete with thesis, method of organization, and examples does not *immediately* drop, do not say, "I can't do it, I can't think of a thing." You can; here's how.

Exercise: Brainstorming

a) Write a word on a piece of paper: shoe, microphone, kayak, purple, money, maple syrup, video shops, swimming, banks, cow, cornflakes, etc.
b) Choose one of these words and for the next 60 seconds write down as many things associated with that topic as you can.

   This is brainstorming. There are only three rules:

1. Don't stop writing things down;
2. Don't think;
3. Don't evaluate.

   You are after quantity, so don't say, "this is stupid," or "this won't work," or "I've already done this." Give yourself one minute and write.

   If you chose the word shoe, your list might look like this:

socks
running shoes
types of running shoes

styles of running shoes
prices of running shoes
deck shoes
hiking boots
construction boots
shoes as weapons
dancing shoes, ballet shoes
cost
materials
style
shoes as accessories
import/export market
uncomfortable shoes
bare feet
cowboy boots
blisters

If you're new to brainstorming, you will need practice to develop speed. Take another word and repeat the process. Time yourself for one minute. Do not stop; do not think; do not evaluate.

Experienced speakers brainstorm all the time to find an idea or a fresh approach that they like and that the audience will enjoy. *Do not ignore this step!* In order to get truly involved in your speech, you need to have a handle on it—an approach that you're comfortable with and that excites you. Whether you are passionately arguing why adopted children should be helped to find their birth parents or more calmly discussing the quintessential Canadian sport, make sure you know the topic, and have the interest, energy, and conviction to follow it through.

I think that's the whole secret. If you are going to be bored, your audience is going to be bored. The secret is finding a topic that interests you.
    (SHERI ALEXANDER—HOSPITALITY STUDENT)

What are the criteria of a good topic?

1. It meets the requirements of the assignment.
2. It interests you.
3. It interests your audience.
4. There is research material available.
5. You can organize it and develop it within the time available.

Exercise: Coffee-time Practice

In your class or over coffee, ask different people to write down single words and brainstorm each one. When you are standing at the bus stop, concentrate on a passerby and list all the things you associate with that person.

Emotional Calm: Free Floating

Instead of desperation, try this calm, free-floating approach to your subject. Let's say you tried to brainstorm on management strategies but could only think of managers:

boss
raise
inventories
personnel
success
unemployment
three-piece suits
Lamborghini
interviews
motivating employees
teams
beast
fire
promote

It is a good list. Which topic intrigues you the most? Remember, the topic is "Successful Management Strategies." What if you don't know any? The boss as a beast appeals to you because you are thinking of a particular person. This is where relaxation is needed. Daydream for a minute. Take a bath. Go into a reverie at the bus stop. Lie down on the couch and tell your family that you're thinking.

Scenario Three: The Double Flip

In the tub you think of extinct animals like the dinosaur, vicious ones like the hyena or weasel, and loyal pack leaders like the wolf. Eureka! You have a topic—the boss as an animal: the dinosaur, out of date; the weasel, cutthroat; or the wolf, a team leader—you have narrowed it down, you have your examples.

This example demonstrates that you do not have to worry about always staying exactly within the topic as it was first suggested: you can think of offbeat ideas. If you have any doubts about this, take the topic to your instructor and see how it works. Look at the criteria. Will it interest your audience? Will the topic interest you? Do you know enough about it? Can you find research material?

Now we can try this with the topic "Resource Management." Wood is a resource, iron ore is a resource, minerals are a resource, but time is a resource too, as are people and money. What else is a resource? Suppose one of your friends is a bird watcher who is keen on birds of prey, such as eagles, owls, falcons, or hawks. She has told you about Canadian efforts to raise bald eagles and ship them to the United States, where loss of habitat has resulted in dangerously low numbers. Can you talk on the need to manage wildlife, especially birds?

You remember a newspaper article in which Canadians are trying to crack down on illegal smuggling of the peregrine falcon. Which other bird needs managing? If you live in the city, you know about pigeons; they certainly need regulating. This could be a good speech. This is an unorthodox but innovative way of getting a topic—the double flip. Take an idea, do some mental somersaults, and come up with a new twist. Instead of water or minerals, you will discuss "Wildlife Resources: Managing Canadian Birds."

Priming the Pump

Crisis scenario: What happens if you brainstorm and still can't find something to talk about? What else can you do? Around you are all the resources you need: your friends, radio, television. Make sure you check the news and issue programs on television. Newspapers and magazines are jammed with interesting current stories. Your local library has a selection on national and local magazines—scan the headings and the articles that appeal to you.

What if they won't like it? Who are *they*? The community group that you're speaking to, your boss, the board of education whose ruling you oppose, your peers? Speakers worry about being liked—with good reason. So much of our being is at stake when we speak. If you are speaking to a friendly group and you follow the advice in this book, your speech will be interesting, you will be convincing, and *they* will like you.

If, however, you are expressing concerns to people who do not like opposition, you're right. They won't like you. If you want to be liked, stay home—there is no right way to speak so that *they* will like what you have to say. On the other hand, if you speak out on behalf of a principle that you and others value, you will have acted with integrity, you'll feel empowered, and changes *may* occur. Your friends, if you tell them that you need support, will praise you for what you said and how you said it!

Exercise: Finding Ideas

Scan the headlines in five recent newspapers or magazines and make a list of several topics that you could use or brainstorm to find a topic. The list can range from baseball strikes to acupuncture to animal rights.

Steely Resolution

Now is the time to control yourself, stop worrying, and *stop researching*. List the five best possibilities and choose one. The most common error that beginners make is to worry and research until the night before the speech. This doesn't work. You need to spend time on the delivery of your speech. After a day and a half, choose the topic: it may not be perfect but it will make a good speech if you work at it.

Assuming you have a week to research, organize, and practise your speech, your schedule should look like this:

THE SEVEN-DAY COUNTDOWN

Day 1: check details
    talk to friends
    brainstorm

Day 2: brainstorm and research
    go inside yourself to discover what
    you really want to say
    formulate a thesis

Day 3: design speech—work on thesis and
    overview of main points

Day 4: add supporting arguments, examples,
    details, etc.
    make notes and start to practise

Day 5: revise notes: practise aloud

Day 6: Practise! Practise! Practise! (aloud)

Day 7: Relax! Review notes one last time.
    Practise introduction and any difficult
    parts once more aloud.

This plan divides your time almost equally into time to plan and time to practise. You *need* the chance to rehearse.

Exercise: Brainstorming in Action

(*allow 30 minutes*)
This exercise gives you practice in finding suitable topics, and narrowing them down to specific ideas for speeches.

a) Choose *two* of the following topics and brainstorm one minute on each. Try to get a list of 10 things for each:
   tattoos
   bush fever
   atomic energy
   black flies
   student loans
   embarrassing moments
   fast-food outlets
   body piercing
   high-speed police chases
   water sports

b) From each list, select the two best suggestions.

c) You now have *four* ideas; for each one make a statement that you can explain, prove, and demonstrate.

d) Choose the best one.

If your topic is too vast for a short speech, concentrate on one specific aspect and use it as the focal point of your presentation.

GREAT CANADIAN QUIZ I

How well do you know Canadian place names, holidays, history, folklore, and political institutions? Here's a quick quiz to get your mind alert.

1. When is Groundhog Day? Feb
2. What is screech? Character from
3. When is Canada Day? July 1st
4. Who invented basketball? Canadians
5. What team was named the greatest Canadian basketball team of the first half of this century?
6. What did Pierre Elliott Trudeau always wear in his lapel?
7. Which province was the last to join Confederation and in what year did it enter?
8. What city was known as Pile of Bones?
9. What Métis hero led the Rebellion of 1885?
10. What is the more popular name of Anne Shirley?
11. Santa Claus's address is the North Pole, Canada. What is the postal code?
12. In which year was the present Canadian flag adopted?
13. Name the political confederacy that was operating before Europeans came to this country, and is still working.
14. The three main transportation passes through the Rockies are named after a bird, an animal, and the hair of a person. What are they?
15. Where and what was Africville?

To test yourself further, consult:

John Robert Colombo, *Colombo's Canadian Quiz Book* (Western Producer Prairie Books, 1983).

John Fisher, *The Complete Cross-Canada Quiz and Game Book* (McClelland and Stewart, 1978).

Sandra Martin, *Quizzing Canada* (Dundurn Press, 1987).

Answers: Great Canadian Quiz I

1. February 2
2. a powerful Newfoundland rum
3. July 1
4. James A. Naismith
5. The Edmonton Grads, a women's team
6. a rose
7. Newfoundland, 1949
8. Regina
9. Louis Riel
10. Anne of Green Gables
11. H0H 0H0
12. 1965
13. League of the Five Nations or League of the Iroquois, now known as the Six Nations
14. Crow's Nest Pass, Kicking Horse Pass, Yellowhead Pass
15. a black section of Halifax, razed in 1969

◑ THE THESIS—THE HEART OF THE PLAN

The next step in organizing a speech is zeroing in on the specific point you wish to make—your thesis. If you plan to do a speech on the boss as an animal, (dinosaur, weasel, or wolf), you need a basic idea of what you're going to prove; your theme, or thesis, is the heart of your speech.

What is a possible thesis for a speech on the manager as animal? How about "Tyrant or team leader? Managers are like animals: dinosaurs, weasels, and wolves. The successful ones are team leaders and, like wolves, their loyalty is to the pack." That is a great thesis, but does it have to be so long? No, it can be very short. Here is a student's thesis on hamburger places: "The things I look for in a burger restaurant are friendliness, atmosphere, and hot peppers." A nursing student doing a speech on palliative care had this thesis: "Palliative care attempts to reassure the patient, ease his or her suffering, and help the patient face impending death."

Mapping Your Success: More on the Thesis and Overview

The perfect plan is like a road map: the **thesis**, or main idea, is your destination; the supporting ideas outlined in the overview are the details of your route. Look at the examples just given. Can you identify the main supporting points in each case?

The preview makes it clear where your speech is going. Have you ever tried to drive someone home and been forced to follow terse commands; "Turn right here! Now left! Quick, left again here! Okay, stop!" Isn't it easier to have someone say, "Go along Burrard Street, and turn right on Pender. Stay on Pender and merge with Georgia at the intersection of Georgia and Pender. Then continue west on Georgia, and you'll run right into Stanley Park."

That is what the overview does: it lets the audience know the main turns that the speech will take as you drive home your thesis. They can anticipate your reasons and work with you instead of wondering where you're heading. To continue the analogy of a journey, a speech with a definite thesis and precise overview enables the audience to recognize the landmarks and appreciate the route.

The overview also makes things clear for *you* , the speaker. Once you have worked hard on the thesis and organized your ideas in three or four main sections, your speech is basically made. You need to fill in the examples and proofs, but the design is clear. That gives you the freedom to devote your efforts to talking directly to people.

Putting It All Together

How well do you understand the process of preparing a speech? If you understood the first three sections on organization, finding a topic, and formulating a thesis and overview, you should be able to demonstrate the technique yourself.

Imagine you have been assigned a two-minute speech on high-rise apartments. Although you don't live in one, you have visited several. Your brainstorming might produce this:

neighbours
condominiums
subsidized housing
high rent
no yard work
rent review board
slow elevators
great view
party rooms
sauna and weight rooms
few play areas for children
security problems
excessive noise
finding a roommate
fear of heights
fire safety
the pool
good location

(Can you see the various points of view reflected on this list?) These are all good topics; however, you must choose one. You decide on security because you have a friend who has had security problems in a high-rise; he will provide excellent first-hand information.

Once you do some preliminary research, you realize that security is still a general heading and you have to brainstorm again. This is an informed list; it reflects the work you have done:

need for better peepholes in doors
cheap locks
keys kept by former tenants
elevators
main foyer door too accessible to strangers
parking garages
poor lighting
theft

muggings
loud fights
balconies dangerous on lower levels
mailbox theft

Finding the Thesis

You need to refine exactly what you want to prove or outline. The thesis is your precise statement of where the speech is headed or what it will demonstrate.

Considering the topic, you have at least two routes: "Why are there so many security problems?" or "what are the major danger areas?" The student who did this speech identified the foyer, elevators, and parking garage as the major danger areas. She also figured out why they were so dangerous. Owing to time limitations, she had to choose whether to discuss the reasons for the lack of security in high-rises or to discuss the main danger areas.

These are the thesis statements she considered; remember, they were prefaced by the grabbers.

Thesis Statement A

"Security problems in high-rise apartments are the result of short-sighted or incorrect attitudes on the part of designers, owners, and tenants."

This thesis statement almost has the overview in place. The following statement is even more specific. It classifies the danger areas.

Thesis Statement B

"The areas of greatest risk in highrise apartments are the foyer, the elevator and the parking garages."

The student went on to discuss the three danger areas in the order given in the overview.

In each case the thesis and overview give the audience an exact outline of the purpose of the speech and the major points. The audience knows where the speech is going and how it will get there.

The One-Sentence Shower Test

How do you know if your thesis is clear? Take the one-sentence shower test. You've worked hard on your speech and you're in the shower. Challenge yourself: **"Can I state in one sentence what my whole speech is supposed to prove?"**

Pass the test and you have a thesis and a speech. If you mumble and ramble until the water runs cold, you had better start narrowing things down and hammering out one precise idea.

WHO? WHAT? WHEN? TESTING YOUR TOPIC

Before you go any further, ask yourself if your topic is appropriate:

for the audience,
for the occasion,
for the time allotted.

◑ MATCHING YOUR SPEECH AND YOUR LISTENERS: THE NEED FOR AUDIENCE ANALYSIS

When Rick Hansen went around the world on his Man in Motion tour, he spoke to hundreds of groups of people. Although exhausted, he always took the time to make his remarks special for each audience. He has a knack for reaching out to establish a link. More than that, he instantly takes notice of people and circumstances. When he visited Bawden Correctional Institute in Alberta, he began his speech like this:

We are all imprisoned in different ways.

The speech was obviously a success: the inmates presented him with a ball and chain.

You too must adapt your speech to each audience and each occasion. An audience analysis is *essential* each time you speak; it is part of your preparation. In most cases, it is also your responsibility. You can do an informal analysis by telephone, asking whoever contacted you questions about the group. In your class, you can make observations and ask questions to add to your knowledge of your classmates and instructor.

Consider these situations:

1. You have prepared a speech on the superiority of country inns and why they are better than large hotel chains. Your audience is a group of managers from several chains. How can you adapt your topic? Would it not be better to speak on the qualities of country inns that are found (or you would like to find) in larger hotels?

2. You are asked to speak to a community group on the life of a college student. Do they know what a community college is? Are they more interested in courses, vocational possibilities, costs, and the level of instruction, or in the personal development you experience while in college?

3. You are a street worker going to the municipal council to ask for funds for shelters for street kids. Will they be more convinced by a discussion of the needs of your clients, or by proof that it is cheaper to care for them before they are perpetrators or victims of crime?

Often, you do not have to change your speech as much as your examples. Imagine that you're talking about investing money and you have used a hunting analogy to explain the difference between safe investments and speculation. When you discover that your audience consists of naturalists, changing the analogy to conservation will make your presentation more effective.

Analysis Checklist

Here are some of the things to check when you do an audience analysis. They may help you to get a clearer picture of the group and the situation. You must guard against making unfair assumptions based on age, income, or education, while at the same time determining how those factors affect the speaking occasion.

Knowledge of the subject
What do they need to know?
Age
Occupational background
Gender
Rural or urban experience
Parents or non-parents
Family composition
Race or nationality
Disposable income
Level of education
Interests and hobbies
Why are they asking *you*?

Warning: Derogatory remarks about race, religion, gender, disability, size, or sexual preference are unacceptable everywhere. Such slurs undermine your credibility and insult your listeners by assuming that they would accept such remarks.

Exercise on Audience Analysis

Exercise: Asking the Right Questions

You are speaking on

a)   retention rates in schools
b)   the spread of the use of crack
c)   hiring a student

What would you want to know about your audience in order to prepare a good speech?

Exercise: Class Analysis

Jan MacLeod, a speaker from St. John, New Brunswick, is coming to speak to your class on "The Deaf Community." Prepare a two- or three-paragraph analysis of your class to send to her. (You may compile your own list of speakers or topics.)

Exercise: Winning and Losing Topics

Based on your analysis of your class, prepare a list of

a)   three topics to generate maximum audience *interest*;
b)   three topics to generate maximum audience *boredom*.

    To see how accurate you are, do a survey. Ask 10 classmates how interesting or boring they find your topics.

Putting Yourself and Others at Ease

Analysing the Occasion

A friend of mine was asked to make a speech to a conference of youth leaders on the need for HIV/AIDS education. This was her specialty and she was pleased to be invited. She also knew the group well and believed that they would be receptive. But things broke down. The audience had no idea that their luncheon address was going to be on HIV/AIDS and my friend didn't realize the group was not prepared for the topic. Both audience and speaker were taken aback. Although the event co-oridnator should have told my friend about the state of things, every speaker knows that she or he is responsible for finding out all the details.

    These insider tips will help you analyse the occasion.

1. **Why are you speaking?** What is the occasion? Is this a formal dinner or an informal gathering? Do you need to persuade your listeners, entertain them, or inform them? Were you chosen because of your reputation for dealing with the subject clearly? Beware of the internal politics of a group. Your reception will vary if you've been billed as a helpful consultant or someone they have to listen to.

2. **Where will you be speaking?** With even a cursory knowledge of basic human needs, you'll be able to make sure that your listeners' needs are met. They must feel worthwhile and respected in order to get the most out of your speech. You should also pay attention to the speaking environment:
    • is there enough air in the room?
    • is it too hot or too cold?

- can everyone see and hear? are there appropriate arrangements for translation and/or signers for the hearing-impaired?
- did someone arrange for coffee, tea, and juice?

3. **When will you speak?** If you speak first, make sure that latecomers feel comfortable entering the room. If you speak last, you may face a tired or hungry group. After a meal, you'll need a high-energy approach to revitalize a mellow audience. If you're scheduled to speak after a discussion that you know will run late and arouse strong feelings, negotiate to speak at another time.

4. **Who else is speaking?** If you are going to be one of several speakers, find out their approaches to the subject in advance. You can then plan a complementary or contrasting position, rather than repeating what has been said. Enrich your listeners rather than bore them.

5. **What format suits the group?** Depending on the occasion, the size of the group, their level of knowledge of the topic and their reasons for coming to hear you, consider these types of presentation. Your own speaking skills and comfort with the subject also influence your choice:

    - a straightforward presentation
    - speech and question period
    - short introduction to a full question-and-answer period.

Talk Without Speaking: What Your Body Language Tells Others

We communicate with our words, our eyes, our bodies. Audiences notice the way you walk to the front of the room, and the facial expressions you use. Although listeners make predictions about your speech from the way you look, they generally withhold judgment until after the first few minutes; your words, after all, are what count.

1. **Psych yourself up**. Bring a sense of anticipation to the exercise—it shows in your eyes and face.
2. **Breathe deeply**. You will look and feel calmer.
3. **Wear appropriate clothing**. Your clothes should be comfortable and send the right signals to the audience.
4. **Practise rising from your chair and walking to the front**. Rise quietly, and walk carefully with your eyes on your destination.
5. **Watch out for stairs**. People who run up the stairs in an exaggerated display of eagerness often make spectacular entrances.
6. **Walk confidently to the lectern, keep your posture erect, and acknowledge other speakers naturally**.
7. **Establish eye contact**. Make the audience feel that they are special.

Find a receptive person to the left, right, and centre of the group and speak to them in turn.

8. **Make your gestures natural**. They should be determined by the content of your speech, and not by nervousness.

9. **Do not dress yourself on stage**. The checklist "On Arrival" (in Chapter Eight) suggests that you allow yourself some private time when you arrive to check buttons and belts, to tuck in your shirt, etc. New speakers, with 45 pairs of eyes on them, often feel the urge to fix their clothes. Control yourself.

10. **Trust your audience**. They want you to do well.

Exercise: Weird Postures to Avoid

This exercise is fun. It is designed to make you aware of quirky postures or gestures caused by nervousness. Speakers are often unaware that they are making them. You may work alone or in small groups, one person performing and the others providing feedback and encouragement.

a)   Choose a card. On each is the name of a weird posture or gesture that nervous speakers use *frequently* (see the following list).

b)   Take three minutes to practise the posture and prepare a 30-second speech of your choice (e.g., "junk food I love"). Exaggerate the posture and get feedback from your partners.

c)   One at a time, go to the podium. A classmate reads the title of the quirk and you demonstrate it during your 30-second talk.

d)   Get these postures out of your system *before* your next speech.

key jangler	one-legged crane
ballet position	the snob
toe tickler	gum chomper
hip shifter	abdominal cramps
dancer	clothes hitcher
tilter	

❶ DEMONSTRATIONS: THE REAL THING

The real test of a chapter on organizing and preparing a speech is for you to use what you have learned. Demonstrations are a good, non-threatening way to experiment; the audience concentrates on the materials instead of you.

A demonstration speech is instructive and interesting if

1.   the subject matches the audience, the time allotted, and the space available;

2.   you know the subject well and have a genuine interest in sharing it;

3.   you organize clearly;

4.   you rehearse until the demonstration and delivery are smooth.

We often make demonstration speeches as part of our jobs. Cooks and bakers show assistants how to make a creole sauce or crème caramel. A technician for the Ministry of Natural Resources helps others make a walkway through a bog. A salesperson sells different lighting systems by demonstrating the advantages of each. A veterinarian shows a group of assistants how to prepare an animal for anesthetic. **The purpose of the speech is *not* to talk about a subject, but to explain it so clearly as you demonstrate that the audience learns the procedure and remembers it**. After your presentation, audience members should remember the main steps, and be able to work on their own.

Actual Topics Used for Demonstration Speeches

How to
>   paint clown faces
>   cut glass
>   pot a plant
>   execute a good golf swing
>   pour beer
>   do a Greek dance step
>   tie a bow tie
>   change a tire
>   use a haki sak
>   choose a ski boot
>   uncork wine
>   read palms
>   buy a good amplifier
>   spike hair
>   stop on roller skates
>   cook pasta
>   prepare squid
>   boost a car battery
>   cast: jig bait casting, imitation bait casting, live bait casting
>   twirl a pen
>   instal a light switch
>   adjust bindings on ski boots
>   bone chicken breasts
>   throw a cream pie
>   diaper a baby

    give a massage
    tie-dye material
    hand-paint T-shirts
    change a washer
    clean a chimney
    choose a canoe paddle

How to make
    a simple table
    duck decoys
    tea
    espresso
    popcorn
    the ultimate milkshake
    the perfect peanut-butter-and-jam sandwich
    Irish cream liquer
    various exotic drinks
    vegetable dip
    carrot cake
    spring rolls
    carrot juice
    Caesar salad
    paper roses
    paper decorator bows

How to use
    underwater breathing apparatus
    instant cash machines
    correct cycling procedures
    a 35-mm camera
    a formal place setting
    army issue camouflage make-up

Demonstration speeches add excitement to the class; you never know what will happen. The smell of garlic draws you to some exotic concoction; speakers in costume intrigue you; clusters of equipment promise hours of variety and interest. I still use recipes I learned from students; in my classes I learned how to prepare squid, use professional corkscrews, and make simple tables.

A Note on Ethical Responsibility

If you demonstrate a procedure involving health or safety—such as boosting a car battery or helping a choking victim—you must be properly trained. Showing an incorrect cable connection may cause an accident. A responsible speaker does not alarm or frighten his or her audience: one student caused an uproar when he suddenly produced a gun (a starter's pistol) during a speech. The class was so unnerved that they couldn't concentrate.

Make the Topic Specific

Limit your demonstration to one procedure, such as spiking your hair or using a microphone. For example, if you choose taking a good picture, too many variables are involved. Limit yourself to framing your subject, using different settings, or choosing a background. Once you have your topic, list all the steps and *discard non-essential ones.*

The Three-Part Plan

Imagine a before-and-after situation: before your speech, the audience knows little about throwing a cream pie; after you're finished, they'll know how to throw a pie, and how to escape.

Your Speech Outline

I. **Introduction**
   Grabber: arouse curiosity
   Thesis: state what you are going to demonstrate and its
                importance
   Overview: outline the major steps—road map to competence

II. **Body**
   Show the steps in order

III. **Conclusion**
   Summary of major steps and a zinger to round off the presentation
   But a Demonstration has More Than Three Steps.

   Stephanie Auld, a junior ranger, was planning to demonstrate a graceful canoe stroke—the solo running pry. She had outlined eight steps:

1. Lean the canoe to the paddling side;
2. Approach the turning point;
3. Change the position of the paddling hand;
4. Insert the paddle blade under the canoe on the paddling side at a 45 degree angle and place the opposite hand on the gunwale for balance;
5. Hold the paddle in position until the turn is half done;
6. Remove paddle from water;
7. Adjust weight to stop turn;
8. Resume paddling position.

Putting the Demonstration Together
1. Make the topic specific
2. Follow the Three-Part Plan
3. Rehearse

When she realized that no one would remember all those steps, she organized them in three major sections: position, stroke, and follow-through.

Her friend, Fred Heidema, however, needed four major sections for his messy demonstration of cream-pie throwing: selecting the pie, approach, delivery, and escape.

Exercise: Making It All Seem Simple

Choose one of the following topics, list all the steps involved, and organize them into three main sections:

a)   Building a simple bookcase or stereo stand;
b)   Blowing bubble gum;
c)   Opening a door silently;
d)   An easy stretching exercise.

Modified Demonstrations

Demonstration speeches are usually done in chronological order from beginning to end. However, what if there is a time lapse while the cookies bake or the glue dries? Will a boring repetitive action like accordion-pleating a piece of paper turn your audience off? The modified demonstration is a technique to use in these cases.

If you plan to bake in class, bring the ingredients to be mixed in front of the group, *and* samples of the finished product. The components of a birdhouse can be assembled up to the stage of glueing, the next example can be worked on until it is time to paint, and then the third complete model is shown. There is nothing more boring than watching someone pleat tissues to use for pompoms; make sure to use a modified demonstration for any action that involves a series of repetitive actions.

Rehearse

Rehearsing with props is essential to a smooth performance. Actors are meticulous about placing and using props, and speakers should be too. Your credibility will be enhanced if you know your subject well and can handle your materials confidently. Use the following checklist as you rehearse your speech; imagine your audience is in the room.

1.   **Rehearse with the materials until you are familiar with them**. This will allow you to give more eye contact to your audience when you actually do the speech.
2.   **Have interesting props**. If you have a collection of materials—ingredients for a recipe, or pots of sequins or nails, put them in separate containers with large, colourful labels. Make the setup interesting.

HAVE INTERESTING PROPS

3. **Check your sightlines**. Set the demonstration up at home, *exactly* as you will do it. Then, walk from your position as speaker to where the audience will be. Is anything blocking your view? Are any bags or materials in the way? This is the most common problem with demonstration speeches. Make sure the audience's view is unobstructed.

4. **Can your notecards be seen at a distance?** Many things require your attention. Practise handling the materials, connecting with the audience, and checking notes all at once.

5. **Practise your movements often**. Can you pour liquids, fold paper, join pieces of wood, or slice mushrooms without your hands trembling?

6. **Repeat key ideas** and include a summary.

7. **Use the audience, involve them, appeal to them**. Make sure they understand.

SPEECH ASSIGNMENT: THE DEMONSTRATION

Choose a topic and prepare a three-part plan to include all the necessary steps. Be prepared to enjoy and learn much during this assignment.

DELIVERY TECHNIQUES TO REMEMBER

For your first speech you were asked to

Pause at the podium and count to three;

Make eye contact;

Pause when you finish.

Now, add the following:

1. Assume a confident posture;

2. Breathe before you start. You will have better control of your voice;

3. Eliminate verbal tics (okay, um, ah).

INTERVIEW

Rich Hansen
Man in Motion

Rick Hansen is a wheelchair athlete, writer, and speaker. Inspired by the example of his friend, Terry Fox, Hansen embarked on the Man in Motion tour around the world in a wheelchair. He covered 24,901 miles (40,073 kilometres) and wheeled through 34 countries. The tour lasted from March 21, 1985 to May 22, 1987, a total of 792 days.

In 1983, he shared athlete-of-the-year honours with Wayne Gretzky; in 1987 he became a Companion of the Order of Canada, and he was the commissioner general for the Canadian Pavilion for the 1988 World Expo in Australia. He is now married to Amanda Reid, living in Richmond B.C., and working as a consultant on disability to the president of U.B.C.

Q

During the Man in Motion tour, you spoke many times each day, and yet you made each group and each speech special. How did you do it?

A

When I am speaking to the public, whether it's one person or 100 000 people, I want them to perceive me as I am feeling. I try to wipe the slate clean of the last speech because every speech is different—different environment, different people. What you have to do is come from the heart, speak from the heart in a way that allows people to gain a sense of what you feel, as well as what you think. They must know that you care about them, that you think they are important.

These days, so many people are getting into public speaking, and becoming proficient at it, even slick. They get mechanical and monotonous or repetitious, sometimes losing the life, and the feeling, and the essence of what speaking is all about. It's storytelling, and communicating, and educating. (I think that part of public speaking has got to be preserved.)

Q

Even when you were exhausted, you made that kind of effort?

A

No doubt about it. There were times when I came in from the road and I was just fried. I'd wheeled 70 miles that day, dealing with headwinds and shoulder injuries, and perhaps be cold and wet. We'd also have to deal with logistical matters and crew problems. Then, I had to turn around, and go out into a town hall where there were 300 people waiting, and they'd been there for four hours. The last thing you feel like doing is trying to overcome what you're feeling—which is a lot of depression, anguish, and pain.

You have to dig down very deep within you, to the essence of what drives you, and come up with not the image of somebody who's hurting, but the image of somebody who is positive, who has a wonderful message that's important for people to listen to. You want to make those people feel important, they're the most important people in your day, in your life, at that time.

Q

What inspired you on the tough days?

A

It's the sum of all the people on the tour that made it the success that it was. No one individual or group was more important than the other, including myself. We were all important, integral parts; we were a team. I had to come up with that. And I think it was my inherent belief in the dream, my commitment to it, and the teamwork around me, that allowed me to perform on those tough days when I didn't think I could.

When you're tired and at the edge, and you don't think you have any more to give, sometimes that's when you come up with your best performances.

Q

How did people respond?

A

That was the magic of the tour. People could relate to it in normal life; it leapt the bounds of disability. Anyone who is setting goals, chasing dreams, dealing with adversity and setbacks along the way, could relate to the message. They realized the value of teamwork, of cooperative endeavour, of the results possible when they challenge themselves.

Q
When you spoke at the Bowden Correctional Centre in Alberta, you started your speech with the line, "We are all imprisoned in different ways." That was a great way to establish a bond. How do you do that?

A
I treat each crowd differently. I never say the same thing. My words reflect a lot of the crowd I'm with. At Bowden, I wanted to say something those guys could relate to. It was important to find an analogy. They have their own personal battles to deal with, and I wanted them to be able to relate to the message, and perhaps, in turn, find inspiration for their own lives.

Q
How long did it take to find that opening?

A
It was spontaneous. I don't like to come into a place with set lines because so much depends on the crowd and the atmosphere. You have to be organized, don't get me wrong, but you also have to leave room to react spontaneously.

Q
What was your message? What were you out there to tell us?

A
What inspired me on my journey was not trying to raise funds for spinal cord injury research, but the inherent message Terry Fox delivered. Terry was a good friend of mine and although he was trying to raise money for cancer research, he created so much awareness of the potential of disabled persons. He brought the country together; he made people feel a way they had perhaps never felt before.

That message of awareness of disabled persons was so important. I thought if I could challenge myself to fulfil an old dream of physically wheeling around the world, and bring that message with me, that I could be a catalyst. I could be a messenger for a better understanding of disabled persons.

Q
What challenges did you issue?

A
I wanted to challenge people in their communities to see how they could remove the many barriers that still remain in the way of dis-

abled persons achieving their potential. Outdated attitudes and physical obstacles have to be removed. We need to instil the idea that it's a community effort. Sometimes people want to slough it off; it's not their responsibility. But it's only a split second away from happening to anyone of us. [*Rick Hansen was 15 when the truck in which he was riding was involved in an accident. As a result of the injuries he received, he is a paraplegic.*]

We have to take that responsibility. We don't want to hand things out to people, but we do want to be compassionate. We want to know how we can help them achieve their potential, to get out and be successful in life again, be productive citizens, enjoy what they can in their own lives. That's the inherent message of my journey.

Q
Did you see evidence of change in your travels?

A
Yes, it was wonderful to see improved facilities, better funding, educational programmes, new legislation, and changed attitudes on the part of the government and the public.

Q

Do you get nervous when you speak?

A

I get nervous when I have to be organized for an extended speech. I don't get nervous when I speak from the heart, but I'm also trying to learn to be organized for a longer presentation. The combination of being organized and maintaining sincerity means so much to me that I get nervous.

I'm new to a more formal speaking style. The message or vision is always clear, but I'm always tired and in a hurry. I want to have enough control so that I can get off a plane and know I can always come through. I don't want to rely on having a good day, but be sure I can do it. Last week, I spoke to an IBM conference; I was well organized and decided to break from the set speech and expand personally on a few points. I expanded from 35 minutes to 50 minutes. It was still quite successful I think.

Q

What speech of yours sticks in your mind?

A

My little speech in B.C. Place. I was home in Vancouver in a stadium and I thought a lot about what I wanted to tell them about Rick Hansen. I wanted to tell them about our dream, the vision that we worked for as a team. My tour is over and yet the challenge is still there. I wanted them to know, and I want each person out there to realize that it's their turn to carry on. I'll be there to support them.

Q

What advice do you have for people who want to speak well?

A

Organize yourselves. Speak from the heart. Be sincere. Give the audience everything that's in you, just like it's your first speech. Have a feeling for the audience and a sense of being with them. If you're speaking to kids, don't revert to old ideas of "adults and kids." Just talk to them so they understand you, and so that you have a feeling for them and what they face.

Rick Hansen
Speech: The Dream is Just Beginning

Rick Hansen and his team took his message to the entire world. These are excerpts taken from his remarks on the road. They show the determination and faith in people that took him 24,901 miles around the globe.

I see myself only as a catalyst. I want to deliver a message to the world, to challenge people to have positive attitudes about disabled persons, and to take action to break down barriers standing in the way of their potential.

We all have perceived disabilities of one kind or another. There are many setbacks in life and I'm wheeling to show that these setbacks *can* be overcome. So never give up on your dreams.

I believe there is a direct link between the physical and emotional rebuilding of one's body. Through rehabilitation, sports, and recreation programs, not only will disabled people be able to get on with their lives, they will be able to re-enter the community and make their own dreams come true.

I'm hoping disabled people will be treated with respect for what they can do, rather than what they can't do. We all deserve the right to live, to be the best we can be. The tour will end in Vancouver but *the dream is just beginning.*

OUTLINE OF A DEMONSTRATION SPEECH

Name: _Hayley Bellingham_

Date of Speech: _Sept_

Purpose Statement: _Demonstration Speech_

INTRODUCTION
~~movie etiquette~~ How to knit

Grabber: mum taught me.

Thesis:

Overview: the major step to knitting a scarf

BODY
Step #1 -planning your scarf

Step #2 - starting
      - knitting

Step #3 - ending

CONCLUSION
Reference to purpose (thesis):

Summary of main steps:

Zinger:

SELF-EVALUATION FORM

This form is to help you evaluate your own speech. It can be kept private or shared with your instructor or peers.

Type of Speech: _____

Name: _____

Title: _____

Date: _____

DELIVERY

Physical Presence

Did I make eye contact with others?

Was my posture natural and appropriate?

Was I aware of my facial expressions and hand gestures?

Were there any distracting mannerisms that I was aware of?

Did I feel good?

Could I feel an energy exchange with my audience?

VOCAL DELIVERY

Was my voice under control?

Did I sound confident?

Was I aware of breathing calmly?

How was my enunciation?

Did I manage to avoid um's and ah's?

Did I sound interested/excited/committed?

How did my voice sound to me?

DESIGN AND CONTENT

How well did the introduction and conclusion work?

Did the framework unify my speech?

Was there a natural progression from point to point?

Did my notes keep me on track? Did I use them?

Did the audience seem to understand the organization of my speech?

Was the information clear?

What was the energy level of the conclusion?

What would I change the next time?

What worked very well?

OVERALL EFFECTIVENESS

Did I connect with this audience?

Did I achieve my purpose?

What do I remember most about making the speech?

What unexpected or unforeseen things happened?

What am I most pleased about?

OTHER COMMENTS

Grade: _____

PEER EVALUATION FORM

Peer evaluation should be done in a constructive and supportive fashion. The speaker may choose people to do assessments or they may be assigned alphabetically. Some groups maintain the same speaker/assessor teams for the entire course; others change for each speech. The instructor may wish to see this evaluation before it goes to the speaker.

Type of Speech: _____

Speaker: _____

Title: _____

Assessor: _____

Date: _____

DELIVERY

Physical Presence

Did the speaker maintain eye contact?

Did she or he establish a rapport with the audience?

Were gestures natural and effective?

VOCAL DELIVERY

Did the speaker sound convincing/spontaneous/excited?

Was his or her voice clear and loud enough?

How did you respond to the speaker's mood?

DESIGN AND CONTENT

Did the introduction interest you?

Did the overview give you an indication of the main proofs?

Did the speech flow easily and logically from one point to another?

Was the conclusion strong and memorable?

Did the conclusion reinforce the thesis and main points?

What was the thesis of the speech?

Were you moved by it?

What was the most outstanding part of the speech?

What changes do you recommend?

What parts should the speaker definitely keep?

OTHER COMMENTS

Grade: _____

EVALUATION FORM

Type of Speech: _____

Name: _____

Title: _____

Length of Speech: _____

Date: _____

Legend: S=Superior   E=Effective   NW=Needs Work

DELIVERY

Physical Presence

Eye Contact

Rapport with Audience

Posture

Gestures

Use of Notes

Appropriate Use of Audio-Visual

Support Material

VOCAL DELIVERY

Naturalness/Spontaneity/Enthusiasm

Clarity

Variety (Tone, Pitch, Pace)

Volume

Absence of Verbal Tics (um, ah, okay, like)

Sense of Control and Calm

DESIGN AND CONTENT

Use of Framework for Introduction and Conclusion

Clear Thesis and Overview

Coherence/Use of Transitions

Strong Finish

Language

Word Choice

Impact on Audience

Grammar

OVERALL EFFECTIVENESS

Treatment of Topic

Intelligent Awareness of Audience

Achievement of Purpose

Impact on/Connection with Audience

OTHER COMMENTS

Grade: _____

CHAPTER

3

Think It Over: The Informative Speech

TIPS FOR SPEAKERS

It is pointless to make an important point in a boring fashion because it may be lost. It has to be made in an entertaining and dramatic way.

(Eddie Greenspan)

1. Use the library and first-hand interviews as research sources.

2. Information is obtained through a process by which facts are gathered, organized, compared, and balanced.

3. Train yourself in speed planning for any topic. A three-part plan always works.

4. A good introduction has a grabber, a clear thesis, and an overview of major points.

5. Visual and audio aids should communicate immediately.

6. There *is* a secret to delivering a good speech—use notes.

7. Save enough energy for a strong finish.

W A R M - U P S

Transportation to Live or Die For—Impromptus on the Move

Divide into groups of two or three people and choose a method of transportation. One speaker will outline the positive aspects of this mode of transportation and the others will discuss its disadvantages. Each person prepares a one-minute speech; preparation time is two to four minutes.

The transportation may be motorized (car, motorcycle, airplane, ship, truck); non-motorized (hot air balloon, glider, bicycle, wagon); animal-powered (horse and wagon, elephant, dog sled); human-powered (walking, skiing, running, snowshoeing, hiking, backpacking); or sports-related (in-line skating, distance swimming, canoeing). You can do your speech on the most dangerous form of transportation or outline the advantages of visualization and psychic travel.

You are encouraged to invent your own data: statistics, examples, personal endorsements, validation by authorities, quotations.

- *Where is the best place to get a charbroiled burger with guacamole and cheddar cheese toppings?*
- *How can you tell the difference between fox tracks and wolf tracks?*
- *How does racism affect our daily lives?*
- *Do you consider the city morgue a possible tourist attraction?*

Any one of the above is a good topic for an informative speech, the purpose of which is to share knowledge and create understanding. If you can find, sort, analyse, simplify, organize, and present your material, you'll be the hit of your company or seminar group. First, there are a few things to learn.

◑ GETTING YOUR SPEECH IN SHAPE

Start by brainstorming the topic and exploring available research resources. Then, move to the general purpose and design of the speech. When you have a firm thesis and outline, concentrate on the introduction and conclusion. They form the framework of your speech and need charity, drama, and impact.

The accompanying flowchart, "Charting Your Success: Preparing a Speech," outlines this process; in this chapter you will learn more of the skills necessary to complete the following steps:

1. Researching;
2. Organizing your materials;

3.   Devising memorable introductions and conclusions;
4.   Making things clearer by using statistics, analogies and audio-visual aids;
5.   Keeping on topic with effective note cards.

As you work through these sections, remember that speeches must be lively as well as informative. As Eddie Greenspan states in the interview that concludes this chapter:

Seize the attention of the audience. Connect with them....Focus on being interesting as well as informative.

Research

Research gives your speech the solidity it needs to be useful and convincing. Once you have a topic, your research will help you discover the essential information you need to know and all the exciting details that will give your work direction and emphasis. There is one warning: Don't go off the deep end! We all know research fanatics who put their anxiety about

Charting Your Success: Preparing A Speech

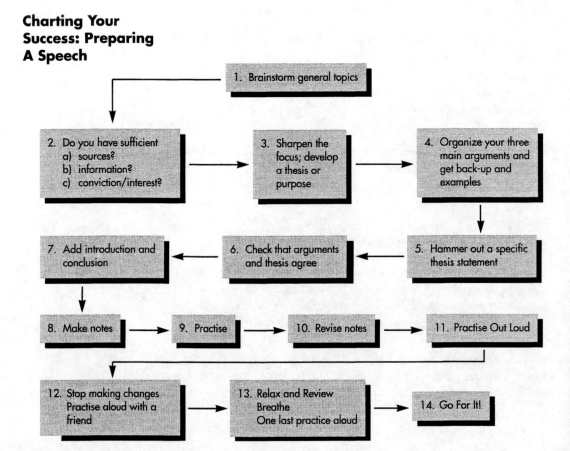

the speech into library hours. They have pages of notes and hundreds of details but no time to practise. Stick to your schedule and control yourself.

Primary Research

Primary research is information you gather yourself. It involves interviews, visits, observation, reading unedited written material (such as scientific reports, trial transcripts, financial reviews). If you are interested in acupuncture, the interviews you do with acupuncturists, doctors, patients, advocates, and critics of the procedure, are primary research. If you have had acupuncture treatments yourself, you are a good source of information.

Secondary Research

The finding, reading, and analysing of written (or taped) material will most often lead you to the library. Stephen Overbury, the consummate Canadian researcher and teacher of research, considers our libraries the best, although most often overlooked, sources of information. In his book, *Finding Canadian Facts Fast*, he writes:

There are at least three things you can be sure of about libraries: they collect information on every subject; the information can always be located; and the librarians who run them have been trained to meet your information needs.
(STEPHEN OVERBURY, FINDING CANADIAN FACTS FAST. TORONTO; METHUEN 1985. P. 85)

Using the card catalogue or microfiche to search for information by author, title, or subject is a starting point. Once you consult these, it may be appropriate to check periodical indexes to obtain the most current information. Your search might proceed like this:

1. Using the catalogues, find and skim a book, article, encyclopedia entry, or vertical file to get an overview of your subject.
2. Ask the librarian about vertical files (up-to-date collections of clippings and articles).
3. Check standard reference books, including the *Canadian Encyclopedia*, the *Encyclopedia Britannica*, *Canada Year Book*, *Consumer Reports*, *Canadian Who's Who*, and so on.
4. Skim or read as much material on your subject as you need to formulate ideas and plans for your speech. Keep in mind the questions "Why am I speaking? What do I hope to explain, demonstrate, or advocate?"
5. Try to zero in on particular issues; this will help you to find information more quickly and lead to a firm thesis. Use geographic areas, specific time frames, or theories to narrow the field.

6.   Check the indexes for articles in magazines and journals. These are often the most recent sources. The following indexes are relatively simple to use; ask the library staff if you need help.
Canadian Periodical Index, Canadian News Index, Canadian Business Index, Microlog Index, Standard Periodical Directory.

7.   If you need still more information, ask the librarian. He or she may suggest an on-line computer search (costs vary), or direct you to the *Directory of Associations in Canada,* a listing of over 8000 associations, which are all potential sources of expert information.

8.   Do you need pungent quotations? Check out all of John Robert Colombo's books: *Canadian Quotations, Canadian References, Canadian Place Names, Canadiana Quiz,* and more.

In all cases, make sure to get the bibliographic details as you work: author, title, date, and place of publication or broadcast. You may not be asked for this information but you must have it.

Evaluate Your Sources

There is no such thing as objective reality. We each select our experiences through the filters of our genes, values and belief systems. Ask a logger from B.C. and a Haida Indian to talk about the importance of a virgin stand of cedar trees or a Bay Street businessman and a person on welfare about taxes and social services. You would swear from their responses that they come from different worlds.

(DAVID SUZUKI. METAMORPHOSIS. TORONTO: STODDART, 1987. P. 5)

"My nation was ignored in your history textbooks."
(CHIEF DAN GEORGE)

Evaluate your material as you work; you may reject a book or article without wasting time making notes, or you may decide to read the work and check it against other sources. As you gather and organize your material, you must evaluate constantly: you will eventually have to make the decision whether to use the material.

For example, Canadian history books written in English before 1960 state that Louis Riel was a traitor; present texts describe him as a leader of the Métis, and a Canadian hero. What accounts for the difference?

Anyone researching AIDS will run into a similar dilemma; various sources will advocate differing, even conflicting suggestions. Take, for example the question of introducing needle-exchange programs for intravenous drug users—a high-risk group. When you read articles or hear debates on this issue, what factors would you need to consider to test the validity of the argument?

You will often have to compare one source to another. This cross-testing will help you make an informed judgement. In deciding whether to accept or reject information, you should start by examining the following:

1. The author. Is the author an expert in that field? Does he or she have suitable credentials? A member of the National Council on the study of HIV/AIDS or a member of a local HIV/AIDS network may have a better grasp of the situation than a right-wing tabloid that opposes all help for, or understanding of, minority groups.

2. The tone. Is the tone reasonable? Is there evidence of scientific proof and fair investigation? Does the author show more interest in solving the problem, or avoiding political and social controversy?

3. The publication. Is the publisher well known, with a reputation for fairness? Does the material come from a professional journal or an inflammatory magazine? Which newspapers, magazines, radio and television shows in your area are
   - fair?
   - known for balanced reporting?
   - biased?
   - more interested in mass appeal or sensationalism?

   As Overbury states: "slanted material is not necessarily unusable—it may be used in context—but you must be aware of the bias in order to make good use of it" (Overbury p. 7).

4. Date and place of the report or publication. Time can make substantial differences in research results, public attitudes, and views concerning social and health issues. Big cities will often pioneer techniques that affect larger numbers of their population long before smaller centres feel the pressure to concern themselves. On the other hand, local newspapers highlight issues, such as the closing of rural post offices, that national journals overlook.

Exercise: Balancing Your Sources

Where would you go to find a fair and balanced evaluation of the following?

How to finance a car

The contribution of Quebec to Canada

Importance of k.d. lang to Canadian music

The housing situation in your city or province

Whether to increase or cut the amount of money available for student loans.

Using Research Correctly

Completing the Process

Gathering the facts does not mean you have finished your research; you must now classify and weigh the material. Stephen Overbury tells of selling a potentially explosive article on the exporting of tank engines to South Africa, a violation of the United Nations arms embargo. Unfortunately for the article, the engines were for trucks, not tanks, and although Overbury salvaged the story, he warns of the danger of faulty assumptions and incomplete research:

Gathering random facts does not necessarily mean obtaining information. Information is obtained through a process by which facts are gathered, organized, compared, and balanced in a logical manner.
   (OVERBURY. P. XII)

Avoiding Plagiarism

If you are preparing a speech about the responsibilities of a fire crew boss working for the Ministry of Natural Resources, much of what you learn may be new to you. All information considered public knowledge can be used without specific acknowledgment. However, if you get into value judgments about techniques used, whether there is enough regulation of fire crews, or sufficient on-the-job training, you must be prepared to acknowledge your sources and give them credit (and blame) for your statements.

Similarly, if you use other people's ideas, even if you do not quote directly, you should give them credit. Although it is hard to know when to acknowledge sources, you should be very careful in this area and err on the side of caution.

Plagiarism occurs when you knowingly pass off the work, works, or ideas of others as your own. It is a mean-spirited thing to do. And it's illegal.

◑ ORGANIZING YOUR INFORMATION: THE PRINCIPLE OF THREE

Organize your observations, arguments, steps, explanations, and exhortations into three manageable, memorable segments.

This organizational method is clear, it's simple, and it works for anything. Are you going to praise the attractions of Peggy's Cove? How will you organize your mass of enthusiastic observations? Try three main categories:

1. The beauty of the Nova Scotian coast;
2. The richness of local folklore;
3. The superb seafood.

This same system will work for the mountain of information you have on the Chilkoot Pass, the gateway to the fabled Klondike Gold Rush Route. If you want to convey the thrill of hiking the Chilkoot, you can concentrate on

1. The history of the Klondike Rush of 1898;
2. Scenery;
3. Climbing adventures.

Each major section has subsections so that you can work a considerable amount of information into your speech and present it so clearly that your audience will remember what you have to say. To do this, jot down significant points for each main section, look for ideas or themes that go together, experiment with mini-plans, and you're ready.

This takes practice; once you are used to taking an idea and breaking it into main ideas and supporting subsections, you'll be able to do it in seconds.

What Determines the Order of Your Main Points?

The nature of your speech, the occasion, and your common sense will tell you how to order the various sections. Your aim is to approach the subject in a way that you and your audience will enjoy pursuing.

1. Chronological order. Events that have a certain sequence, such as a marketing strategy or medical procedure, should be outlined in the order they occur. Reverse chronological order is also a clear way to organize your points.
2. Flashback or flashforward. Add a little drama by starting at one point, and casting forward or back in time to present the material.
3. Spatial order. If you're discussing the design of a recreation centre or the safest, most efficient arrangement of machinery in a small manufacturing plant, spatial ordering is most logical. Geographical order is easy to follow if you're outlining national concerns like weather or trade patterns, or tourist concentrations.
4. Cause-and-effect order. Do you want to illustrate the unquestionable link between a smoke-free workplace and the reduction of employee sick days? Are you advocating the use of incentives to increase productivity or performance? How about free trips to Hawaii guaranteeing better examination results? Audiences are intrigued by this very clear and interesting approach.
5. All-things-being-equal order. Sometimes all the factors are equal and anything will work. It's up to you to decide on an approach that will

The principle of three: environmentalists ask people to "Reduce, Re-use, Recycle."

be logical and interesting. If you're giving the orientation speech for new counsellors at a drug rehabilitation centre and you want to talk about the major times for vigilance, you might decide to work from the most to least obvious times of stress. Use the approach that makes sense and interests you.

6. Climactic order. Saving the best for last is a method you've used many times. Whenever you argued with a younger brother or sister about whose turn it was to clean up, the arguments went: "it's only fair to share the job; most of this is your stuff; if you don't do it, I'm going to tell you came home late on Saturday." That's climactic order; choose the most convincing reason and save it for a strong, energetic finish.

7. When you're desperate. If nothing works, remember you can always discuss anything using the categories of physical, emotional, and psychological. It's an overused strategy, but you may need it as a last resort. For example, the physical, emotional, and psychological
   - appeal of colour on cereal boxes;
   - impact of portable radio headsets in the workplace;
   - benefits of pets in senior citizens' centres.

Smooth Transitions

How do you move from point to point smoothly? If you watch a relay race, you'll see that the switch-over is a crucial moment that runners practise often. In your speech, you need that same grace to move naturally from one idea to the next. If your overview is clear, your audience will know your main arguments and be ready for the switch. Here are words speakers use to make clear, logical transitions.

TRANSITIONAL DEVICES

Adding a point

and	another	furthermore
also	a second point	in the same way
besides	likewise	in addition
next	too	
or	as well as	
again	in addition	
further	by comparison	
moveover		

Emphasizing a point

above all	in fact	especially
certainly	to be sure	in particular

chiefly
doubtless
indeed

without doubt
unquestionably
for sure

even more important
to repeat

Showing similarity
in like manner
in the same way
similarly

Introducing examples or details
for example
for instance
as you can see
to illustrate

namely
such as
that is
the following

specifically
in particular
for one thing
in fact

Restating a point
in other words
in effect
similarly
that is

to put it another way
in short
that is to say
if we look at it from a different perspective

Introducing a contrast or qualification
although
but
conversely
however
in contrast
nevertheless
nonetheless
on the contrary
on the other hand
otherwise
still

unlike
while
yet
despite
surely
unfortunately
conversely
granted
even if
occasionally

whereas
after all
admittedly
in spite of
if

Showing result/cause and effect
as
because
for
for that
reason
since
accordingly
as a result
consequently

then
therefore
thus
it follows that
hence
so

Showing connections in time

before	next	when
previously	tomorrow	thereafter
formerly	immediately	lately
once	soon	eventually
earlier	in the future	subsequently
now	shortly	ultimately
presently	at the same time	final
meanwhile	simultaneously	in the past
at this time	at this time	
at present	after	
nowadays	afterward	
then		

Indicating chronology or sequence

finally
first, second, third...
first, secondly, thirdly...
    (do not use firstly)
next
in the first place, second place...
at first
to begin with
next, also then, moving along
at the end, at last, finally

Concluding

(try to aim for something more original than "in conclusion.")

in brief	as a result
to sum up	therefore
on the whole	consequently
finally	accordingly
all together	to conclude
as we have	thus
seen	
lastly	

With thanks to Robyn Knapp, Centennial College

Exercise: Group Speed Planning

1. To develop your skills in breaking down a topic into sections and sub-sections, convince your friends to play this game. Make sure that everyone understands the three-part, step-by-step method outlined in this chapter and make a list of topics. You can do this by brainstorming together, using the first five ideas you see in the newspaper, or covering your eyes and pointing at part of a list in this exercise. Remember, all topics are fair game. Everyone gets the same number of topics and the same amount of time.

2. Now, spend five or ten minutes working out plans and then read them to each other asking for comments, criticism, and praise. The criteria for evaluating a plan are the same you would apply to a speech:
   a) Is it clear?
   b) Is it complete?
   c) Is it coherent?
   d) Is it convincing?

3. Ready for a practice? Take an example from a social service worker's speech on the correct response to an abused child. The three main sections are attitude, tone, and words. In two minutes, think up the subsections for each. Attitude might include respect, care, belief; tone will include caring, reassurance, encouragement, protection; words will tell the child that the worker is sorry that it happened, that it isn't the child's fault, and that help is on the way.

4. Need topics to start you off? Try these:
   censorship on the Internet
   safer sex
   minimum wages
   running shoes
   tanning salons
   diet centres
   importance of sunlight
   high-performance cars
   "hot" vacation spots
   stereotyping
   junk food
   domed cities
   Star War addicts
   STDs
   student discounts for travel
   meaning of dreams

Exercise: Thesis Olympics

By now, you should be ready to challenge the other members of the class. Your instructor provides suitable prizes: stale doughnuts are a favourite.

a)   Divide the class into four groups, sitting in clusters.

b)   You are given one minute to choose a general topic.

c)   Write the topic on a piece of paper.

d)   On a given signal, pass the paper clockwise to the next group. At the same time, you will receive your topic.

e)   Take two minutes to hammer out the thesis statement and an overview of three main points. The instructor may award bonus marks for a precise, complete thesis and overview.

f)   Once you are accomplished at this game, step (e) can be amended so that the first group finished, in whatever amount of time, wins.

Students quickly learn to give their competitors challenging topics. Recent games have yielded the following subjects: eyeware, volcanoes, guaranteed minimum income, nuclear submarines, female police officers, gasoline, endangered species, daycare for farm families, radioactivity, centrifugal force, and monkeys.

Street Practice

Use the time walking or driving to work or school to practise on your own. Whatever you pass, whatever comes to mind, chart it into a workable plan. Is there a street musician on the corner?

Instruments: guitar, accordion, saxophone.
Success: Money, crowds, general appearance.

Did someone cut you off at the intersection?

Reasons: Type A, fatigue, mindless wonder.
Personality changes in a car: Mean machine, ruthless competition, status.

Having coffee in a doughnut shop?

Doughnuts: calories, freshness, sugar powder on your face.
Sociological studies possible: Workers getting a sugar boost for the drive ahead, the aimless and homeless putting in time, the regulars gathering for gossip and neighbourhood analysis.

Eventually, you'll be so good at this that the division of major topics will go smoothly.

Once your thesis and overview are in place, and the order of your supporting arguments established, you can add examples. Then it's time to design a framework for speech: the introduction and conclusion.

◑ GETTING IN—GREAT INTRODUCTIONS

Seize the audience's attention. Once they are listening attentively, deliver your thesis and overview. Good speakers experiment with openings that actively intrigue listeners. These openings are called grabbers and have two main functions: to seize the attention of the audience and make them want to listen; and to give both the speaker and the listeners a chance to locate each other. It takes a few minutes for people to become attuned to your voice, observe your body language, focus on you. If you're in a good room, you will have a chance to gauge the audience, sense their mood and their responsiveness. Grabbers are worth the time you spend designing them—they set the mood of your whole speech. When you're planning the grabber, remember these pointers:

- **Your Audience:** Who is out there? Why have they come to hear you speak? How can you reach them?
- **Yourself:** Like your own speech. Believe in yourself and what you have to say. Find a grabber you feel good about.
- **Frame Your Speech:** Think of a picture frame with the main body of your speech inside the frame like the canvas. The frame itself consists of the grabber and your conclusion—if you link the grabber to the conclusion, you achieve a sense of wholeness. The audience thinks, "Hey, that final example relates back to the story in the introduction." They enjoy the sense of completeness.
- **Be Entertaining:** How do you make the proposal for an industrial park lively? Why not take in three briefcases: a traditional attaché case, a bright green case, and a backpack. Each bag relates to a part of the presentation: the attaché case holds the technical outline and financial overview; the green case has the environmental background of the project; and the backpack has the section of the report that details community benefits. Put the appropriate overheads inside each bag. This simple technique, as well as providing colour and suspense, also gives the audience a memory aid—they associate the arguments with the appropriate bag. (If you think this might be "gimmicky," try the word "interesting" instead.)

Choosing Your Grabber

Getting in as a speaker is like getting in as a swimmer; depending on your style, and the climate of the group, you can ease in slowly, dive in gracefully, or jump in feet first. Usually, you can't decide to forget it and go make a sandwich. Here's a list of common grabbers—all are effective in the right circumstances.

- Stories and Examples

- Real Stuff
- Direct Approach
- Unusual or Startling Statement
- Quotations
- Humour
- Music
- Historical References
- Special Occasion

Stories and Examples

Stories touch people. No matter how sophisticated your audience or your topic, telling a story intrigues your listeners. A baseball story or camping memories make the discussion more human and immediate.

Have you ever dreamt of inventing, developing, and marketing a product that absolutely sweeps the market? The passion, the dedication, the sheer gall of what it takes was summed up by Ron Foxcroft, inventor of the Fox 40 whistle—the unbelievably loud, "pea-less" whistle, marketed as the ultimate referee's whistle and the loudest street-safety signal. Foxcroft started his presentation by describing the fear he once felt for his life at a pre-Olympic basketball game in Brazil. He had blown a conventional whistle to declare the ball out of play but the ball or pea in the whistle jammed. When the crowd found out that their team's basket did not count and play had to go back to the point where he had made his ruling, they rioted onto the court. Foxcroft vowed that if he got out alive, he would invent a never-fail whistle.

I love this story. I remember it years after I first heard it and I remember almost all of the presentation. Desperation drove him to his most daring marketing move. He went to the Pan-American games with two prototypes of the whistle in his pocket; it had cost him $150,000 to get that far and if he didn't get orders, he was doomed. In the middle of the night, he blew the Fox 40 in the hallway of the coaches' dorm. They all responded to the noise and immediately placed orders for the incredible whistle. Fox 40 was a hit!

What happens to people when they tell a story? If they've chosen wisely, they relax and get involved in the telling. What happens to the audience? They become interested and are eager to hear more. Audiences are tired of fancy bar graphs and reams of stats; they're either inundated with expert opinions or don't believe them. Stories work.

Diane Francis, business commentator and analyst, uses anecdotes to explain financial matters:

"Business is as interesting as watching paint dry. It's full of details and numbers. But it's the people who do business that are interesting...Business is like sport— it involves people and action."

Where do you find stories? All around you. Remember the things you see that you consider significant or touching. Jot down examples that you read or hear on the radio or television. Ask your friends and colleagues. And remember, use stories that mean something to you; you'll be able to tell them better than anecdotes you plucked at random from a reference book.

Real Stuff

This is my own term for three-dimensional objects that you place in front of your audience as you speak. These things embody each of your main points and they provide visual appeal as you speak. For the most part, they are "found" objects, discovered in the back of your cupboard, garage sales, offbeat stores. How do they work? Last year I gave a speech to educators on the "elements" of elementary school. As I discussed the traditional elements—earth, air, fire, and water and related them to values, creativity, passion, and life force—I unrolled colourful banners. The technique added suspense: what did each colour represent? The banner also provided a great conclusion; when I had finished, I had the basis of a rainbow and children are the rainbow, the promise of our world.

For a workshop with workers in a women's shelter entitled "Being There When Things Are Tough" the props fit in a bag: a statue of a robin hunched down in its feathers, a lucky rock, and my coffee mug. The robin reminds us to listen bravely, hunkered down in the storm. The rock is for staying grounded, being there, listening. The mug is for making tea, a simple way to care for someone. Each prop introduces one of the strategies; people remember real stuff and the concepts that it embodies.

Why use this technique? It's fun. It's a change. Sometimes speakers won't use the simple examples all around them; they go for complicated abstractions and everyone gets lost.

Suggestions for Real Stuff

- a child's top that plays tunes —used to show that traditional toys can have a new "spin,"
- an onion used to show that people may pretend to be dry and crusty on the surface but are tender and they weep on the inside.
- a new version of stacking dolls—a cob of corn that opens down the back; inside are smaller cobs of corn that also open to reveal mini-cobs.

Direct Approach

Faith Popcorn is a dynamic speaker who has predicted the major trends of the 1980s and 1990s. *The Popcorn Report,* starts with the sentence:

These are bizarre times.

The next few sentences outline the socioquake that will change mainstream consumer America. This is an example of the direct approach. If your topic is so dramatic or your commitment so intense, the sincere or direct approach is often the best.

Do not use this type of grabber lightly; it only works if the topic is serious and your commitment to it obvious.

Unusual or Startling Statement

Sheri Alexander, a travel counsellor, surprised her audience to attention with this grabber:

If malaria, yellow fever, and hepatitis don't mean anything to you, maybe the words "lawsuit," "reputation," and "unemployment" do. It is your legal responsibility as travel agents to make sure that the health requirements of your clients have been outlined before their departure.

Questions can be used to intrigue your listeners. "What word are government officials forbidden to say?" (The answer is recession.)

On a more serious note, last month I heard a man from Northern Ontario begin his talk with the stark statement: "A better air ambulance system would have saved my son's life."

Statistics

Statistics must be brief and breathtaking to work as a grabber. In Faith Popcorn's discussion of "Down-Aging," she says that in the 1989 New York Marathon over 10,000 runners or an incredible 42 percent were over 40! The numbers amazed me as much as the feat.

CRISIS CONTROL:

Your statement may be unusual or challenging but it cannot be insulting or your listeners will retaliate by closing their minds. Telling a group that they are the most poorly motivated, coffee-swilling underachievers that you've ever encountered is a turnoff, not a grabber.

Quotations

Which quotations work? How do you fit them in? After years of hearing speeches I have one plea: do not use encyclopedias of quotations simply to get a remark that relates, however obscurely, to your topic. It is stilted to start a speech about light rapid transit with the phrase: "As Descartes so aptly put it." Or discussions of marketing strategies that refer to Cicero, Masefield, or Hegel. Where are the people we recognize and value—Alice Walker, Nelson Mandela, Martina Navratilova, Gandhi, Michelle Landsberg, Martin Luther King Jr., David Suzuki, Gloria Steinem, Elijah Harper, Svend Robinson, Erica Ehm, Lily Tomlin, Thomson Highway?

Use quotations that have internal resonance for you and your audience. And once you've used them, refer to them later in your speech to make it clear why they were chosen.

Build your own reference file; when you listen to the radio or scan the paper, copy down quotations or lyrics that impress you. Several of my favourites are

Friends take you along but they don't always bring you back. Miss Eva John always said that.
(GARTH JOHN—STUDENT, CENTENNIAL COLLEGE)

Early to bed, early to rise, never get tight and advertise.
(TIMOTHY EATON, FOUNDER OF EATON'S DEPARTMENT STORES)

We don't kill people who talk about self-esteem by beating them to death like they did to Steve Biko. We kill them with ridicule.
(GLORIA STEINEM)

Free your mind and the rest will follow.
(k.d. lang)

Trust in God but tie your camel.
(SUFI SAYING)

Women have cleaned up things since time began, and if women get into politics there will be a cleaning up of pigeon holes and forgotten corners...The sound of the political carpet-beater will be heard in the land.
(NELLIE L. MCCLUNG)

I am convinced that intelligence, patience, and eloquence can, sooner or later, lead the human race out of its self-imposed tortures provided it does not exterminate itself in the meantime.
(BERTRAND RUSSELL)

Humour

Why is humour so far down the list? Because it is such a dicey subject. Experienced speakers use humour in the form of stories or shared experiences that everyone in the group can laugh at. But for too many people, humour means jokes; indeed books for the old way of speaking recommend starting your speech with a few jokes. And the examples they give are often racist or sexist or homophobic. How many times have you heard generally decent people start a speech with a string of one-liners that fall flat? They do not intend to be offensive; they are unconsciously repeating old and hurtful patterns.

Humour involves stories that build a feeling of recognition. A sort of "thank god, I'm not the only one; it's happened to you too" feeling. Imagine a circle, everyone is in it, laughing together—rather than insiders laughing at outsiders. For example, Susan Faludi, author of *Backlash,* said that she was so afraid of public speaking that she once stood "knock-kneed and green-gilled before 300 people. Was it too late to plead a severe case of laryngitis? I am Woman, Hear Me Whisper."

Music

Books are not your only source of quotations; "Give Peace a Chance" and "We Shall Overcome" are familiar to all of us. From k.d. lang to Woody Guthrie or Sweet Honey in the Rock, from Judy Garland to Prairie Oyster, music can enliven a speech and provide just the right words. Quote the lyrics or put the song on a tape and watch the looks of delight and surprise on the faces of your listeners. Be sure to clarify how the words and music relate to your topic.

Historical References

Events in the lives of great people such as Martin Luther King, Jr. or Amelia Earhart can provide a good starting point for your talk. You can refer to specific national events or to environmental turning points. Make sure to choose an historical event that means something to you. One student used the example of Norman Bethune to open a speech on inventiveness: Bethune was so determined to cure his own case of tuberculosis that he pioneered a new surgical procedure and experimented on himself.

Special Occasions

Often our speaking date coincides with an important occasion: Person's Day, Deepavali, summer solstice, Groundhog Day. When you're asked to "make a few remarks" or "bring greetings" (such terms!), make those comments worthwhile. Referring to a special day and talking about it can add interest and substance to your greetings. Examples?

Person's Day. Canadian women were declared persons on October 18, 1929—what does it mean to be a person? Do we have full and equal rights under the law today?

Deepavali. The Hindu celebration of light. What kinds of light would you celebrate: street lights in dangerous places, spotlights on the unheralded, lamps of learning, candles for hope?

Summer solstice. What does the ritual change of season bring to the world?

Groundhog Day. While you had the television cameras of the world hovering to see if you cast a shadow, what would you say to them?

What Next?

After the grabber, you need a transition—a statement that leads into your thesis and overview. Such a transition might be

"And one of the issues that stands out in this instance is the need for...."
"As so many people have observed recently...."
"And what Greenspan has said applies to all of us..."

Exercise: Changing the Grabber to Suit the Audience

Grabbers change with your topic, your style, and your audience. As a class or group, decide on a single topic. Every member of the group then has eight minutes to decide on a profile of his or her audience and a great grabber. The time allotment includes practice. At the end of eight minutes, everyone stands and delivers; the audience provides encouragement and helpful feedback. (This is a good exercise to videotape.)

◑ FINISHING STRONG—DYNAMIC CONCLUSIONS

Distance runners know the secret of a good race—finish strong. If you watch a 1500-metre race, you'll see the best runners work for a position at the front of the pack; they hold that spot until the last lap when they give a final great push to pull ahead and fly to the finish line.

It takes planning and practice for speakers to save enough material, enough conviction, and enough strength to avoid petering out and **finish strong.** Don't put all your energy into the body of the speech and conclude by saying something like, "Well, I guess that sums it up and I can sit down now." Or worse, repeating every single point you've made until you've exhausted your resources and your audience.

Remember the frame—the idea of your grabber and conclusion tying your arguments together in a solid package? If you started with a story, outline a further development; a startling statement or humourous remark, refer to it, perhaps mentioning another aspect.

Sheri Alexander's feisty conclusion tied in well with her grabber:

Dr. Azouz is here today to make you aware of what you and your clients may be up against once they leave the country. And how you can save their lives— and your neck.

Building Your Conclusion

The function of the conclusion is to reinforce your thesis, review your main points—if necessary—and finish solidly. You and the audience should think, "there, that feels complete." If you have already reviewed your arguments, a complete summary may be unnecessary. Your aim is to remind the audience without boring them. You may wish to urge them to action or point to future possibilities. If it's appropriate, tie in your remarks with the rest of the evening or conference. Whatever you choose to do, end your speech. Wrap it up well and then sit down! Do not ramble or repeat yourself. Finish!

Ending on a high note may come naturally to you. There are also a number of sentence patterns that help your sentences rise to a crescendo. You can build your conclusion with alliteration, a series of parallel questions, or repetition. Jesse Jackson used alliteration in when he promised to "compete without conflict and differ without division." Eddie Greenspan concluded his speech on the futility of the death penalty by referring to Donald Marshall, a New Brunswick native person convicted of a crime he did not commit. Greenspan asked:

"Which of you, sitting here today, could have pulled the bag over his head? Which of you could have fastened the rope around his neck? Which of you could have sprung the trap door which sent Donald Marshall to his death?"

Rose Anne Hart, in a speech found in Chapter 8, urged her audience to pause:

"When you meet someone who is different from you because of nationality, or colour, or religion, obesity, handicap, or sexual orientation, before executing that clever imitation, before making that witty remark, before issuing that curt dismissal—think."

Listen to Your Conclusion

When you practise your speech, listen to your final words. Do you sound clear and strong? Do you sound like yourself? Do **you** sound convinced?

TED MOREAU'S SPEECH—MIDNIGHT HEROES: THE INDEPENDENT TRUCKER

Ted Moreau was asked to speak on an aspect of contemporary work. His aim was to show how the independent trucker used to be a folk hero like the cowboy before technology and societal changes altered the job.

This speech shows how a strong introduction and conclusion can frame a speech and intrigue an audience. The main points are clearly presented and the speech flows smoothly.

1 Introduction

Grabber: "It was 4:30 in the morning. The dimly lit yard was mystical with all the sleeping steel horses lined up in a row. Dad parked the pick-up and slowly we walked towards his rig. The smell of diesel fuel floated up and into me from the oil-soaked gravel lot. Dad opened my door and lifted me high onto the seat. The soft smell of leather, the view and all the knobs and gadgets enchanted me. This was it! The experience of a lifetime."

Thesis: The independent trucker, like the cowboy, was a folk hero. Now, three things have altered this image:

Overview: mobility
           gender roles
           independent status

ll Body

1. mobility:
   —influenced by changes in technology
   —remote area access
   —cost of maintaining remote area access
2. gender roles
   —society has been a major influence
   —changes in trucks make strength less of a factor
   —equal rights
3. independent status
   —primarily influenced by the economy
   —larger companies
   —have to work for others—megacompanies
   —secondarily influenced by technology

III Conclusion

Review: the plight of the trucker today

Zinger: "The independent trucker used to be like the cowboy. He travelled over good roads and bad, in all types of weather, and had the strength to handle the iron horse beneath him. While sitting in a roadside truckstop, drinking strong black coffee and smoking endless cigarettes, he was the essence of the modern hero. My dad, the epitome of the old-time trucker, has retired now and I regret the passing of the trucker hero."

Exercise: Finishing Strong

Using the same topic you prepared for the exercise on grabbers, prepare a strong finishing statement. Together that introduction and conclusion

"Where does the power come from to see the race to its end? From within."

(*Chariots of Fire*)

should form a framework that strengthens your speech. If you need new topics, you might consider

- the importance of water
- the fitness level of Canadians
- are steroids banned substances or part of every athlete's training?
- what's wrong with caffeine?
- chocolate is my downfall
- a personal hero

◑ MAKING THINGS CLEAR: STATISTICS, ANALOGIES, AND VISUAL AIDS

Statistics are numerical facts; they can be clinchers or clunkers in your presentations.

When you use a string of statistics, even if they are impressive, the audience forgets the numbers even before you have finished. Try for one or two outstanding statistics that the audience might remember. Even better, use numbers on a human level. Consider these guidelines.

1. Do not overuse statistics. In her book, *Outrageous Acts and Everyday Rebellions*, Gloria Steinem confesses to "a habit that might be okay in articles but is death in speeches: citing a lot of facts and statistics." Her friend and lecture partner Florence Kennedy told her kindly: "Look, if you're lying in the ditch with a truck on your ankle, you don't send somebody to the library to find out how much the truck weighs. You get it off."
2. Make sure statistics are accurate. Check different sources to make sure that the statistics you are using are fair and unbiased.
3. Use statistics comparatively whenever possible. If you want to stress the plight of the beluga whales found in the Saguenay River northeast of Quebec City, it is not enough to say that there are fewer than 500 left in this area, unless you point out that a century ago there were 5000.
4. Statistics should mean something to the audience. Isolated numbers will not make an impression but examples will. In the case of the belugas, which is a marine mammal at the top of the food chain, recent autopsies have shown levels of PCBs (cancer-causing agents) so high that the beluga corpses should be considered hazardous wastes.

Analogies

Analogies help to make a point by offering the audience a parallel example and asking them to make logical connections. In a speech about the criminal justice system and whether it should rehabilitate criminals or just warehouse them, Greenspan used the analogy he heard from a cab driver:

"The whole process [political activity] is sort of like doing dishes. They're never done—there's always another dirty dish. And it never stops. We have to continue to be vigilant."

(Gerry Rogers)

"Putting people in prison is like putting clothes in the wash without any soap. The clothes get wet but no dirt comes out."

A sports analogy works very well for public speaking. Good skiing and speaking have a lot in common; it looks so easy when you do it well. Only the speaker or skier knows the importance of practice, technique, coaching, and pacing. Only she or he appreciates the rush of adrenalin just before you start. It's that rush that gives you the edge, the desire to go for it and win.

Exercise: A Sports Analogy

Using any sport, develop an analogy to convey how you feel about speaking in public and how you prepare yourself to do well.

Audio and Visual Aids

Audio and visual materials (A-V) can add colour and drama to your speeches. You can use anything from the clunk-clunk, one-at-a-time slide show, to multi-projector images synchronized with music, to short video clips. There are only three rules to consider.

1. Back-up material is just that; it can never replace a good speaker.
2. Do it well or skip it.
3. Never make your speech entirely dependent on any piece of equipment. In an emergency, you must be able to make your speech based on your own knowledge and enthusiasm. Too many speakers tell sorrowful tales of the computer slideshow that wouldn't work.

Be careful about the support materials you select.

The graph	must say something.
The overhead	It must communicate
The object	to the mind, or to emotions,
The video/audio clip	or to both.

Visual aids are used to imprint an image so strongly in the minds of an audience that both the picture and the statement are unforgettable.

The usual advice to beginners is to concentrate on your speech and don't become caught up in the preparation of extravagant audio-visual material. A good rule is to make sure that you spend most of your time designing and practising a clear, coherent, thoughtful speech. Then, if support A-V would *enhance* your delivery, an unprecedented amount of superb material is available. Choose carefully and sparingly.

You are the best judges of good A-V: ask yourself if the material you are considering fulfils the following criteria:

1. Is it necessary?
2. Is it big enough?

3.   Is it clear and colourful?

4.   Is it a grabber?

Materials that are poorly produced, hard to see, used as fillers rather than reinforcement, can detract from your speech.

Types of Visual Aids

1.   Graph, map, or chart. Line graphs, pie graphs, and bar graphs are good ways of illustrating a speech in which numbers are used; they transmit information with immediacy and ease. Look at the examples to see which subjects go well with the different types. Some graphs also make use of pictures to add drama and interest to the presentation; good examples are in all major magazines and newspapers.

Charts are graphic representations of material that compress much information into a form that is easily read and understood. You might use a chart to show the organizational plan of a group or company, or to illustrate the steps in the manufacture of a product.

Maps are often used to indicate patterns: weather movement, immigration, import/export trends, tourism. If you draw your own map, or use one that is already available, make sure that the information you wish to convey is emphasized, that you colour the map to focus on selected detail.

When using graphs, charts, and maps, ensure that the colours are sufficiently vivid and contrasting to communicate easily, that the size of the letters is adequate for viewing from a distance, and that you provide clear, interesting, lively interpretation.

2.   Slides and overhead projectors. Many topics, especially those related to tourism, or to a process or a product, are naturals for slide back-up. Use your own, or part of a collection provided by a resource library. Make sure that the slides you use are simple and uncluttered. It is more effective to use several, vivid pictures to get the message across than to rely on a dense, confusing shot. For all presentations involving A-V equipment, consult the checklists. For now, remember only the most important advice.

 •   Practise your speech with the slides several times in advance;

 •   Never use material you've never seen or rehearsed with;

 •   Always carry an extra bulb, your own extension cord, and, unless you really trust the contact person, your own projector;

 •   Keep your upside-down or out-of-focus pictures for your own private shows.

 •   Explain the material as you use it. It may not seem as obvious to everyone else as it does to you.

For some inexplicable reason, people refuse to arrive early or to carry spare parts and extensions. Often the first part of any speech by a novice that requires slides involves protracted and painful apologies, pleas for parts, and general bumbling. Do it well or skip it!

Overhead projectors are portable and easy to use. By combining computer graphics, good colour, and clear lettering, you can create excellent transparencies. Many photocopying machines can produce transparencies directly from printed material and will enlarge or reduce the size. Used in moderation, overhead projectors are helpful. Remember, however, that your face is far more interesting than an endless repetition of diagrams and charts.

3. Pictures and sketches. If you can't bring your Clydesdale to school to demonstrate how to shoe a horse, the next best thing is a sketch or diagram. These take work to do well, and the person who holds up a tiny, smudged drawing immediately loses credibility. Make a clear, colourful drawing and then, just as in your demonstration speech, put the picture at the front of the room and go to the back to check its effectiveness. Can you see it? Can you read it? Never be guilty of introducing an obviously inadequate scrap of paper with the apology: "I know you can't see this very well at the back but...."

4. The blackboard (or whiteboard) is a standard piece of equipment in most lectures and board rooms. Before you use it, ask yourself whether your speech really needs it. Will you spend more time talking to the board as you work than you will explaining things to your audience? Would a chart or picture prepared ahead be better? Can you get to the room ahead of time to put your material on the board before you start? If you use the board, make it brief, and face the audience at least some of the time.

5. Actual objects. You will use objects, such as ski boots, for your informative speech on how to buy downhill equipment to add interest and appeal to your presentation. Make sure that they are large enough to be seen by all and can be carried and handled easily.

6. Video tapes and music. Music can change the pace of your speech as well as make a point. The audience doesn't expect it and are delighted to recognize songs or musicians. Use only as much as you need. To attract attention or reinforce your argument, you need 20 to 30 seconds of a song; don't give in to audience pleas to "play the whole thing."

Well-produced video tapes can also add an extra dimension to your presentation. Again, figure out why you are using it and show only as much of the tape as you need. Your audience will always catch you if you try to fill dead space with second-rate video clips.

"IF YOU CAN'T BRING YOUR
CLYDESDALE TO SCHOOL"

Video tapes are used to reinforce your ideas, to accentuate your speech. They are not used to provide a break from a boring experience. You, the speaker, and your message are most important—the visual and audio aids are back-up.

7. Storyboarding a speech. Storyboarding is a technique used in film to note the shots required for the script; in speaking it refers to matching the key points of the spoken material with slides—dramatic, clear, lively, funny, poignant pictures. If you are promoting the use of puppets to explain surgical procedures to children, or speaking about management's effort to improve employee relations in your company, try to arrange enough lead time to enable you to take slides of the actual people you'll be talking about. Audiences delight in seeing themselves—use discretion in your selection of slides.

8. Human assistants. As sophisticated as we are, an audience is always intrigued by the use of a group member to demonstrate a technique. If you rehearse thoroughly so that the demonstration and the message are clear, and your assistant uses expressions appropriate to the movement, your audience will remember your speech for some time.

Human models also add a sense of theatre: when two helpers act out, for example, showing effective counselling techniques, the speaker can get the message home far more emphatically than is possible with a straight how-to lecture. This approach gives your audience the information they need, and adds drama and the unexpected to your speech.

Keep this type of back-up short. Make the point with the demonstration and stop. It is your job as speaker to outline, clarify, and review. The technique is good as long as it is not overused.

Final Reminders About Audio and Visual Aids

1. Use speaker back-up materials only when necessary, and then only as long as you are talking about them.
2. Use your aids to improve pacing as well as understanding.
3. Do not overuse speaker back-up—too much of anything becomes predictable and boring.
4. Talk to your audience, not the object or picture. If you're using a ski boot, make sure your eyes are directed on the audience, not the inside of the boot. This is harder than it sounds.
5. Make sure that everyone can hear, see, and understand.
6. Move to the screen to point out something on a slide, overhead, or film clip. Don't fumble with pointers or little flashlight arrows; the audience wants to see more than the top of your head as you bend over the work.
7. If you have an assistant to help with the projector, make sure that she or he knows the material and is familiar with the equipment.
8. If you are going to pass around materials, make sure that passing it won't distract your audience.
9. Does the back-up material add clarity, colour, and impact to your presentation?

Exercise: Evaluating Audio-Visual Material

a) Divide into small groups.
b) Choose one or two types of visual aids described in this chapter.
c) Draw up a list of criteria for good examples of the back-up material you selected.
d) Search the building and return with a good example of the material you have chosen. (You may also wish to bring a bad one.)
e) Prepare a presentation using the example(s) you have found.
f) Present criteria for a good example of the back-up material that your group has concentrated on.

◑ NOTES THAT HELP

There *is* a secret to delivering a good speech: use notes.

Everyone gives better speeches, sounds more relaxed, more confident and more sincere when we use notes. It takes practice to do it well, and courage. But it is ultimately much more convincing.

There are two vital reasons why you should not read from a written script:

- **it's boring.** Written language sounds different. The audience knows you're reading and they drift off. They want the speaker to talk to them.
- **it's isolating.** Your only relationship is with the page—your interest in the material is secondary to getting the words out in the order you wrote them. Your first-hand experience, your involvement, your humour, your emotions, are all dulled by the reading. And you can't look up. If you do, you'll lose your place. Eye contact is impossible; how do you know the audience is still there? As Dave Nichol, former President of Loblaw International Merchants, said about poor speakers, "They hang onto that script, they read it—I mean, they shouldn't have chairs, they should have beds for the audience!"

The ideal notes are the ones that work for you. They may vary in style, but you must have them. Notes consist of the main details of your speech written in brief point form. They

- keep you on course;
- provide reassurance;
- rescue you from total blanks. (Have you ever seen a speaker look up at a full auditorium or a video camera and go blank? It won't happen to you.)

Why Notes?

Why use a point-form outline instead of reading from a thick bundle of papers? A speech is a speech; it is not a memorized piece, nor is it a reading—you are talking to the audience, and should sound fluent and natural. Some speakers don't have notes because they researched for so long, they didn't have time to make notes and rehearse.

You have to make a choice. Do you want to be a good speaker or not? If you do, practise using notes. Use your nervousness as a catalyst to get you to rehearse. You don't really need to read the details of where you live and how you got your first job—you know those things! Make clear notes and remember to use them. Pause in your speech, take a breath, look down, and concentrate on where you are.

How do the experts do it?

I work only from notes. I write in note form, sometimes full sentences, on folded pieces of white paper. Never any longer than five sides of notes. Just one word will sometimes remind me of a story. I take care with the opening and the end.

> —JUNE CALLWOOD

Yes, I always use notes rather than writing out a speech word for word.... To write it out word for word, you might as well send a letter. There are things you think of or ways you express yourself while you're standing there. The atmosphere and the circumstances change what you say.

> —GLORIA STEINEM

Here are basic criteria for effective note cards. Experiment and discover what works for you.

MAKING CLEAR SPEECH NOTES

- These are notes, not novels; have a maximum of five to seven cards.
- Put the notes on heavy paper or cards to eliminate shaking.
- The size is up to you—larger cards cut down on the number required.
- Writing must be large and legible—visible at a glance from at least 50 centimetres away
- Use point form.
- Number your arguments. Use a highlighter or coloured pen to highlight key words and arguments.
- You may wish to write essential lines out in full.

(I like to write out my conclusion and any line I worked hard on and consider *essential*, perhaps two or three of these per speech, maximum. When I reach these lines, I don't read them. I make a natural pause, review the exact phrasing, then look directly at the audience, and give them my best shot.)

- Include statistics you might forget.
- Write out punchlines to jokes.
- Number your speech cards.
- Use one side only. (When some people get nervous, they tend to shuffle the cards as they use them. Their careful ordering goes haywire and they never find side seven.)
- Don't have too many cards—know your speech better or use bigger cards to eliminate a constant turning of notes. Your eyes should be on the audience.
- Keep an emergency set of notes at home or in your car.
- Give yourself delivery cues at the sides of the card:

  pause

  relax

  slow down

  smile

  eye contact

  stop dancing

  use visual

  breathe!

- Improvise a podium at home by putting a box on the kitchen table and practise your speech with the cards. Do they work? Is the print large enough? Is revision necessary?

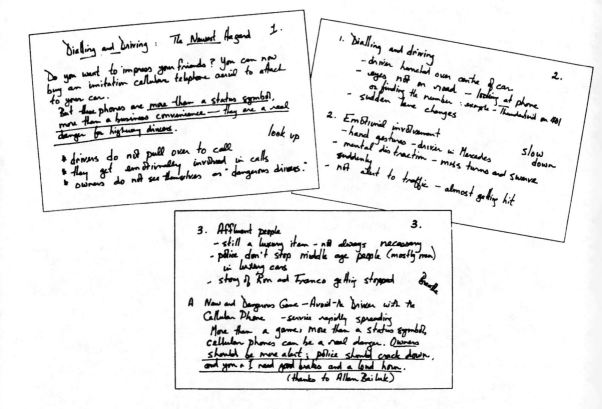

A Note to the Confident

If you know your speech cold and want to dazzle your audience by appearing to wing it, go ahead, but tuck in a set of notes, just in case. Sometimes overconfidence can trip up a good speaker. You may know your speech well when you rehearse it the night before, but the day of your speech may be hectic. You may have to

- take your sick dog to the vet;
- settle a family argument on the way out;
- do a last-minute review for a test;
- go to lunch to celebrate a friend's new job;
- check with the A-V technician that the equipment you need is ready.

Everyone's day is busy; you need good notes. They are your insurance.

Questions To Ask Yourself

1. When do you make your notes? How important is it that you practise with the same notes you will use for the speech?

2. Can you see the cards when they're on a lectern 50 to 60 centimetres from your eyes?
3. Can you find the main points and important examples and statistics when you're excited?
4. Have you used colour to accentuate key ideas?

◑ USE YOUR OWN LANGUAGE

As you prepare your speech, you should be able to hear yourself talking. Do you sound natural? Whether you are describing the operation of a commercial snowmaking machine, explaining a simple process to assistant bakers, or outlining the various options for building an investment plan, you want your audience to understand. That depends on your language. You need to be precise, and use terms correctly. However, do not turn a good talk into a boring lecture full of jargon, careful qualifications, and gutless abstractions.

Use your own language; you should be able to deliver your speech and feel it at the same time. Find your own words; if anything is forced or staged, alter it so that your personality comes through. Remember that speaking from the heart means using words you understand and mean.

Here is advice from the best:

I would try to think of how I would explain it [a scientific paper] to my parents so they could see why it was exciting or important. It's very simple really, but scientists tend to get caught up in fine details and try to qualify everything to be accurate. Too often, the central question and the passion and excitement are drained away.
(DAVID SUZUKI, METAMORPHOSIS, P. 133; SEE ALSO INTERVIEW)

Speakers...use those words to impress others with their knowledge and erudition, and it's absolutely ineffective. Lawyers do it; they love to use words like "purport." Now, I've never sat in a bar and heard anyone use the work "purport" in general banter. And so, I never use that word. I don't need to hide behind my words, to say words that make me sound smart.
(EDDIE GREENSPAN)

Each of us has a way of saying things that is unique: no one else can say them.
(GLORIA STEINEM)

◑ WHAT CAN YOU LEARN FROM A VIDEO TAPE OF YOUR SPEECH?

It's time to see what you do and how you do it. A video tape will show you how you look and sound. Students generally make the following statements; "Is that me?", "I never noticed that I....stood on one foot....said 'um' that many times...looked that confident." You will notice that you look calmer than you often feel; the tape will establish some of your strengths. It is your voice that you hear and it is different from the voice you normally consider yours, because of the sound reverberations in your head. Accept it and find the good aspects of it to emphasize and the weaker ones to correct. Some of you may prefer to start with an audio tape and progress to video. Either way you will be able to assess your voice and pacing as well as the content. Concentrate on what you want to say and the taping will be less obvious.

Taping Exercise: Dynamic Intros and Strong Conclusions

Prepare a dynamic and complete introduction (grabber, thesis, and overview) and a convincing conclusion for one of the following topics:

a) Canada's National Animal Should Be...
b) The Biggest Rip-Off...

Omit the body of the speech; your overview will outline the main supporting reason for your choice. When you replay the tape you can assess the clarity of your organization and your delivery.

Suggestions for Taping

The taping should be a positive experience. The camera operator can place the video camera at the back or side of the room and use a good microphone closer to the speaker, but not at the lectern. Try to include close-ups and distance shots, and views of the speaker's hands and face and even feet. If you use an audio tape recorder, the microphone should be as inconspicuous as possible and the tape long enough so that no one has to interrupt the speaker to flip a tape.

The exercise is short, and if the class is supportive it can be taped and played back in one session. It is important that class members identify with each other and offer praise and encouragement. The individual student can then select the details that he or she would like to improve. Some people like to review the tape in private and submit an evaluation sheet, but at this stage, working and reviewing as a group can be instructive and fun.

◑ THE INFORMATIVE SPEECH

It's time to combine research skills, delivery techniques, and good design in an informative speech. Plan your speech so that your audience will understand and remember your presentation. These guidelines should help:

1. Generate interest. Devise a good grabber. Follow it with convincing reasons why people should listen to you.

2. Make sure the audience understands. If the material is new or complicated, you should check that your listeners are comprehending. Are they nodding their heads in agreement? Are there rumblings of confusion? Ask if you need to clarify a point. Precise suggestions about the application of the information will help.

3. Answer all the basic questions. Who? What? Where? When? Why? How? How much?

4. Emphasize your main ideas. Organize your speech according to the principle of three and make sure your audience follows your progression from point to point. Use transitional remarks such as "having dealt with the need for more jelly in the doughnut, we can examine the third and final problem—messy sugar coatings."

5. Repeat the key ideas. Most teachers know that the secret of getting people to remember is to repeat key ideas three times in different ways: "if you breathe calmly and deeply just before you speak, you'll avoid embarrassing squeaks and breaks in your voice;" "we've all run to the telephone first thing in the morning and, without taking a breath, have answered. What an embarrassing sound comes out." And a few minutes later: "the impression you make will be much better if you remember to take several slow, deep breaths just before you start to speak."

6. Are you excited about your own topic? If you did research that opened up fresh possibilities, or thought of an entirely new approach to a familiar subject, your energy will attract and engage your audience. If you are interested in your material, your enthusiasm will give liveliness and conviction to your performance. That in turn will help your audience become interested, absorb the information, and remember it. The test of a good speech, its organization, research, and delivery, is to see whether the audience can remember the main points the day after they heard it.

7. Are you on schedule? Chapter Two provides a seven-day countdown; here is 24-hour countdown. Let's assume you are speaking at 10:00 on Wednesday morning.

24 HOUR COUNTDOWN

24 hrs. to go	Tuesday	10 a.m.	– make a final copy of notes
		11 a.m.	– rehearse with those notes
			– make sure of examples
			– wow your partner, friend, or cat with your delivery
		11:30 a.m.	Stop Changing Things!
			– Experimenting is over: this is it!
			– Concentrate on delivery
22 hrs. to go.		12 noon	– daily living
			– take care of yourself
14 hrs. to go		8 p.m.	– your lucky friend hears the speech again
			– which anecdotes work best?
			– can he or she identify thesis and overview?
			– you need praise and feedback
12 hrs. to go		10 p.m.	– relax-Stop Practising!
2 hrs. to go	Wednesday	8 a.m.	– get ready:check notes are in order
1 hr. to go		9 a.m.	– start deep breathing for control
			– If speech is short, have a quick run-through; if it's long, just rehearse the introduction, conclusion, and any hard spots.
Blastoff!	10 a.m.		– Breathe, Relax, Good Luck.

SPEECH ASSIGNMENT: THE INFORMATIVE SPEECH

Prepare a three-to-five-minute informative speech.

You may generate the topics yourself or use one of the following suggestions:

1.   Choose an event, a disease, or a discovery that significantly changed the nature of our society. Describe your choice and outline its impact.

2.   Praise or Pan: A Review
Visit a restaurant or hotel in your town or city and prepare a review. The restaurant may be a gourmet place or the local fish-and-chip place, but your review must bethorough and organized according to the Principle of Three outlined in this chapter.

You do not need to stay at the

hotel, but can review its public rooms on the basis of decor, atmosphere, etc. Be sure to include all the basic information (location, cost, etc.) that your audience will want.

3. A Local Treasure

Visit a local spot that is significant for its social, cultural, environmental, historic, or entertainment value. Describe it and outline its worth.

To prepare for this last assignment, brainstorm with a group to get ideas; one group extolled the pleasures of such diverse attractions as a romantic skating rink at the local park, Kensington Market, and the former morgue now used as a police museum.

Brainstorming will help you to develop thoughtful questions:
- When is the spot open?
- When is the best time to visit?
- What group of people would enjoy it most?

- Do you need tickets?
- Is it suitable for all age groups?
- Is it safe? What about fire exits?
- Is it physically demanding?
- Is it suitable for the differently abled?
- Is it wheelchair accessible? Completely or partially?

DELIVERY TECHNIQUES TO REMEMBER

1. Psych yourself up: take deep breaths, anticipate the challenge.
2. Use audio-visual aids naturally: handle them gracefully and address your remarks to the audience.
3. Use energy to build to a strong finish.

INTERVIEW

Eddie Greenspan
Lawyer and Author

Edward Greenspan, Q.C., is a defence lawyer renowned for his championing of the underdog and his outspoken opinions of the Canadian justice system. He is an entertaining speaker, and his clarity and wit make him a favourite as the host/narrator of *The Scales of Justice*, a CBC docu-drama on famous Canadian criminal trials.

Q

What makes a good speech?

A

It must entertain. It is pointless to make an important point in a boring fashion because it may be lost. It has to be made in an entertaining and dramatic way.

A good speech must be made in fairly simple language. It's senseless to use words that are not generally understood. Maybe it's my training as a lawyer; I recall using the work "surreptitiously" when I was addressing a jury, and I saw glazed looks on the faces of the jury that caused me to conclude that they didn't understand what I meant by that word.

When I'm addressing a gathering, I assume that I'm talking to bright high-school students, always. In law school, in writing law exams, we're told to write as though we were trying to explain complicated legal principles to a bright 13-year-old. That's a good rule when you're speaking—speak to a bright 13-year-old. Don't talk down to an audience but don't speak in such complex language or leave the ideas hanging in so complicated a fashion that people simply won't understand your meaning.

Making an analogy is vitally important to making your idea understood. It helps people know precisely what you mean.

Humour is something I always try to inject. No matter how serious the speech, even when I was debating the death penalty, if it was apropos I would make a humourous reference. In the case of topics that are simply not funny, like the prosecution of a hatemonger like Ernst Zundel, no jokes. There are things that are too serious for any levity at all. For some reason, occasional jokes during the death penalty debate were acceptable. But wherever humour can be injected, I will take advantage of it. I won't use constant one-liners, but I will inject humourous remarks to lighten the seriousness of what I am saying in order to keep my audience listening. If you lose your audience, speaking is a waste of everybody's time. When I structure my public speeches, I often begin with three or four humourous anecdotes, to put the audience in a good and receptive mood.

But if you're going to use humour, the depth of the rest of your speech has to be that much better. You cannot keep the speech at a superficial level or you're underestimating your audience.

Q

How do you prepare for a major speech?

A

Because I speak often, if I am attracted to an analogy that I read in the press or in a book, or if I hear it on the radio or on television, I will make a note of it. I collect what I think are good examples of whatever point is being made. Of course, it is always on legal matters. If I am given the task of addressing a group on a certain subject, the first thing I do is gather up the major works on that subject and I read them, so that I'm not missing some issue or point relevant to that topic. I also read minor works or essays so that I am fully aware of competing or opposing views, and take from that material quotes that best sum up what the writers are trying to say. I dictate a summary of my interpretation of what I have read. Then I outline in point form, what the key issues in the area are, pro and con, and from that, I determine what my views are relative to all views on the subject. That is, I look at the popular position on any issue and look to the position of its detractors and dissenters and I try to determine where I stand. I end up with a summary of the main issues and a clear statement of what my views are on the subject. I then go to the material I have collected to see if I can find any quote or story that is appropriate and then I sit down and dictate my speech.

Q
Do you like to know about your audience in advance?

A
I like to know the type of people I'm speaking to, in a general way, so that I know where their interests lie and what part of the community they reflect. Oftentimes while I'm there and I sense the mood of the audience, I may change some of the examples that I intended to use. I always speak to the head-table guests to get a flavour of the organization and the audience.

Q
Why did you spend all that time and energy in the late 1980s speaking against capital punishment?

A
It happened to be an issue

that I was vitally concerned about as a Canadian; it went to the very heart of what I believe. The death penalty was a moral and social issue that I could not remain silent on. Had I done nothing and the death penalty been restored, then I would have been a party by my silence to a significant legislative change that would have been, in my view, a serious step backward. I could not sit silent.

I happen to believe that Canadians are just and decent; the death penalty is neither a just nor appropriate measure for a civilized state to take against crime. Canadians did not seem to know that the death penalty would do nothing to decrease our murder rate.

Q
How do you explain unfamiliar terms?

A
If I'm talking about a concept, like a rehabilitation model of punishment, I won't use any expression unfamiliar to the general public. Or, I'll stop and explain, I'll go back historically. If I'm talking about the rehabilitation model, I'll go back and explain how prisons began and why we have them. For a long time, we thought pris-

oners were sick and needed to get better.
Those theories have been questioned over time. I don't assume that the audience is familiar with the subject of the speech.

Q
What errors do speakers make?

A
Speakers often use terminology that they assume the audience understands when, in fact, they don't. Speakers lose their audiences that way. They use those words to impress others with their knowledge and erudition, and it's absolutely ineffective. Lawyers do it; they love to use words like "purport." Now, I've never sat in a bar and heard anyone use the word "purport" in general banter. And so, I never use that word. I don't need to hide behind my words, to say words that make me sound smart.

Q
Do you get nervous?

A
I get anxious every time I speak. When I stand up, it's a question of trying to win the audience. For the first five minutes of my speech, I run the big risk of telling jokes; there's nothing worse

than a joke falling flat; recovering from it is very difficult. Yes, I'm apprehensive about every public speech I give. I want the audience to be entertained and informed. Working towards that, I will always look at my entire audience as often as I can, trying to bring them all into the speech.

Q
Do you have notes?
A
I have notes. I write my speeches out in longhand or dictate them and they may go through two or three revisions. I learn my speeches. I also have very good peripheral vision; I can look at an audience and see my notes at the same time.

Q
Can you tell if a person is telling the truth?
A
No better and no worse than anybody else. I don't think that I'm any better or any worse than anybody else at the difficult task of trying to figure out who is telling the truth. Every person has to make those decisions every day; if you talk to a car salesman, you have to determine if he's telling the truth or not; if

you ask a waitress or waiter what's good on the menu, you have to decide if they're telling the truth or not. You have to learn to trust or not to trust what's being said to you by the demeanour of a person or other things that help you in your truth-seeking mission. When you watch television, you have to decide if you're being told the truth or not during every news report.

Q
Have you heard a good speech or speaker lately?
A
Nice question. I am impressed by a device that Conrad Black uses when he introduces speakers; his knowledge of the speaker's background including pertinent years, dates, positions, titles, events, all given without reliance on a single note, truly impresses me. It is a very effective device; he obviously has a magnificent memory and he utilizes it effectively and absolutely wows the audience. He works without a single note and without ever looking down. Very, very impressive.

Q
What don't you like?
A
I don't like the heaviness of

some speeches in which people wade through statistics. If you can't prove your point simply by making an analogy from the statistics, and you go on and on, the audience just listens to large numbers.

Q
What are the qualities of a good speaker?
A
In terms of a dazzling speech, the Diefenbaker form of address is the very best. But who has it today? I think Trudeau had it; he was a marvellous, effective, at times spellbinding speaker. Stephen Lewis is an excellent speaker. You have to have something you can't learn or acquire: charisma.

Q
What speech did you enjoy giving?
A
I enjoyed speaking to the Empire Club about the role of the defence lawyer. There was a good feeling in the room, and the Empire Club is the World Series for a speaker. In fact, I said that to them, that I could now die and go to heaven having reached the height of a speaker's goal, addressing the very prestigious Empire

Club. I think people really liked that. They like honesty, humility, sincerity, and self-deprecation—a very Canadian characteristic. I think it's important to make the audience happy and feel good.

But let me also point out that I've said things to audiences that they clearly don't like; in fact, I may infuriate and I may upset. But they don't walk away not liking me or not talking about what I've said. I think it's important to be controversial and to cause an audience to think about how they feel about the subject matter. I will never hold back from my audience my true feelings on a subject and I will not tone down my language to the point where my beliefs are not crystal clear. I will call it as I see it. I owe that much to my audience.

Eddie Greenspan
Speech: The Futility of the Death Penalty

In 1987 Eddie Greenspan spoke out against the death penalty in a series of nationwide appearances. In today's climate, this speech is once again pertinent. Note especially the power of the conclusion.

In Canada, capital punishment was abolished in 1976, but it has never lain still in its grave, and continues still to raise its ugly head from time to time. Each time a police officer or prison guard is killed, we hear a clamour for its return. After little Alison Parrot's death, the *Toronto Sun* had a front-page editorial calling for the return of the death penalty.

It is my purpose to hopefully persuade you first, that capital punishment is no deterrent to crime and therefore an unjustifiable weapon to deter potential murderers, and second, that the state wants to continue to kill its victims, not so much to defend society against them—for it could do that equally well by imprisonment—but to appease the mob's emotions of hatred and revenge.

...To attempt to abolish crime by killing the criminal is the easy and foolish way out of a serious situation. Unless a remedy deals with the conditions which foster crime, criminals will breed faster than the hangman can spring his trap. Capital punishment ignores the causes of crime just as completely as the primitive witch doctor ignored the causes of disease; and like the methods of the witch doctor, it is not only ineffective as a remedy, but is positively vicious in at least two ways. In the first place, the spectacle of state executions feeds the basest passions of the mob. And in the second place, so long as the state rests content to deal with crime in this barbaric and futile manner, society will be lulled by a false sense of security, and effective methods of dealing with crime will be discouraged.

Even now, are not all imaginative and humane people shocked at the spectacle of a killing by the state? How many men and women would be willing to act as executioners? How many fathers and mothers would want their children to witness an official killing?

I have always hated capital punishment. To me it seems a cruel, brutal, useless barbarism. The killing of one individual by another always shows real or fancied excuse or reason. The cause, however poor, was enough to induce the act. But the killing of an individual by the state is so deliberate and cold, without any personal grievance or feeling. It is the outcome of long premeditated hatred. It does not happen suddenly and without warning, without time for the emotions to cool and subside, but a day is fixed a long way ahead and the victim is kept in continued, prolonged torture up to the moment of execution.

...And yet some people misperceive rising crime rates and say that if we had capital punishment—if we could literally put the fear of death into these criminals—the problems would all go away. Now that doesn't make sense, of course. Crime rates have nothing to do with capital punishment. In this capital punishment debate you will hear lots of statistics. You will hear people talking about crime going up and crime going down when there is or is not capital punishment. This is not a topic where it is possible to find the one definitive study which concludes, once and for all, that capital punishment is a deterrent, has no effect, or, indeed, that it cheapens life and encourages people to kill.

...It is easy to be in favour of revenge in the abstract. But if something happened to someone you know, and that person got angry with another family member, went out and purchased a weapon and killed his victim, would you really want that person—automatically—to be hanged? Don't think about it in the abstract; think about a real person. We don't hang abstractions, we hang real people.

...Now some people say capital punishment is justified because it prevents a murderer from ever again committing the same crime. In Canada, less than 10 people who have been found guilty of murder by a Canadian Court, were ever convicted of murder again. Former Prime Minister Trudeau, in the debate of Parliament to abolish the death penalty, said, "In order to be absolutely sure that no murderer would murder again, we would have to take the lives of all persons convicted of either first- or second-degree murder, even though the probability is that an infinitesimal percent of them would ever commit murder again if allowed to live. That's an unacceptably high price to pay in

human lives for a sense of security insignificantly greater than we have now." No one knows whether visualizing and hearing the effects of punishment of one deters others or induces others; or whether, even if it served to deter in this particular way, it might not render men, women, and children callous to human distress.

Only one thing is certain about capital punishment or its effect—that it is administered for no reason but deep and fixed hatred of the individual and an abiding thirst for revenge. Are we so lacking in hope for the human race that we are ready to accept state-sanctioned vengeance as our penal philosophy?

Capital punishment is too horrible a thing for a state to undertake. We are told, "Oh, the killer does it, why shouldn't the state?" I would hate to live in a state that I didn't think was better than a murderer.

There isn't, I submit, a single admissible argument in favour of it. Nature loves life. We believe that life should be protected and preserved. The thing that keeps one from killing is that emotion they have against it; and the greater the sanctity that the state pays to life, the greater the feeling of sanctity the individual has for life.

We stopped taking human life in 1962—24 years ago. That's the last time the hangman in Canada practised his terrible trade. And for those of you who regret that situation—who lust for the return of that rope, let me remind you of this: Donald Marshall was convicted for a crime he did not commit. Which of you, sitting here today, could have pulled the bag over his head? Which of you could have fastened the rope around his neck? Which of you could have sprung the trap door which sent Donald Marshall to his death? Because that is what capital punishment is all about. It's not just another news story on page 10 of your newspaper. It's the coldblooded killing of a human being. The next time you hear that bloodthirsty cry for revenge, I ask you to remember that.

OUTLINE OF AN INFORMATIVE SPEECH

Name: _____

Date of Speech: _____

Purpose Statement: _____

INTRODUCTION

Grabber:

Thesis:

Overview:

BODY

Supporting Argument #1

Supporting Argument #2

Supporting Argument #3

CONCLUSION

Reference to purpose (thesis):

Summary of main steps:

Zinger:

SELF-EVALUATION FORM

This form is to help you evaluate your own speech. It can be kept private or shared with your instructor or peers.

Type of Speech: _____

Name: _____

Title: _____

Date: _____

DELIVERY

Physical Presence

Did I make eye contact with others?

Was my posture natural and appropriate?

Was I aware of my facial expressions and hand gestures?

Were there any distracting mannerisms that I was aware of?

Did I feel good?

Could I feel an energy exchange with my audience?

VOCAL DELIVERY

Was my voice under control?

Did I sound confident?

Was I aware of breathing calmly?

How was my enunciation?

Did I manage to avoid um's and ah's?

Did I sound interested/excited/committed?

How did my voice sound to me?

DESIGN AND CONTENT

How well did the introduction and conclusion work?

Did the framework unify my speech?

Was there a natural progression from point to point?

Did my notes keep me on track? Did I use them?

Did the audience seem to understand the organization of my speech?

Was the information clear?

What was the energy level of the conclusion?

What would I change the next time?

What worked very well?

OVERALL EFFECTIVENESS

Did I connect with this audience?

Did I achieve my purpose?

What do I remember most about making the speech?

What unexpected or unforeseen things happened?

What am I most pleased about?

OTHER COMMENTS

Grade: _____

PEER EVALUATION FORM

Peer evaluation should be done in a constructive and supportive fashion. The speaker may choose people to do assessments or they may be assigned alphabetically. Some groups maintain the same speaker/assessor teams for the entire course; others change for each speech. The instructor may wish to see this evaluation before it goes to the speaker.

Type of Speech: _____

Speaker: _____

Title: _____

Assessor: _____

Date: _____

DELIVERY

Physical Presence

Did the speaker maintain eye contact?

Did she or he establish a rapport with the audience?

Were gestures natural and effective?

VOCAL DELIVERY

Did the speaker sound convincing/spontaneous/excited?

Was his or her voice clear and loud enough?

How did you respond to the speaker's mood?

DESIGN AND CONTENT

Did the introduction interest you?

Did the overview give you an indication of the main proofs?

Did the speech flow easily and logically from one point to another?

Was the conclusion strong and memorable?

Did the conclusion reinforce the thesis and main points?

What was the thesis of the speech?

Overall Effectiveness

Did you learn something new or worthwhile from the speech?

Were you moved by it?

What was the most outstanding part of the speech?

What changes do you recommend?

What parts should the speaker definitely keep?

OTHER COMMENTS

Grade: _____

EVALUATION FORM

Type of Speech: _____

Name: _____

Title: _____

Length of Speech: _____

Date: _____

Legend: S=Superior   E=Effective   NW=Needs Work

DELIVERY

Physical Presence

Eye Contact

Rapport with Audience

Posture

Gestures

Use of Notes

Appropriate Use of Audio-Visual

Support Material

VOCAL DELIVERY

Naturalness/Spontaneity/Enthusiasm

Clarity

Variety (Tone, Pitch, Pace)

Volume

Absence of Verbal Tics (um, ah, okay, like)

Sense of Control and Calm

DESIGN AND CONTENT

Use of Framework for Introduction and Conclusion

Clear Thesis and Overview

Coherence/Use of Transitions

Strong Finish

Language

Word Choice

Impact on Audience

Grammar

OVERALL EFFECTIVENESS

Treatment of Topic

Intelligent Awareness of Audience

Achievement of Purpose

Impact on/Connection with Audience

OTHER COMMENTS

Grade: _____

C H A P T E R

Thinking On Your Feet—Impromptus and Interviews

TIPS FOR SPEAKERS

1. A real impromptu is a surprise—never *forget* to plan a speech.

2. Make use of your speaking time—don't just fill it.

3. Skid-School lessons help you deal with unexpected questions.

4. Always check the microphone yourself.

5. Rehearse for an interview: get your ideas and your voice ready.

WARM-UPS

Winging It: Impromptu Persuasives

Divide into small groups (of two to four students) and select one of the following topics. Then, as a group, design a two- to three-minute speech to prove or disprove the statement. Each group member is responsible for delivering *one* section of the speech. Thus, after five minutes of preparation, each group presents its argument. The goal is to have speakers follow each other smoothly so that the speech seems strong and unified.

You are encouraged to invent all supporting data (examples, quotations, validation by authorities, historical background).

1. Thirty-five should be the minimum age for people to marry.

2. God is a woman.

3. Men should wear women's clothing to liberate themselves.

4. The world is actually flat.

5. Canada should appoint its own Maple Leaf Sovereign and dispense with elections altogether.

6. Pigs are beautiful.

7. To avoid burdening children with parental expectations, newborns should be switched at birth so that we never know their genetic background.

8. Bicycle tire jewellery is the trend of tomorrow.

9. University degrees should be handed out at the end of kindergarten.

10. North America should be divided into two countries with east/west boundaries rather than the existing north/south border.

You arrive at a reception for your regional humane society and one of the directors spots you hovering at the refreshments. Knowing you have five cats and a keen interest in banning product-testing on animals, he asks if you would fill in for a speaker who couldn't attend. "Just a few minutes," he says. "Talk about anything on testing—I'm sure we'll find it interesting."

How do you react? "I don't—I forget nine-tenths of the English language," was the response of one person I coached. She is a potter whose work has been displayed around the world. Her creativity didn't help her in all situations, however; when she consulted me several years ago, a request to speak turned her feet to clay.

Consider the impromptu the main window—it gives access to a variety of speaking opportunities. This chapter will help you become adept at thinking and speaking on your feet. As you improve your reaction time, you'll feel more confident in interviews and community events.

◑ WINGING IT: THE IMPROMPTU SPEECH

Impromptu speeches are a challenge. Like overtime in a play-off game, they demand all your skills and nerve. You can handle an impromptu if you remember that it's like any other speech; it requires a thesis, a clear design, and a strong finish. You just have to think faster. Consider the following techniques; they've been tested many times by people who have earned their wings.

1. **Be Prepared.** This old motto works well for speakers. Predict when you may be asked to speak. If you are well known in your community, have recently received an award, or can be depended on in a tight situation, you may be called on to speak. Acquire a speaker's ear for the perfect story: news items, conversations in elevators, talk shows, university events, radio interviews, children's questions. When you read magazines, make a mental note of interesting items. This doesn't have to be complex; you may have just heard a documentary on being successful and having a good personal life. How about a speech on what success means to you, or how to balance business and personal time? Next time you're waiting for the meal to be served at a conference, plan what you would say if you were given just five minutes to prepare.

2. **Make Use of Your Time.** You will probably have a few hours or at least a few minutes to gather your thoughts. Don't panic! Instead, follow the procedure you would for any speech:
    *   think of your subject. Choose one that's important to you and right for your audience.
    *   establish your thesis. Pause and find out what you think. Determine one clear main idea. Be specific.
    *   think of one or two supporting statements and examples.

3. **Work Out a Brief Outline.** This is a speech—it needs a grabber, a thesis, points to prove that thesis, and a strong conclusion. Once again, keep it simple. For the grabber, use something you've observed lately. Tell a story to set the mood and introduce your topic. Did your car get sideswiped yesterday? That leads into speeches on the importance of friends, insurance, reflexes, and chiropractors.

One good plan for an impromptu is past, present, and future. What is the history of the group you are addressing? How have they worked together in the past? What present challenges do they face? What are their future resources?

This outline can apply to many situations. Madame Jehane Benoit, a superb chef and prolific author, offered good advice to cooks and speakers alike:

I feel a recipe is only a theme, which an intelligent cook can play each time with a variation.

Think of specific examples or details to support your main statements; no one expects you to have exact statistics but some concrete data will help. Tell one story for every point you wish to make. As you become more experienced, you will have a good reserve of examples.

4. **Jot Down Your Notes.** Take time to write down a few words to keep you on track.

5. **Breathe and Enjoy Yourself.** Nervousness always gets you in the throat. *Breathe.* A good deep breath will clear your head and make you sound confident. At the same time, look as though you are enjoying yourself. Even in an impromptu situation the audience needs to know that you like talking to them. Express your pleasure, "I'm surprised but happy to be able to share this time with you—I've always valued this organization." Then get on with the speech.

6. **Stick to the Plan.** Use your plan to speak with confidence and conviction. Don't ramble. Inexperienced speakers get so nervous, they forget to coach themselves and ramble in an attempt to fill time. Instead, channel your nervousness into planning your speech. Say what you want to say and stop.

7. **Be Brief.** You're not expected to know everything so unless you were hoping for the chance to speak and actually have a speech in your pocket, make your main points and stop.

8. **Finish Strong and Sit Down.** Although this may appear to be an obvious point, watch nervous speakers—they never know if they've "said enough." So they repeat themselves, add unrelated points, and stretch out their talk unnecessarily. Once you've covered your main point, told stories to illustrate it, and made a strong final statement, you're finished. Sit down.

9. **Have Speeches and Quotations in Reserve.** Take a lesson from Gloria Steinem—she makes several speeches a week, often impromptu, and tries to make each talk special for the group she is with. She suggests that you treat sections of your speeches as building blocks and use them to design an impromptu speech quickly. It helps to keep a few quotations on hand. Although I'm not good at memorizing, I have several short quotations that I've used many times, altering a word or two to suit the group. Here they are: the first one is often attributed to Bobby Kennedy—proof that he too had a good stockpile of versatile quotations.

You see things, and you say "Why?" But I dream things that never were, and I say, "Why not?"
  —*GEORGE BERNARD SHAW*

It takes trouble and it takes courage to be free.
  —*FERRON*

Every writer needs a built-in, foolproof, crap detector.
        —ERNEST HEMINGWAY

Human compassion is equal to human cruelty and it is up to each of us to tip the balance.
        —ALICE WALKER

CRISIS CONTROL:

A real impromptu is a surprise. It is not a speech that you decided to forget about. Never plan to speak impromptu. And never bore your audience with endless apologies about how surprised or unprepared you are. They can handle a few rough spots but get impatient with the fifteenth declaration of "gee, if I'd only known I was going to speak, I think I could have done some great research on fish eggs. It's really hard up here and I'm a bit embarrassed and I also sat on my glasses...."

Five-Minute Workout

Spend a few minutes reading or listening to the news. Select several topics that interest you and plan a three-minute speech on one of them. Give yourself 10 minutes to plan and then try it out loud. How well does it hold together? How confident do you sound?

The Good News On Impromptus

You do get better! The potter with feet of clay called me recently and told me that she enjoys speaking much more. She tries to think of an idea that starts with art and relates to a wider audience. She also said she's much faster on impromptus. When we first worked together, she considered an impromptu to be a request made the night before or morning of an event. Now, she's calm when they greet her at the door with, "We were hoping that you would say...."

A Few Words

When you speak, you have a tremendous obligation to your audience— these people are giving you their time.... Most people just try to fill time, fill up their twenty minutes...I try to get excited and get others excited. You aren't going to die during the speech.
        —DAVE NICHOL

Make your time count. If you are often asked to bring greetings or make a few brief remarks before the guest speaker begins, think of a way to make your few minutes interesting for you *and* the audience. An easy way is to see what significant event happened on the day you are speaking. Did

South Africa have its first free vote? Is it the anniversary of Joey Smallwood's birth? What about James Naismith—do you know when he invented basketball? How does that relate to the group? Choose a quotation from a book you're reading and challenge the group to apply it to their organization. In other words, don't fill time—use it. A quotation or example you give may be as interesting to the audience as the speech that follows. Every speaking opportunity counts.

● SKID-SCHOOL LESSONS FOR UNEXPECTED QUESTIONS

Have you ever panicked when your car started to skid? Quick responses can save your life. Skid schools—driving programs that teach you how to handle treacherous situations—force you to perform well under stress. The rules are simple, and they also apply to speakers facing slippery conditions. The primary rule is *avoid the skid*. Predict the situation and take precautions to avoid going out of control. However, if you do start to slip, follow these three rules taught at skid-school courses:

1. Don't panic.
2. Take your foot off the brake and steer.
3. Steer in the direction you want to go.

Translated into speaking terms, they read:

1. Don't panic: Breathe—get oxygen to your brain.

Pause—assess the situation.

2. Get your brain in action. *Think* of what you want to say, *Breathe*.
3. Have a thesis—one main idea—and *steer* toward it.

For those people who do a few spins before they acquire the knack, the best thing about Skid School is the large expanse of uncluttered lawn. The classroom is your protection. Don't worry if you freeze the first time; follow the rules.

Handling Unexpected Questions on the Spot

Questions that you didn't anticipate or are slightly offbeat may upset you. If you forecast questions, you have a good chance to develop and rehearse your responses, but if you're caught off-guard, the following technique works.

1. **Pause**. Don't panic at a silence. A pause is good for your image. You appear thoughtful rather than glib, and show respect for the question. Get comfortable with a pause.
2. **Clarify**. Ask questions to clarify the matter. This gives you more time to think. It also ensures that you are on the same track as your

WHEN IN A SKID, DON'T PANIC.

"Look wise, say nothing, and grunt."

(Sir William Osler)

questioner. If I ask, "When is civil disobedience acceptable?", you may ask me to clarify what I mean: nonviolent actions? in time of peace or war? public or private objections?

If it is clear that you are totally ignorant, *don't bluff.* You'll sound as if you are. Admit you're not sure, (you needn't apologize) and promise to get back with an answer within a specific time.

3. **One point plus amplification**. Make a clear statement, with some examples or explanation. In effect, this is a thesis and one or two supporting points. (Three *would* be excellent but this is under pressure.) *Do not babble. One point is sufficient.*

4. **Involve the other person**. Ask for a comment in response. This works well to turn attempted confrontation into communication. Under pressure it's hard to remember phrases that elicit a response: Stockpile a few of these: "This works well in our agency, how do you handle it?" or "Does this hold true in your situation?" or "Will this suggestion work?" or "Does this match your experience?"

Exercise: Handling Unexpected Questions on the Spot

In this exercise, it is important that the class be supportive.

a) Together, class members generate a list of questions. These are placed on a table.

b) Each class member chooses a partner. One person goes to the table, and selects a question that his or her partner will find challenging, yet manageable, and asks the question.

Alternative method: The instructor selects a student, then points randomly at a question.

c) The speaker answers from his or her desk. Arranging the desks so that class members can see each other may help the group to focus their attention.

d) Practise the technique. Answers can be one or two minutes long, sufficient to experiment with the process. Remember that this is a learning experience; the instructor may take time to coach the speaker through the four steps: pause, clarify, make one point plus amplification, involve others.

Students generated these questions:

- What should be done about people who push on buses and subways?
- Should the government give more funding to college and university students?
- What do you think of daytime drama (the soaps)?
- Should there be more choice in your college program?
- Should sex be taught in elementary schools (grades 1-8)?
- Is there an improvement in the number of non-smoking areas?
- What's wrong with capital punishment?
- Who would you choose as a Canadian hero and why?
- How far should free speech go?
- Should students work a minimum number of years between high school and college or university?
- How do you feel about impromptus?
- What do you think about people who help themselves to bulk food while shopping?
- What was your most memorable disaster?
- Are summit meetings worthwhile?
- How much does the Royal Family mean to you?
- Should surrogate mothers be forced, if necessary, to give up their babies?
- Should escort services be allowed to advertise in the yellow pages?
- Is Christmas too commercialized?
- Is Sunday shopping a benefit or a detriment to society?
- What part of Canada is the most intriguing place to visit?
- Are food banks a benefit to society?
- Is drug abuse common in professional sports?
- What do you think of condom commercials on public and private TV stations?
- If a major disaster occurred, and you had approximately one hour to live, how would you spend your time?
- Should the minimum driving age be raised?

- If you had to cross rough water, would you prefer to use a sailboat or a canoe?
- Knowing what you know now, if you were to live your life over, what would you do differently?
- Should a woman have a baby if she wants children but does not want to get married?
- Do high-performance cars have a place on our highways?
- Do you dress for comfort or for success?
- How do they get the gooey caramel into the Caramilk bar?
- Should you lie in job interviews?
- Should young offenders accused of major crimes be charged under the Young Offenders' Act or in adult court?
- Is there a place on television for garbage talk shows such as Geraldo Rivera's?
- Cheat sheets or students' salvation: what's your opinion of *Coles Notes*?
- Is big-name wrestling a sport or a soap opera? Why is it so popular?
- Should we have no-fault insurance?
- What one course would you love to take?
- What one course would you rather not take?
- Should funeral services advertise in the media?
- What's a good way to answer the following question in a job interview: "Are you planning to stay with the company or is this position just a stepping stone?"
- Should police require a search warrant to enter a building or should the law be changed to allow them to enter on suspicion?
- Does an accent make a difference in your chances for success?
- Would you rather be called "bland" or "pushy"?
- Is Elvis alive?
- If you found bags of money on a highway, would you try to return them?

◑ TIME OUT! MANAGING CONFLICT

The title tells it all. In order to resolve conflict, you must acknowledge that it exists and take the time to work it out effectively and honestly. People rarely plan to have conflict arise, so the skills you learned for impromptu speeches will come in handy.

Identify, Outline, Explain, Resolve

How do you talk out your differences? Let's look at a meeting of students living in a university residence. Eighteen people have gathered to discuss the problem of racist and homophobic slogans that were spray-painted on building walls. There is considerable difference of opinion: some students think it is not their problem; others are very concerned and want to prevent a recurrence; still others want to look at underlying attitudes; and a few wish to call in the police.

1. Identify. The first step is to identify the problem; that is the obligation of everyone in the group. To identify, you have to speak clearly and honestly. You must also respect the feelings of everyone concerned; the emotional content of the meeting is as important as the problem. Often people think they can ignore the conflict and "get on with the job." This approach doesn't work. Group members may sabotage each other or drift away to escape the situation.

2. Outline. Someone—not necessarily the leader—must outline the situation without taking sides. (Try for open-ended questions.)

    "Raoul, what reasons do you have for thinking that there is a racist undercurrent in this residence?"

    "Michelle, how would it be if you spoke to all of us, instead of making asides to Patrick?"

    "Kam, how can we stop arguing and make this residence a safer place—emotionally and physically?"

3. Explain. When individuals decide to present their ideas, they need a fair hearing. You may not all agree with each others' opinions but people need to be heard without being attacked.

4. Resolve. Individual and group needs have to be met or everyone in this situation will feel unsafe. This gathering has a lot of work to do. They need to define and list the various problems, generate possible solutions, evaluate them, make decisions, and try for consensus. Once they carry out their plans, they should evaluate the process, so the next problem-solving meeting will be easier.

Why Bother Touching All the Bases?

This is a time-consuming and difficult process. External conflicts such as fussy clients, the budget cutbacks, and equipment malfunctions, are easier to deal with than internal conflict. However, you must work through the process or individuals may resort to sniping and sabotage, and the group may collapse. Conflict is normal. It happens. Talk it out.

Exercise: Managing Conflict

Divide into four groups and choose one of the scenarios below to act out. You must think of your role, your approach to the situation, and your language. Your words reflect your attitude and your personality. The characters outlined in the various scenarios would naturally hold a variety of opinions—as a group make sure that variety is present.

You may work through a situation separately, and then present it to the class, or showcase them one at a time. You may decide on your role, and your attitude either by consulting with your group or by choosing a piece of paper on which your character and stand are outlined. Your aim is to resolve conflict.

Scenario 1: White-Water Rafting

You are the coordinator of youth programs for 14- to 18-year-olds in a middle-class neighbourhood. Your group is going to Vancouver as part of an exchange program, and the participants have raised money to go white-water rafting on the Fraser River. Now there's a problem.

Several parents are concerned about the dangers of river rafting and have planned a meeting to cancel the activity—maybe even the whole trip. One parent has contacted you to express concern and two others have phoned your supervisor. You are now at that meeting.

Scenario 2: Industrial Waste

You have worked for Sludge Chemical Co. for 15 years and have recently been appointed manager of emissions control. Your job is to oversee the dumping of industrial waste into the Rideau River to make sure that the chemical content is within government guidelines. You have discovered that the chemical wastes have been "unsafe" for several months and have come to a meeting of senior management to persuade them to reduce the dangerous emissions. This would mean shutting down the plant, which employs 230 people, for three weeks, and incurring heavy financial losses.

The basic conflict is whether Sludge Chemical has an ethical responsibility to stay within recommended but non-mandatory guidelines or whether its primary responsibility is making money.

Scenario 3: Hospital Services

A hospital committee, consisting of representatives of the board of directors, nursing staff, administrators, doctors, and patient advocates, is holding a meeting. As members of that board, you must decide how much of your allocated budget and available space should be given to a counselling service for people involved in surrogate motherhood arrangements.

Scenario 4: Is a Medical Condition a Drawback?

Your college/university outing club is planning a backpacking trip to hike part of the Cabot Trail in Cape Breton. One of the club members has epilepsy. You are having an executive meeting to discuss whether she should go. She is not present at the meeting. Who decides?

Evaluation

1. Did people sound as if they wanted to resolve conflict or get their own way?
2. Which words or phrases helped the situation and which did not?

GREAT CANADIAN QUIZ II

Chew on a Maple Leaf for inspiration and test your knowledge of Canadian places, dates, and characters.

1. Which Canadian hero started out on a "Marathon of Hope"?
2. What are the three levels of government in Canada?
3. Other than the Green Party and the Rhinos, what are our major national political parties?
4. In what year was slavery outlawed in Canada?
5. What is a furry Arctic owl doll called?
6. Who was the first woman from the western hemisphere to successfully climb Mount Everest?
7. Who is the singing and stomping musician who wrote "Bud the Spud"?
8. Which national park was the first to be established?
9. Name two legendary creatures that haunt various parts of the country.
10. What schooner is pictured on the dime?

To test yourself further, consult
John Robert Colombo, *Colombo's Canadian Quiz Book* (Western Producer Prairie Books, 1983)
John Fisher, *The Complete Cross-Canada Quiz and Game Book* (McClelland and Stewart, 1978)
Sandra Martin, *Quizzing Canada* (Dundurn Press, 1987).

Answers: Great Canadian Quiz II
1. Terry Fox
2. Federal, provincial, local
3. Conservatives, Liberals, NDP, Reform
4. 1834
5. Ook pik
6. Sharon Wood, mountaineer and guide, in 1986
7. Stompin' Tom Connors
8. Banff
9. Sasquatch, Ogopogo
10. The Bluenose

◑ OPEN NEGOTIATIONS AND DETERMINED BARGAINING: THERE'S ROOM FOR BOTH

Negotiating is an open process in which you are prepared to put something forward in return for what you get; it is rewarding for both sides. Bargaining is more one-sided; you are clear about your needs and are determined to achieve them. Neither technique involves arguing, yelling, or intimidation. Both rely on the way you speak as well as what you say.

Negotiating

Two international food fairs are being held this year for the hospitality industry. As the catering manager for a large hotel chain, you are expected to attend one food fair; your boss will attend the other. One food fair is being held in San Francisco, the other in Fredericton. Unfortunately, you both wish to go to San Francisco—time for negotiation.

For this process to be effective, you both have to offer something in return for what you get. Since both parties are giving something, both are sure of winning. If you go into the meeting determined that you are going to San Francisco, it is not negotiating; you have to be more open about the result. In this case, your supervisor is also willing to negotiate, and you look at various possibilities. Can you both go? No, one of you must be in the office. Would you be willing to go to the national food fair this year, and the international one next year? If one of you goes to San Francisco for the food fair, the other could have first chance at the big tourism convention being held in Italy next year. In this case, your supervisor agrees to go to Fredericton; next year she'll be in Naples and you'll visit St. John's, Newfoundland.

This is negotiating; you both have a shared concern for the business, and personal interests to satisfy. If you negotiate, the work gets done, and you both win.

Bargaining

Many times, you need to get something done; often the other parties involved are not cooperative. This technique can be used to deal with any of the people you encounter in arranging the business of daily life: your family, your bank manager, your employer or employees, your teachers or the teachers of your children, the municipal roads board, etc. You can be successful without resorting to bullying, arguing, or demanding.

Imagine this situation. You have signed up to give your major persuasive speech next Friday. Your instructor has been clear in his discussion of responsibility; you must give the speech on the date you choose. It is a firm commitment and no cancellations are allowed. That afternoon, the personnel manager of a company you have always wanted to work for calls to offer you a job interview for a summer position. Guess when the only available appointment is? You know what your public speaking teacher's reaction will be—no sympathy. What can you do? Request an appointment, and with an air of polite assurance, enter his office and use the following techniques:

- fogging;
- positive strokes;
- shared responsibility.

Fogging

Prepare and practise a phrase that expresses what you want or need and keep repeating it:

"I need to make an alternate date for my final speech."

Your teacher may respond with,

"I think the conditions were very clear."
"It wouldn't be fair to the others."
"But I told you."
"It's impossible!"

Each time, nod agreeably (because what he says is true) and say, "Yes, I agree but...I need to make an alternate date for my final speech." Allow him a chance to work through all the stages of frustration involved, and at the same time, state your case.

"No, I don't want to fail. It's just that...I need to make an alternate date for my final speech."

Fogging fills the room and the listener's mind with your request. It's especially useful for people who

- give up when someone says "no, of course not; absolutely not!";
- get nervous when others raise their voices;
- crumble when someone attacks them verbally;
- remember all their good lines after they get home.

Positive Strokes

Agree with the other person. Your teacher says,

"This is terrible!"

Immediately you reply,

"I agree with you; you are absolutely right."

Now how can anyone argue with you, when you agree with him? If you can honestly do it, say positive things about the other person.

"Your course was worthwhile, and I don't want to jeopardize my mark."

Shared Responsibility

Request feedback from the other person and offer positive suggestions of your own.

"I have some possible solutions and want to know if you think they're worthwhile."

Here's a surprise: few people expect you to ask for their opinions or help. In most situations, people go in with demands; here, you offer suggestions and ask for cooperation in resolving the problem fairly.

Warning! Do not give ultimatums or walk out in anger. Avoid insulting others, making "or else" statements that you're not prepared to carry out, or slamming the door on the problem.

Here's another scenario. You share the housework with another person—a partner, a parent, or a sister. In this case, your sister has not done any cleaning in the past four weeks and the dust balls are bigger than your cat. You've had it.

Do not insult your sister. Instead, prepare your fogging statement:

"I want you to do the housework this week. It's your turn."

She may lash out with a personal insult ("What do you know—you're only 5'2") or oft-repeated excuses ("But I work hard all day"). Do not retaliate or walk out. Instead, fog:

"I know your job is exhausting but...I want you to do the housework this week. It's your turn."

When she moans that she hates housework, use the second technique and agree with her.

"You are so right; housework is wretched but..."

If she tries to escape with the excuse that she's busy all week, go immediately to shared responsibility:

"I agree it's a problem. How do we solve it? What do you suggest?"

Remember, you aren't going to give up or forget. You are going to persist.

What Happens When Someone Uses the Technique on You?

When I went to my bank to get a consumer loan, the rates quoted were far too high; the bank next door offered a much better deal. Preparing my fogging statement, I went to the manager of my own branch:

"I want a loan rate that proves to me that I am a valued customer."

To my surprise, the manager came back with positive strokes and shared responsibility,

"I agree there's a problem. How can we solve it?"

Fogging was the answer. It gave me time to remember the alternatives that I had considered before the meeting. I came out of the manager's office with a loan rate that was 3.5% lower than the original offer.

When Do You Negotiate and When Do You Bargain?

Negotiation is a cleaner, clearer experience. It is possible when people are willing to seek solutions in an atmosphere of cooperation and mutual respect. But there are many times when you have legitimate requests that other people will not consider: the principal of your child's school refuses to arrange testing to detect a suspected learning disability; the marina owner will not give you access to your boat after the season is over; your doctor is reluctant to discuss the result of blood tests. Fogging, positive strokes, and shared responsibility may help you.

Exercise

Should you negotiate or bargain in each of the following situations? Decide on your technique, and carry it out.

1. You want a cat; your partner thinks that, as a couple, you are too busy to care for a pet.
2. You want the hotel where you work to establish smoke-free public rooms. The other managers think that clients might be annoyed.
3. You want to take your holidays during the first three weeks in July; two other people also want their holidays at that time. Only one person can be absent at a time.
4. Your mother wants to buy an artificial Christmas tree; you want a real one.
5. You and three friends are going to the southern United States during study week. Two people want to hit the beaches; the other two want to stay somewhere with more variety.

Evaluation

1. How did you decide which technique to use?
2. Were you able to avoid intimidation or bullying?
3. Which is more important—words, tone, or body language?

◑ JOB INTERVIEWS

How well do you communicate at the interview? Whether you are applying for a new position, working your way up the corporate ladder, or representing your company in its campaign for new clients, you need to speak well. Let's assume that you have done your résumé, researched this particular company, dressed well, and made it to the location promptly. What next? *Breathing exercises:* they'll help you relax and get your voice ready to perform with assurance. When you are shown into the office, approach your interviewer, introduce yourself, and shake hands. You make an immediate impression with

- eye contact
- the tone of your voice (courteous, firm, relaxed)
- your handshake (warm, firm, and fitting)

It is important *to behave as you wish to be treated.* If you want to be perceived as a person of worth and talent, have confidence in yourself. Your inexperience can always be remedied. Decide what you want and act appropriately.

There are two scenarios to note. The first is the *one-minute wait.* When you enter the interviewer's office, he or she is on the phone. (It's always Los Angeles or Boston, never Charlottetown or Kapuskasing.) You are waved to a seat and wonder what to do. Do *not* pick lint from your clothes or adjust your trouser legs. If you feel nervous, pull out a pen and make a note, review the plans you made on how to fix your car—look efficient and busy, fidget administratively. When the interviewer finishes the call, go back to the intro-and-handshake routine.

The second—and very common—scenario is the *weak-female routine.* Women are waved to chairs by gallant men who say, "Here, take a seat." People rarely collapse from the long walk across the office. If you want to be perceived as competent, ignore the gesture, and introduce yourself with a pleasant handshake.

During the interview, you may be asked some unexpected questions. For instance, "Do you enjoy socializing with co-workers outside the office?" or "How do you define a team?" This requires discernment on your part. Is the question appropriate? If it is, take time to answer it honestly and thoroughly. You have no idea what has happened before you arrived and perhaps no indication of the real challenge of the job. If two departments are merging, the company may need someone who is good at promoting cooperation and teamwork. Although these skills may not be on the job description, they may be in the mind of the interviewer. Remember the Skid-School lessons for unexpected questions.

◑ MEDIA INTERVIEWS

One of my friends joined a protest to stop the construction of a logging road through old growth forest. At one point, she chained herself to a huge pine tree to stop the loggers. A television interviewer asked if she was ready to die to save a tree. My friend was indignant. "He didn't even ask why I was there—I wanted time to give background on the situation." It was hard to explain to her that being chained to a tree with police officers all around is not exactly background time. The reporter wanted a newsbite, not a summary.

This is the challenge of interviews: how does our purpose jibe with the interviewer's needs? How can we get our message across and feel confident in the process? Here's a sample of suggestions from people on both sides of the microphone. They can be summed up in four phrases that apply to all interview situations:

- be yourself
- think of the audience
- practise
- breathe!

Remember that an interview is a speech: **organize, rehearse, relax.**

In their efforts to be immediate, radio stations want to talk to people directly connected with a news story. Thus, the scientist at a nuclear power plant can no longer assume that management will handle all interviews; direct answers have more credibility. Similarly, hotel and restaurant workers are contacted about the impact of international summits on their industry, and union stewards go on the air to discuss negotiations between management and labour.

Although the following pointers will help you in dealing with all media, they relate particularly to radio interviews.

Preparation

- When someone calls to request an interview, make sure they are setting a date in the future, not recording your remarks immediately. Insist on a chance to prepare.
- Pause: is it appropriate for you to do the interview? Do you know the details? Are you the logical choice? If it is not appropriate, say no or suggest someone else.
- Ask the researcher who calls you about the format of the interview. How long will it be? What usually happens? Will you be speaking live via telephone or in the studio?
- Cover all bases. If a sensitive issue is involved, make sure you have called your employer—or in the case of associations, your colleagues—to outline your point of view. You may not have essential information, and it's humiliating to be corrected in a subsequent interview.
- If you are not familiar with the show on which you will appear, start listening. You usually have at least one day. If not, call a friend who listens to the station. Research the usual format of questions—confrontational, "what is your opinion?" "is it true?" etc.

On Air

- **Be sure of your one main point and three supporting arguments.** Try the one-sentence shower test described in Chapter 2. The interviewer takes care of the introduction and conclusion.

- **It is easier for the interviewer and the audience if you number your reasons.** "Well Joe, I think my dog Annie should be the next mayor. She has the three essential qualifications: she's smart, she photographs well, and she loves catered receptions." Then elaborate.
- **Use notes—a few key words or phrases.** This is no time to wing it. This is pressure.
- **Speak clearly.** This is a radio audience. Breathe in order to get your voice into a mellow range, and hold on. Don't get so excited that you tighten up and race to the end. Radio can be very hard if you're in a studio for the first time; it's a hectic place with people signalling and moving all at once.
- **Make eye contact with your interviewer.** Use the same speaking techniques you would with a larger group—remember, they are out there. If your interviewer is looking at the traffic reporter or the control room, imagine someone at home listening to you and talk to that person.
- **Keep the interview on track.** Consider this advice carefully. You know a lot about your subject; that's why you were asked on the show. To the station, you are just one of many interviews: they are not experts. So, when the interviewer asks something that is not relevant or seems to be filling time, say, "Yes, that's a possibility, but there are other considerations." Don't wait for the interviewer to give you space; you have only three to five minutes, and the time flies by.
- **Practise at home.** Get your friends or partner to ask you all kinds of questions at you to see how well you handle them, and how well *you work in your main point.*
- **Rehearse your first line.** The first line is crucial. You always sound better when you've warmed up. If you are contacted over the phone, someone will call, ask you to hold, and suddenly the next voice is the interviewer's and it's live. While you are waiting on the phone, breathe, and rehearse your opening line *out loud, exactly as you want to say it.*
- **Sound like yourself.** Don't be overly formal. Use everyday examples.
- **Don't:**
  - knock the media on air;
  - say "no comment":
  - be tempted to speak about things beyond your area of knowledge;
  - give yes or no answers
  - lie;
  - let other people put words in your mouth. Say "no, that isn't an accurate picture. Let me tell you what really happened";
  - hog the limelight: give others credit if you are part of a group.

More on Interviews

Be Yourself

Talk to an interviewer as you would talk to your neighbour—try for a conversational tone. Take your time and explain things. Sound as though you enjoy being interviewed; it makes the interview go smoothly and helps the image you project. In the first minute or so, explain clearly why you are speaking; it's important that you sound as committed as you really are. If people don't believe what you're saying, they won't listen to you.

Think of the Audience

How much does the audience know about the subject? I've found that interviewers want either a general discussion or a firm position. Quite often when I arrive, the interviewer needs a briefing on the topic—despite the fact I've already submitted it. As one broadcaster said, "I should have more questions ready but it's hectic here. I just want a general overview of the subject and we'll get to the meaty part later. My listeners need to know the person first. They want basics—not a lot of background." Relax, explain the basics, give them a sense of yourself.

If you're speaking on a hot topic such as contract debates or civil disobedience, be ready for the hot-seat questions and use them. If you're part of a work slowdown, you might be asked if you're overworked; if you're in favour of gun control, the interviewer may wonder if you're too selfish to think of the needs of those who hunt to eat. Prepare for the hot questions.

Relax

- Sound like yourself. Understand and use inclusive language. (See Checklist 19, Chapter 8.)
- Co-operate with the interviewer if possible. Get to the station early enough to meet him or her, and come prepared with a short (4-6 lines) biography; it saves work for both of you. Prepare a brief statement of your main points for the interviewer—he or she may or may not welcome it.
- Arrive early enough to get used to the activity of a radio or television station. Concentrate on speaking to the interviewer and ignore the bustle around you.
- Centre yourself. In extreme cases—you will either be put on the spot or no one will remember who you are and they will have lost your press kit—focus on why you are speaking. Things will work out.
- Talk to people—don't sound like you are reading assembly instructions. If you listen carefully to radio shows, you'll be able to hear when

others read their remarks; it sounds like an address. Their vocabulary and cadences are not as natural as normal speech. You'll also be able to watch television novices following the teleprompter; their look of concentration gives them away. When you are interviewed, centre your energy and your thoughts, and be yourself.

- Take care of yourself. If you're on a phone-in show, crank calls can slip in and you can be subjected to an harangue. Stand up for yourself and look to the host for help.

Breathe

A deep breath is the best thing in the world; it calms you and helps your throat muscles relax. Before you speak, breathe in to a count of 2-3-4, out-2-3-4. If you think you have to rush to get through everything, do the opposite. Stop, breathe, and slow down. You may say fewer words but your audience will hear more. No one listens to a speaker who rushes from nervousness. One good breath can clear everything in your head and make you feel and sound solid.

Be Proud

You'll always hear or see glitches that you wish you could erase. Never mind. You did your best to present information or a point of view; the very fact that it made it on air is important. Learn from your experience and remember to feel good about the time you took to speak.

◑ IS THIS ON? USING EQUIPMENT

Picture this—a speaker walks jauntily up to the microphone, blows into it and bellows, "**IS THIS ON?**" The audience reels in pain at the noise. Why do most experienced speakers take the time to do an equipment check and the people who need the help that a good sound system offers, never give it a thought?

Here is my best advice—if you want to be a good speaker, **check your equipment.** The corollary to that is—**use the equipment.**

How often have you seen speakers approach a microphone, look at it, and then stand back a full foot? You can't hear them at all. Details like this can derail your speech. I often sit in audiences and feel so bad for speakers who have good things to say but are inaudible. Why *won't* they step up to the microphone? Don't they know some microphones don't work from the side? It isn't rude to check the equipment; despite eveyone's best efforts, things do go amiss. Good speakers practise—often.

It's Your Speech—Do the Work

All the preparation in the world won't help you if the equipment isn't working. Beginning speakers are often undone because they assume that someone else has made all the necessary preparations. Just remember, this is your speech—if the mike isn't working when you stand up, who will look like a jerk—you or the person who said, "Don't worry; everything's taken care of"? Experienced speakers check every detail. Here's some insider advice. You may not believe any of these things really occur—until they happen to you.

a. **Take a private moment.** Arrive in good time, perhaps 30 minutes in advance to get yourself ready, meet the group, and do an equipment check. As soon as you arrive, and before your hosts introduce you, go to the washroom to arrange yourself. You may not have another chance. Comb your hair, check your clothes, make sure your notes are handy. Halfway through your introduction is not the time to make sure your zipper is done up.

b. **Check the microphone.** The most common response to a request to test the microphone is a vague but pleasant, "Oh, I'm sure everything's all set."

Understand that the organizers of an event believe that, "everything's set" when the speaker arrives and the meal is ready. They've

> "Trust in God but tie your camel."
>
> —Sufi saying

done their part. It is your job to check equipment essential to your presentation. The microphone may have been ready two hours ago when the technician went home. **Check it yourself now.**

c. **Is the slide projector or computer working?** Now is the time to en- sure that your slide holder fits, the bulb works, and the cord reaches the outlet. Say to the technician, "I'd like to check the first three slides. May I see them please?" If anything's wrong, you have time to get help. If you're using a film, video, or computer-generated graphics, be sure the equipment is ready to go and you understand the controls.

d. **Don't hold back!** If the equipment isn't available yet, or the technician is on a break, stay there until everything is in place. You may need to return in a few minutes. Don't be distracted if your host seems im- patient; he or she has other things to do. Assure them you'll be along as soon as all is well. If it requires time to get things as you wish, take it. You are the speaker—it is your job to ensure that everything re- lated to your speech is ready. It is not rude to insist on changes or a sound check—it's responsible.

More On Using the Microphone

We're all familiar with movie images of people horseback riding, canoe- ing, and using microphones. These activities look so simple, we assume anyone can do them with ease. It is a shock when the horse runs away and the canoe zigzags endlessly. People approaching the microphone for the first time often look foolish as they crouch low or stand on tip-toe to speak. The microphone seems too close, pushing into their faces, so they step back and become inaudible.

Modern technology has made microphones more sophisticated than ever. This means that everyone can be heard; public speaking is no longer the domain of the person who can boom to the back of a hall. You can lower your voice to sound confidential; you can hold conversations with your audience. But microphones only work well if you use them properly.

• **Ask for a microphone when you make your arrangements.** Microphones make public speaking possible for everyone. People with soft voices may be wonderful speakers; people with strong voices no longer have to strain them in order to be heard. A whole range of ex- pression is possible. However, some groups still belong to the traditional holler-and-boom school of speaking. As a speaker, you deserve equip- ment to make your job possible.

To become used to using a microphone, bring one into the classroom and acquaint yourself with the following features:

• Microphones are either on floor stands or lectern clamps. In both cases, the necks are flexible.

- Floor stands have a centre join that will loosen to allow you to adjust the height a foot or more. Grasp the stand with one hand and, with determination, unscrew the centre join. Adjust the stand and tighten.
- Handle the microphone firmly: tilt the head smoothly.
- Once the mike is adjusted, lean into it. It may be hard to get used to this object between you and your notes, but you can do it.
- The sensitivity of the equipment varies. Some mikes are omnidirectional and will pick up your voice from all sides and the top. With others, you must speak directly into the head, at close range. You've seen singers who seem ready to kiss the microphone; they do that to get maximum amplification. You can whisper into good equipment and be heard perfectly if you do it right.
- **Do not tap, or blow and puff, into the head of the mike.** To check for power, say clearly "check 1-2-3-4." This allows the technician to test for volume and feedback.

Exercise: Microphone Competence

Looking confident, walk to the microphone. Pause, adjust the floor stand, and raise or lower it. Then, adjust the head with a firm smooth action. Speaking directly into the mike, make a brief comment on

a) the ideal weekend;

b) why reggae is so popular;

c) why newscasters always smile so much on television;

d) the need for a law to ban the keeping of exotic pets such as cheetahs and ocelots.

Speak long enough so that you can explore the range and power of the equipment. You will also need to get used to *leaning into the mike*, instead of retreating from it.

This exercise is more challenging if, before you resume your seat, you angle the head, and adjust the stand to an awkward height for the next speaker. Some day, they'll thank you.

Handle the microphone firmly and smoothly. If you appear unhurried and capable, your credibility with the audience is increased.

A Note on the Exercises

These exercises are designed to get you on your feet, speaking with coherence and vitality. There are various methods of organization; for several consecutive classes, your instructor may ask some students to prepare an impromptu for that day. You may all get the topic at the same time, or, using the envelope technique, you can try the one-minute drill. The suggestions range from lighthearted themes that everyone can manage to more complex subjects. Enjoy the challenge and use that nervous energy well.

SPEECH ASSIGNMENT: THE IMPROMPTU

1. The Envelope Please

Each student writes down one or two general topics on separate pieces of paper. The instructor collects the topics, reads them aloud to give everyone an idea of the subjects, and discards any that are too obscure. There should be at least as many topics as there are students present. All pieces of paper go in an envelope and one volunteer selects a topic, without looking. He or she has one minute to prepare an impromptu that should only last 60 seconds (a timer may indicate the 45- and 60-second marks). As the first speaker begins, the envelope is passed to the next person, who draws a topic and starts to plan. The second person can prepare until the first speaker concludes. At that point, the second person goes to the front, and the envelope is passed to the next student, and so on. This exercise is fun. Everyone faces the same challenge and the class is generally very supportive. You'll be surprised at how well you do. Doing this exercise several times over a few weeks will help you develop skills.

2. Considered Topics

You will need a list of topics concerning a subject you are studying or current issues that you are all familiar with. You may prepare the list as a class or your instructor may supply it. Choose a topic and following the time limit (5-15 minutes depending on the class and the material), prepare an impromptu.

You may wish to use some of the following suggestions:

- are dreams real?
- should you require a permit to buy a pet?
- is bribery common in business?
- dressing for work
- buying Canadian
- cults
- pregnancy and young teens
- a current movie
- high-performance cars
- music in the workplace
- travelling by yourself
- butter or margarine?
- why not to swallow your gum
- is collusion inevitable in baseball?
- missing people

- parental assistance for a child living away from home
- do people regret tattoos?
- flexible work hours
- dyeing your hair
- the best roller coasters
- drug testing—who and where?
- the best investments
- adventure holidays

DELIVERY TECHNIQUES TO REMEMBER

1. Listen to yourself: are your words and tone working for you? Do you sound the way you want to?
2. Are you interesting and clear? Do you speak decisively and stop effectively?
3. Are your stories and examples effective?

INTERVIEW

Roberta Bondar
Physician, Astronaut

Roberta Bondar is a physician, astronaut, researcher, and pilot. Her medical specialty is neurology and she was the payload specialist for NASA's 1ML-1 mission—the space shuttle that orbited earth in January 1991. Her humour and energy make her a popular speaker; she goes to the core of her intellectual and emotional being and speaks to people from the heart.

Q

Is it true that you had to make a speech as part of the final selection process for the Canadian space team, when you and 19 others out of 4300 original applicants made it to the final cut?

A

Yes, they wanted us to do a talk for 10 minutes on one of four topics without the use of audiovisual. It was not easy, but I never really thought of being nervous. We had one week to prepare for this thing. The topic I chose was the "Role of Science and Technology in Society." I had very little time to prepare, and I hadn't given many public speeches other than for medical reasons.

I always use slides; I like talking to people as though we're watching home movies, but this speech was to be done without any use of audiovisual equipment, and I hate writing speeches. I find that I can't be spontaneous because the talk is something I prepared when I was in mood A and now

I'm in mood B; I've met people and decided the tone should be slightly different. So, I guess it was supposed to be a written speech and I tried. But after two pages I stopped, and started just making notes about what I could talk about when I got to the lectern. In terms of the subject material, because I didn't have much lead time, and because I had chosen how society perceives science, I went back to the early days of the American flight program when I was in public and high school. I looked at old *National Geographic* magazines that my parents always got, and noted all the advertisements that had something to do with the space program, because that's how society was perceiving the space program and how we could use space technology.

The selection committee were all told not to smile at any jokes we cracked; they were just dead pan. It wasn't a normal audience. By the time I was finished the first seven minutes I thought, "Well, these guys don't look like they're having much fun, and I don't feel like I'm having much fun." So I started straying a bit to other things I had thought I might want to say. I deliberately did not look at the person holding the big sign that told you there was one minute to go, so he kept moving it down the table. I must say that I don't like giving talks unless I'm going to have fun doing them.

Q.
In other words, spontaneity is very important to you?
A
Very much so, because when I use point form, it's like a conversation with people. When you have a written text, if you try to memorize it, and not look at the notes, you can forget a line and you're really in trouble. That is absolutely devastating.

I had a hard time in school with memory work, spitting back words that someone else had said. I liked science because you could explain it in your own words, and this approach is better for communicating ideas, presenting them in a creative way.

I'm interested in being able to speak to other people about science. When I was in university, and went home at Christmas to the Soo, communicating my ideas to people who had no science background at all was very difficult. So at Christmastime I would really make an effort to tell them.

Q
What is your personal style in groups?
A
I listen. It's amazing how many people tell me I'm a quiet person. I'm a listener; I observe how people are interacting. I try to figure out where they're coming from, what they're trying to get out of the group, or what points they are trying to get across. And I adjust my level of contribution to that. If it's a really aggressive group, and I know I'm not as aggressive as the rest, I know I'm going to have to pitch in and not be nervous about things.

When I first started all this, I was really inhibited because everybody else had such wonderful things to say...It takes a while to get over that and be able to contribute. When I get into a group, I want to make sure I've got those feelings out of my head, and when I speak, it's going to be something positive.

Q
How can you, Dr. Roberta Bondar, astronaut, be inhibited?

A
I never think of my position; I think of what I can contribute, what my value is. What is Roberta Bondar's value here, what can I do, what can I give to the group from my personal repertoire? In terms of communication, I'm very direct. I try not to mess around.

Q
Do you have any problems in groups?

A
When I'm nervous, I start speaking quickly and that does me in. My pronunciation goes down, and my thoughts don't come out clearly enough. I have to slow down and enunciate.

Q
You use audio-visual material extremely well.

A
If you're giving a general lecture, slides with a lot of writing can be distracting but if you're giving technical talks, it's much easier to have the information on the slide, than ruffle through your notes to see if you've memorized something properly.

Q
Is it easier to speak now than when you first began?

A
When you give a number of talks on the same subject—now I'm not saying that all my talks are the same: I try to make them different or I'll be bored—you get so familiar with the material that it gets easier for you. And it appears easy. The average person looking at someone who talks a lot may be overwhelmed, but it's like everything else in life—it's rote learning. You're not born with all the medical knowledge. It's just going over and over it.

The first time I use a new slide or new information, I may make an error. If I realize it, I'll correct myself. But unless there's an expert in the audience, they may not even remember what you said. And you're got to remember that someone listening to you only takes home a fraction of what you've said. I've done 18 years of university and I'd hate to tell you how much I've forgotten.

You don't expect your audience to remember everything, so if you do

make mistakes or you do forget things, you shouldn't get sweated up about it while you're at the lectern. If you remember afterwards during question period, you can bring the material back in. So you shouldn't get so nervous; you should have a main message and have interesting slides to support it.

Q
How do you practise?

A
If I'm on a plane, I think about things and make notes. Then I try to take something local and incorporate it into the talk. If I'm at a school, I talk to the teachers or principal about what the big topics are. I try to make the crowd know I'm interested in them, to include something personal.

Q
How do you deal with sexism in the industry?

A
It depends on what your background has been, how you've been beaten or scarred by various things. I've had to deal with a lot of it, and it's surprising where it comes from. Sometimes sexism surfaces on occasions when you don't want it to surface and you get

angry. And that's the danger point. If you try to deal with things from an angry state, then you put yourself in a much worse position. The main thing is to try to be cool, to come back with short one-liners to put people in their place but not in a vicious way. If you're vicious, you'll just get it back again.

Q
You've seen a lot of speakers. How do we as Canadians measure up?

A
We use fewer gimmicks than people in other countries. In the United States, people use jokes a lot more. And some people, Canadians and Americans, use pointless jokes, ridiculous stuff that is completely out of context. And jokes with inappropriate sexual connotations are beyond the limit. I remember one lecturer talking about dermatology with all these slides of women—they weren't about dermatology at all. So the women, over 50 per cent of the class, walked out. That's how we dealt with that.

Q
What advice would you give to people making their first speeches?

A
Being nervous may be the most distracting thing. I've told people who wear glasses to take them off but that's not such a hot idea. You have to have a good night's sleep and know the material. The other thing you have to realize is that people are there to hear what you have to say, not win the lottery based on how many "ah"s you use. As long as you're interested in what you're doing, your audience is interested in what you're saying.

Keep the level of enthusiasm up throughout the whole speech: there's somebody out there who is as interested in minute 15 of your speech as in minute one. I've heard a lot of speakers trail off; keep the interest level up.

Roberta Bondar

The following excerpt is from a speech Roberta Bondar gave when she was Honorary Director of an International Event held by the Girl Guides of Canada. Over 3500 women and girls attended the event, representing 48 countries.

Speech: A Responsibility to the World

I'm delighted to be here. Three years ago, when I was asked to be honorary director of this camp, I thought it was a dream come true. All my life, I've wanted to be a physician, an astronaut, and a camp director....If I had had this opportunity at your age, I'm not sure which choice I would have made. I understand you have 101 choices for today. That's absolutely amazing. This might be one of the few times you can speak to people with real expertise in various fields. You are going to be in small groups to help you approach people, talk about important things, discuss issues...It's *so* important to share information. None of us would be experts in our fields if we have not discussed things with other people. There's nothing wrong with asking.

All the workshop leaders are volunteers, sharing with you because they think it's important. I want all of you to remember that you are important. Each of you has a responsibilty to the world. Each of you has to carry something away from today and make it important to you because you have to share it with others. You see, I don't have any children; you people are my bridges to tomorrow. You have no idea who you will be touching in your lives, even in a small way, that will affect them forever.

OUTLINE OF AN IMPROMPTU SPEECH

Name: _____

Date of Speech: _____

Purpose Statement: _____

INTRODUCTION

Grabber:

Thesis:

Overview:

BODY

Supporting Argument #1

Supporting Argument #2

Supporting Argument #3

CONCLUSION

Reference to purpose (thesis):

Summary of main steps:

Zinger:

SELF-EVALUATION FORM

This form is to help you evaluate your own speech. It can be kept private or shared with your instructor or peers.

Type of Speech: _____

Name: _____

Title: _____

Date: _____

DELIVERY

Physical Presence

Did I make eye contact with others?

Was my posture natural and appropriate?

Was I aware of my facial expressions and hand gestures?

Were there any distracting mannerisms that I was aware of?

Did I feel good?

Could I feel an energy exchange with my audience?

VOCAL DELIVERY

Was my voice under control?

Did I sound confident?

Was I aware of breathing calmly?

How was my enunciation?

Did I manage to avoid um's and ah's?

Did I sound interested/excited/committed?

How did my voice sound to me?

DESIGN AND CONTENT

How well did the introduction and conclusion work?

Did the framework unify my speech?

Was there a natural progression from point to point?

Did my notes keep me on track? Did I use them?

Did the audience seem to understand the organization of my speech?

Was the information clear?

What was the energy level of the conclusion?

What would I change the next time?

What worked very well?

OVERALL EFFECTIVENESS

Did I connect with this audience?

Did I achieve my purpose?

What do I remember most about making the speech?

What unexpected or unforeseen things happened?

What am I most pleased about?

OTHER COMMENTS

Grade: _____

PEER EVALUATION FORM

Peer evaluation should be done in a constructive and supportive fashion. The speaker may choose people to do assessments or they may be assigned alphabetically. Some groups maintain the same speaker/assessor teams for the entire course; others change for each speech. The instructor may wish to see this evaluation before it goes to the speaker.

Type of Speech: _____

Speaker: _____

Title: _____

Assessor: _____

Date: _____

DELIVERY

Physical Presence

Did the speaker maintain eye contact?

Did she or he establish a rapport with the audience?

Were gestures natural and effective?

VOCAL DELIVERY

Did the speaker sound convincing/spontaneous/excited?

Was his or her voice clear and loud enough?

How did you respond to the speaker's mood?

DESIGN AND CONTENT

Did the introduction interest you?

Did the overview give you an indication of the main proofs?

Did the speech flow easily and logically from one point to another?

Was the conclusion strong and memorable?

Did the conclusion reinforce the thesis and main points?

What was the thesis of the speech?

OVERALL EFFECTIVENESS

Did you learn something new or worthwhile from the speech?

Were you moved by it?

What was the most outstanding part of the speech?

What changes do you recommend?

What parts should the speaker definitely keep?

OTHER COMMENTS

Grade: _____

EVALUATION FORM

Type of Speech: _____

Name: _____

Title: _____

Length of Speech: _____

Date: _____

Legend: S=Superior   E=Effective   NW=Needs Work

DELIVERY

Physical Presence

Eye Contact

Rapport with Audience

Posture

Gestures

Use of Notes

Appropriate Use of Audio-Visual

Support Material

VOCAL DELIVERY

Naturalness/Spontaneity/Enthusiasm

Clarity

Variety (Tone, Pitch, Pace)

Volume

Absence of Verbal Tics (um, ah, okay, like)

Sense of Control and Calm

DESIGN AND CONTENT

Use of Framework for Introduction and Conclusion

Clear Thesis and Overview

Coherence/Use of Transitions

Strong Finish

Language

Word Choice

Impact on Audience

Grammar

OVERALL EFFECTIVENESS

Treatment of Topic

Intelligent Awareness of Audience

Achievement of Purpose

Impact on/Connection with Audience

OTHER COMMENTS

Grade: _____

You've Got a Friend: The Social Speech

TIPS FOR SPEAKERS

1. Get the name right. This is the essential rule of the social speech.

2. People look forward to social speeches; combine enthusiasm with preparation and practice. Your friends deserve the best.

3. Clear patterns for the introduction and thank-you, presenting and accepting an award, the tribute, and the toast.

4. Breathe! You'll feel better and sound great.

5. Good speakers show respect for lifestyles other than their own.

Be prepared! Know the content. The most nervewracking thing in the world is not being sure of what you're doing.... The audience yearns for you to do well, they're totally on your side, and there's very positive energy going for you.

June Callwood

WARM-UPS

Impromptus of Praise

Our National Dessert

You have three minutes to prepare a brief speech outlining the merits of the sweet dish we should adopt as our national dessert. Describe the dessert and why it deserves to be our national delight. Be inventive—the dishes can range from bumbleberry pie to jamoca almond fudge jello. Your mood is both persuasive and celebratory.

Animal of Honour

You have three minutes to prepare a brief speech in honour of the animal that has done the most to enrich your life. Your choice can be a pet, a working animal, or a creature that has contributed to our health, national pride, or comfort. You can use the species or an individual animal—be sure to highlight specific traits and to speak sincerely.

A 17-year-old inventor named Rochan Sankar bounded to the microphone to accept the YTV Achievement Award for Innovation. With television cameras focused on him and thousands of people in the audience, he was affable, enthusiastic, and funny. Eyes shining, he thanked his parents and the sponsors of the award and went on to talk of the excitement of having an original idea—the energy and the rewards it brought him. He was a superb speaker. Not so the bureaucrats who presented the gift. They had to read directly from the teleprompter—for statements like "It's wonderful to be here tonight."

Special occasions hum with spontaneity and goodwill. Why do some speakers find it necessary to inflict empty phrases and wooden delivery on their friends and associates? If you are asked to introduce a speaker, make a toast, or present an award, concentrate your energy on connecting with the people in front of you. If you're nervous, reach out. Look at them. This makes all the difference. Know your material well, and draw on the vitality and joy you carry inside. Your speech will make the event richer.

Social speeches are often much shorter and more informal than business or persuasive speeches. Some people assume, therefore, that less preparation is needed. This is not true. If you spend so much time on a class presentation, shouldn't you concentrate more on a speech for your friends? Speeches for special occasions—the introduction, the thank-you, the presentation and acceptance, the toast, the tribute, and the after-dinner speech—all require diligence and preparation. They also need a sense of the occasion and personal warmth.

Your voice adds that depth, that feeling of joyous spontaneity. In the section on voice and gesture you'll find exercises to help you develop a fuller range of vocal expression.

◗ THE ONLY RULE: GET THE NAME RIGHT

Can you imagine mispronouncing Sinead O'Connor's name? What about Elaine Wabi, Foluke Akinremi, Laurene Boileau, Iggie Praught, or Duc Banh? What we consider easy to pronounce depends on where we live and what we hear in the media. During Olympic competitions, we talk about various athletes as though they were old friends—and never once consider their names difficult.

Getting the name right is always essential, but even more important when the whole purpose of your speech is to introduce or honour the person concerned. Don't rely on someone else's version of the name or even your own experience—my friend Iggie pronounces her last name Pratt; her cousins say Prowt. It's spelled Praught. Find out for yourself.

The following names were taken from the class registers of a community college. How would you pronounce them?

Bourner	Sardella
Tzouhas	Deviatiarov
Tonnerre	Gottlieb
Atagi	Luong
Riel	Mattice
Belliveau	Sernoskie
Ayuyao	Rouse
Kearns	Zaida

Strategies for Tracking Down Correct Pronunciation:

1. **Advance warning**. The president of a retail shoe chain, Arch Heels, asks you to introduce the speaker at the annual sales convention. Your boss hands you a sheet with a few details about the speaker, an expert on orthopedic design, and gives her version of the name. It's an easy one: Haley. What is your next step? It would be a good idea to phone the speaker to check the background information and the name. Haley looks easy, but is it pronounced Hal-ee like the comet or Hay-lee like the author? If you mispronounce a name in front of 200 people, do they care that your boss gave you wrong information? Check the name.

2. **Surprise—you're it**. Your boss meets you at the registration desk with the news that you will be giving the introduction. What next? Remember the outline given in this chapter, organize your thoughts, practise your breathing exercises, wait by the door for the speaker to arrive, and check the name as you say hello.

3. **Smooth work**. You're on the stage and the speaker is late arriving. As the regional sales manager outlines the year's success, the orthopedic expert enters and walks to the stage. Slipping smoothing from your chair, you move to one side of the stage, greet your guest in a courteous fashion, and *check the name*.

4. **Deceptively daring**. This is the situation that makes even experienced speakers check their pulse rates. You're on the stage, the guest appears before you can make a move, and suddenly you're called upon to introduce a speaker called Haley (or Praught or Ayuyao). You have several choices: guess; do it wrong and apologize (reaping scorn from everyone who knows these strategies); embarrass yourself for life with a remark like "Gosh, I've never seen a name like this;" or walk over to the guest, shake his or her hand, and very quietly ask, "Do you pronounce your name Hay-lee?" Guest speakers always help you out because they know how much you want to get it right.

Exercise: Get the Name Right

Group members put two or three names, which they can pronounce, on slips of paper and sign them. Exchange lists and take two minutes to determine the correct pronunciation of the names. Taking turns, each person stands and with enthusiasm and confidence, gives a concert welcome. "And now, let us welcome—Jay Haley!!!" (*tumultuous applause*)

Cities and Towns Also Need Research

Last week, the production crew of a local radio station mocked the new announcer who referred to Gan-ann-ook: that's Gananoque (Ga na nok way) to most of us. It's unnerving to stand up to introduce representatives to a conference and discover that the list of cities represented reads like a quiz in pronunciation. How would you manage with these: Nanaimo, Port Coquitlam, Ucluelet, Tuktoyuktuk, Kluane, Kananaskis, Okotoks, Esterhazy, Batoche, Fort Qu'Appelle, Dauphin, Gimli, Sault Ste. Marie, Penetanguishene, Etobicoke, Kapuskasing, Stouffville, Percé, Chibougamau, Rimouski, Miramichi, Antigonish, Margaree, Malpeque, Middle Mosquodoboit, Baie Vert, Souris, Port aux Basques? Try calling your local reference library for assistance.

◐ GUIDELINES FOR SPECIAL OCCASION SPEECHES
Never Miss an Opportunity

Most of us will never get the Order of Canada, but we will still be touched when someone takes the time to express appreciation of our work or our lives. If you're asked to make a speech, don't hesitate because you are embarrassed. Focus your efforts on the other person and make use of an opportunity that may never come again.

Imagine your grandmother has her 80th birthday, and your family says to you, "Say, you took that public-speaking course; *you* make the speech." If you toss away the opportunity with an offhand remark like "Great going, Nana," how can you be sure that there will ever be another time for your family to acknowledge to your grandmother and to each other how much she has meant to you? The effort you take to speak is a tribute in itself.

Be Brief, Sincere, and Spontaneous

Social speeches are short and specific; they pave the way for the main event, wrap up the proceedings, or accentuate an important occasion. If you are well prepared, you can be brief, and the occasion will retain its excitement.

The key to sincerity is finding the appropriate tone. Avoid trite or exaggerated remarks such as "this cherished heritage building," "our valued customer," "this priceless collection." Speak simply and with warmth.

How can you be spontaneous and well prepared at the same time? On social occasions, your audience expects you to know the person you're talking about, and to be enthusiastic. You should not use notes when giving the speaker's name or referring to the recipient of an award. If you need to look at your notes to remember that you are delighted that Fred's work has finally been recognized, your good wishes seem a little forced.

Research

You get information for a social speech in the same way you do for other types: *Research*. Specific, concrete examples enable your listeners to see the value of a co-worker, or understand the amount of work done by the coordinator of the Heart Fund. You must dig for stories, examples, numbers, quotations.

Ask family members, friends, and colleagues for details to illustrate your remarks. Support your speech with concrete data. If your grandmother came over as a war bride, recall her experience of getting off the train at a northern settlement.

If your classmate is receiving the George Wicken Writing Award, find out who Wicken was and why the award was established.

Research also involves common sense. If you're presenting an award to a blind co-worker and it's appropriate that you mention that she's blind, what's the most considerate thing to say? How do you find out? Ask the person. That's research.

◐ PATTERNS FOR SOCIAL SPEECHES: THE ADDED TOUCH

Social speeches follow the same general outline given earlier:

- seize the attention of the audience and outline your topic or thesis;
- deliver the goods;
- reinforce your point and make a strong finish.

The added touch is a very specific *signal.* The audience is given the cue to applaud, the guests are given the words of a toast, the spectators are given the motion to start.

The Introduction

Quirky, unpredictable, boring. The speech of introduction is one of the hardest speeches to predict. It's often assigned at the last minute and no biographical material is available. But you can make the difference. You can give a good speech that arouses interest in the guest speaker and presents an idea in a clever way.

Your job is to establish a link between the audience and the speaker. You should make the speaker feel welcome in that group and give the audience notice that they will benefit from the speech to follow. You can help the speaker by outlining the appropriate credentials and creating an atmosphere of anticipation. How long should the speech be? In most cases, two to three minutes is appropriate.

Pattern

1. **Address the audience**. What does everyone in the room share in common? Are they students interested in employment possibilities, or club members who share an interest in hot-air ballooning? Establish some common ground for the meeting.

2. **Direct attention to the speaker**. Mention his or her name early and repeat it two or three times in your introduction. Remember, the audience is hearing it for the first time and wants to know *who* the speaker is, *what* his or her credentials are, and *why* they should listen. You might want to ask the speaker what credentials to mention and choose ones appropriate to the group; do not repeat the entire biography found in the program notes.

   The surprise technique. If your guest is well known or you wish to surprise your audience, you can use the mystery approach; give all the significant details and then say, "and now, may I present...."

3. **Focus on the topic**. In the example on page 76, Sheri Alexander made sure her co-workers would pay attention. She wanted them to know

that tropical disease is as much a matter of concern for travel counsellors as it is for doctors and adventurers.

4. **Give the signal—in this case, the name**. Use your voice to build to a climax, and incline your head to the guest or make eye contact. Then, speaking *directly into the microphone*, give the cue: "It is with pleasure that I present Dr. Fred Azouz."

A Special Note on Titles

When you introduce the Governor General, you'll refer to "Her Excellency, the Right Honourable…," the archbishop of the Greek Orthodox Church as "His Eminence, The Archbishop of the Greek Orthodox Church of North and South America," your English teacher as "Dr. Kent," and the police officer in charge of community relations as "Staff Sergeant Pulford." How do you find out the correct form of address? Libraries have books that list various forms of address in current usage in Canada. If you're stuck, ask the person directly, or his or her executive assistant. Do *not* rely on popular opinion. If you are introducing a couple, check both their names.

Blunders to Avoid

1. *Introductions that say too little or too much.* A remark such as, "and now here is Howell Gottlieb, a man who needs no introduction" is difficult for the speaker. Howell has to think fast or the audience will have no idea why he was asked to speak. Similarly, long introductions can be embarrassing. If you have ever had to sit through someone reading out every course taken, job held, award won, you know it can be a case of overkill. You can revive the audience with a touch of humour: "The detail that most impresses my cat Kodiak is how fast I operate the can-opener."

2. *Don't make a speech about yourself, how you know the speaker, or how difficult it is to make a speech about a person you admire.* If you do know the speaker, mention it briefly and modestly.

3. *Don't make the speaker's speech.* Perhaps you were asked to do the introduction because you are interested in the topic. State its importance with sincerity. Then stop. Do not cover material the main speaker may have built into the speech. Stick to the basics: who is this speaker? what is the topic? why is it relevant to this group now?

4. *Keep the humour low-key.* For some reason, we tend to blurt out inappropriate remarks when we become nervous. Our attempt at humour can alienate both the audience and the speaker. If someone is

speaking on employment equity, now is not the time to poke fun at the inclusive language policy. Stick to the basic information and be as gracious as possible.

5. *Don't forget the name of the speaker.* Write the speaker's name in big bold letters to save you if you fumble. If your speaker is accompanied by a partner or spouse, make sure that person's name is also given in full. Do not use trite references to " lovely wives" and "distinguished husbands."

6. *Demonstrate active listening.* The audience's gaze will occasionally shift to you during the speech; your body language speaks volumes. Don't make an introduction and then spend your time making notes, whispering asides to colleagues or checking details with servers. Keep your eyes on the speaker and generate support and appreciation.

The Speaker's Response

Gloria Steinem replied to a warm and admiring introduction by saying, "I know what I'm going to do with the rest of my life—live up to that introduction." She had listened carefully to the introduction and replied generously.

It's surprising how many people ignore the comments of the people introducing them and come with their thanks written out ahead of time. Good speakers are recognized by their very first words. Leave time at the beginning of your speech for a reply to the introduction. The secret to a gracious and obviously spontaneous response is listening. Focus on the welcoming remarks and find a reference, an image, or word to pick up on. If you can do it smoothly, you will distinguish yourself as an accomplished and thoughtful guest.

The Thank-You

These are short but sincere remarks. Your preparation may involve advance research or on-the-spot attention.

Pattern

"Time is not the same for the speaker as for the audience. To the speaker it is too, too brief for what he has to say. For the audience it is a grim foretaste of eternity."

(Marshall McLuhan)

1. **Reason for thanks**. If you are thanking a speaker, your function is clear. You need to mention one or two points from the talk that you found helpful or interesting, and remark on them *without* repeating or interpreting the original address. If you are thanking a conference or group coordinator, you need to give the audience a specific idea of this person's function. Statistics are sometimes amusing: 386 air flights booked, 2300 meals planned and ordered, 465 name tags lettered.

2. **Try for a balance of brevity and sincerity**. Whether you have advance notice or must plan your thanks in two minutes, take time to make thoughtful, specific remarks. By concentrating on the concrete, you avoid rambling. The key is sincerity. Focus on the idea you found appealing and let your enthusiasm show.

3. **Signal—Thank the person by name** and pronounce it correctly. Finish your speech, then turn and applaud the person concerned.

How do you thank an unpopular speaker? If someone has come to justify the government's plans to close the local hospital, that person will not receive a pleasant welcome. Your job is to thank the government representative for the time spent with your community group. Although you may not like what was said, you can appreciate the time and effort that individual gave.

Presenting an Award

When you combine your own enthusiasm with some clear organization and add the sparkle of goodwill, you have a good speech of presentation. If you outline clear cause for the award, the audience will not only perceive the worth of the recipient, they will also enjoy the energy of your speech. Its function is three-fold: to honour the recipient, to present the actual award, and to give the person being honoured a chance to express thanks. The speech should be three to five minutes in length; brevity is the key.

Why was the local owner-operator of a cycle shop voted citizen of the year? If the announcement of the award is the main idea or thesis, what follows? Three supporting reasons, which must be illustrated with anecdotes, quotations from neighbours, telling examples.

Pattern

1. **Set the stage**. Discuss the background or history of the award and the conditions concerning its presentation. Brief the audience on how recipients are selected.

2. **Talk about the recipient**. Use concrete examples that you discovered during your formal or informal research. Be sincere in your remarks. You may point out how you know the award winner but do not go on about yourself.

3. **Explain the award or gift as a symbol of the group's esteem**. Even though everyone contributed 50 cents for the present, you need not dwell on the gift itself. Be sure that everyone knows that it is an honour for you to present the award and that you are paying tribute to the recipient.

4. **Give the signal**. Ask the cycle-shop owner to come forward, give her direct eye contact, and perhaps a personal word. Then, speaking directly into the mike, address a few words to her, such as, "All of us think that Regina is a happier, more free-wheeling place to live because of your contribution to our community. It is with pride, Kit Creek, that we present you with this award."

5. **Help the recipient with the gift**. It takes practice to speak into the microphone, make eye contact, shake hands, and present a gift in one smooth motion. It is even harder to accept a six-kilogram Inuit sculpture wrapped in three metres of paper. *Help with the gift*. In many cases, it is expected that the person being honoured will unwrap the gift; in that case, and depending on its size, a small table would help. As the presenter, you might assist by holding the gift while the recipient unwraps it. Quite likely the person is surprised and a little flustered; lend a hand and add to everyone's enjoyment.

Accepting a Gift or Award

No one expects you to have an acceptance speech planned and rehearsed; that might seem just a little too slick. If you have been notified in advance, prepare a general acceptance but try to keep your words spontaneous. If you are completely surprised, keep in mind that the audience must hear every word you say, and take the opportunity to make a short, warm thank-you.

Pattern

1. **Express appreciation in simple, direct language**. Be sincere and pause, if necessary, to think. One or two sentences is enough.

2. **Don't apologize for being unprepared**. You are not supposed to be prepared. Enjoy the honour, and be yourself.

3. **Thank the key people who helped you**. Most successful efforts are the result of teamwork. Share the praise but do not list every person you've ever met.

4. **Again, thank the organization presenting the award**. A citizenship award is established to recognize and promote community awareness and participation. What impact does receiving the award have on you? If cash is involved, how will you use it?

5. **Open the gift if that is expected**. A group may have gone to great trouble to find something to delight you. Join in the spirit of the occasion by unwrapping the object as gracefully as possible. Respect the efforts of the organization that is honouring you.

6. **Accept the gift and say thank you once more**.

LESSONS FROM A PRO

When Rochan Sankar appeared on television to accept the YTV Innovation Award for inventing the cardiogauge, he was told to prepare a speech that would appear on the teleprompter. But he was also told it would be better if he worked only from a plan and tried to be spontaneous. Rochan heard other winners give long lists of thank-yous and decided to try a different approach: "I really wanted to give a message, something personal that applied to other people in the audience. So after the first few sentences on the teleprompter, I winged it. I spoke from my experience about what I really felt. It came from within."

Speaking directly to the audience, he shared his vision and his humour:

"There is nothing more precious than an original idea; seeing it translated into reality is truly an exhilarating experience. It's extremely rewarding—intellectually *and* financially."

The Funeral Tribute

This speech taxes your heart. On one hand you want to give a final gift to a friend or colleague who has died. At the same time, you must find enormous personal reserves to put your memories into words. It is the speaking aloud, the actual words, that make a friend's death so real and so hard to talk about. But it is a tribute, a remembering that each person deserves. Take heart when you are asked to do this speech—and take time to work through the process.

In formal terms, this speech is a eulogy. Traditionally, it dwells on a person's attributes and accomplishments, and is sincere and simple. The following example outlines the characteristics, achievements, and charm of a very devoted teacher. It was delivered at his funeral by a colleague.

A FUNERAL TRIBUTE TO GEORGE ROBERT GRENFELL WICKEN

Given by Dr. David Kent

Toronto

George Wicken was many things, variously accomplished. He was a remarkable person in so many ways. His profound sympathy for other people—that reaching out from himself to the other we all experienced in relating to him—that sympathy was at the heart of his teaching gifts.

...He was a trusted, valued person. No one who knew George was neutral about him. Everyone liked him. The presence of students here today tells us in what affection he was held by those he taught.

But reaching out is tiring when combined with such a sense of responsibility and duty as George had. In his book on the Canadian poet Wilfred Campbell, itself a major contribution to scholarship on Canadian major lit erature, George writes of the "personal spiritual experiences in nature" that Campbell's poetry describes. His annual vacation at the family cottage must have brought George the kind of self-losing experiences which gave him peace, rest, and renovation. This communion with nature allowed George to return to the academic wear and tear each August with renewed vigour.

Sympathy, or identifying with the other, is probably related to George's love of the theatre, too. He delighted in organizing a theatre outing for students and faculty. The greatest artistic ecstasy for George was attending a Broadway musical; in it were joined language, drama, and his other love, music. We all loved to listen to his reports of a trip to New York.

George was a sociable person. He loved to tell jokes. He certainly had a sweet tooth. He took great joy in rounding up tardy faculty and heading for Hospitality Place, the college restaurant. Or, he liked to use his powers of persuasion to convince us that there could be no more convivial place for lunch than at "Feathers," the English pub on Kingston Road. One of my dearest memories is the sight of George moving from cubicle to cubicle in our department office, greeting each one of us and stopping to chat as long as we wished.

Above all, George was a teacher. He loved teaching. It was his vocation, his calling, his fulfilment. Out of that love came ideas, innov-

ative techniques, and imaginative exercises, all of which he generously shared with his colleagues. We all remember his students eagerly searching out information about their dates of birth in the newspaper microfilms or becoming genuinely excited about doing research on the Confederation poets.

...Another remark George made in his book on Campbell is pertinent here, and a reflection of his own personality. George wrote: "Commitment to others, through loyalty and love, can give life meaning." In that sentence George is still speaking to us now, speaking of commitment, dedication, enthusiasm, love. Those are values he embodied.

...If we could have told George something a few days ago, I wonder what each of us would have said. I'd like to end with a quotation out of a letter Leigh Hunt sent in 1822 to Joseph Severn, the man who was caring for the dying English poet, John Keats. I think some of us might have wished we could have said this to George, even if through an intermediary. I say it now on behalf of us all: "Tell him (Hunt wrote to Keat's friend) that we shall all bear his memory in the most precious part of our hearts...

Tell him that the most skeptical of us has faith enough to think that all (of us) are journeying to one and the same place, and shall unite somehow...again face to face, mutually conscious, mutually delighted. Tell him he is only before us on the road, as he was in everything else, and that we are coming after him."

You can also prepare a shorter, more personal statement. Obviously, it's a hard thing to do. Dave Duggan, when asked to make a speech for a friend killed in a car accident, said he wanted to do it because his friend's parents had asked him to, and he wanted "to say in public how special he was to all of us." To prepare a funeral speech, consider the following suggestions.

Pattern

1. **Honour the person**. Your speech, even if it's hard on you, is a way of paying tribute to someone you liked and will miss. It is a chance to say how much that person meant to you.

2. **Make a plan—and tie your speech to something solid.** How do you see your friend in your mind? Did he or she have a hobby or a job that you can base your memories on? A neighbour of mine gave a tribute to the father of a friend who was an enthusiastic gardener. She started with a memory of him tending his plants and finished by saying that for many people, he was the pick of the crop. Do you have one outstanding picture that can form the base of your talk? Make a plan to help yourself get through the speech and give it a framework.

3. **Outline how you knew the person**. Were you friends at school? Did you attend the same camp or play on a community ball team? Establish your connection for family and friends who don't know you.

4. **Select specific memories that bring your friend before you**. Your job is to give yourself and others a glimpse of your friend and his or her special qualities. Choose one or two good memories: a joke shared, a camping trip, the time you were lost in Paris and your friend decided to spend the night in the police station. It's all right to smile as you remember the good times; it's a way of keeping that person in your life.

5. **Keep it short**. Don't strain your emotional reserves. Present your memories, say that you will miss your friend, and *finish*. That's often the hardest part. Dave Duggan ended his speech with the words, "John Robert was my best friend and I will miss him always."

Crying is all right. More than that, it's common and can even occur in what should be happy speeches. In the case of funeral speeches, you should be prepared to feel the constricting of your throat, which means tears are on the way. If you *practise*, you will know which words and phrases are likely to trigger tears, and you will be ready. Pause. Breathe. Tell yourself you're okay. People will wait. This is a hard speech, but the students I know have been determined to do it well.

The Toast

Toasts are ceremonial tributes given on special occasions; the most common are a toast to the Queen, an impromptu toast, and a wedding toast. Making these speeches can be a pleasure if you remember to brainstorm, plan, and practise.

It is essential to include the signal and the verbal cue.

Patterns

A Toast to the Queen or her representative. The Protocol Office of the Secretary of State provides a simple outline for a toast to the Queen. The person proposing the toast raises his or her glass and says, "Ladies and gentlemen, will you rise and raise your glasses in a toast to the Queen: the Queen—la Reine."

The toast usually occurs after dessert and before coffee.

An Informal Toast. Often, when you're present at a celebration or dinner, someone will say, "Let's have a toast," and look straight at you.

1. **Be prepared**. If you can form three-part plans as you stand in line for a concert, you are used to being ready. During the soup course of a celebration dinner, you will think of one or two thoughtful and complimentary things to say. You should also think of the cook; make your remarks brief, or speak *after* dinner. Never let a fine meal cool.

2. **Relax**. Take the opportunity to express appreciation or congratulations; focus on the person you are speaking about. Your friends look forward to your words, so enjoy yourself.

3. **Breathe**. This is an informal setting but you still need a well-modulated, resonant voice. Breathe.

4. **Make one or two sincere remarks**. If your friend has just received her pilot's licence, wish her adventure and freedom. Compliment the sense of adventure and attention to detail that led to her success. You might use stories from her training to illustrate the challenges she faced.

5. **Give the signal**. Raise your glass and address your friend directly: "Congratulations on your pilot's licence, Valerie. We wish you good weather and smooth landings: [*the cue*] To Valerie."

Wedding Speeches

Speeches are the landmines of the wedding reception. Too often, the bride and groom wait until the day before the wedding to ask someone to host the reception or make a toast. In the midst of the excitement and partying, there is little time to prepare. To compound their nervousness and lack of preparation, would-be speakers listen to friends who advise them to have a drink to "loosen up." What often results is a five-minute mumble of semi-humourous anecdotes, insults more suited to a roast than a toast, and remarks that show no regard for the families present. To make things worse, the verbal mayhem is recorded on videotape—so the humiliation lives on.

How can this happen? How can families spend thousands of dollars on a reception and not insist on speakers whose skills and thoughtfulness they trust? If you think I'm exaggerating, consider the following examples.

- a man proposing a toast to the bride and groom said that for them it was love at first sight. They hopped into bed the night they met and didn't emerge for two days. True perhaps, but not a good choice for a family gathering.
- in toasting the bride and groom, the best man enthusiastically recalled meeting the groom's boss Ben and his talented wife Zora. Too bad Ben was there with his present wife Olivia.
- another speaker joked, "It's nice you decided to make it legal, James. I was afraid she'd be a live-in for years." The bride's father did not look pleased; he was there with his common-law partner of eight years.
- the MC proposed a toast to the parents of the bride. Because the bride's name was Hope St. Jean, he assumed that her parents were called Mr. and Mrs. St. Jean. Their names were actually Marie and Jack Boddam and they were irate. The MC had embarrassed and infuriated the people who were paying the bills.

Everyone deserves a happy wedding day with speakers who respect the occasion and say kind things. If you're asked to do a toast, follow these rules of common sense:

- Honour the families and their guests. Respect the value of the people present. They don't need shock treatment or x-rated gags. The reception is not a roast or a time to embarrass others.
- Be sensitive. This is a very emotional occasion for everyone. Prepare in advance and find out who will be present and what is considered appropriate. If you're in doubt about some of your material, leave it out.
- Leave past histories and family composition alone! This is the most dangerous landmine. Do not assume anything about the relationships of the people present. Ask them how they want to be mentioned; check their names carefully and omit all references to ex-mates and past history.
- Don't elevate yourself at the expense of others. Too many people speak to get a few laughs for themselves rather than to please the wedding party.
- Bring up happy, positive memories. Tell stories that outline the lives of the bride and groom in a considerate way. It's fun for the families to recall highlights of their lives and interesting for guests who don't know the couple well.
- If you can't speak—don't!

Turning Landmines Into Goldmines

Choose an MC you trust to keep the speeches moving and share the microphone wisely—a friend or relative who is a good speaker and an affable host. The groom's childhood friend might be a great best man but a terrible speaker; get someone else to be the MC. He or she should enjoy large groups and be able to control access to the microphone in a friendly way. Insist on a good speaker.

What are you supposed to say in a toast to the bride and groom? It is a speech to wish the bride and groom happiness, and share stories that give a sense of the couple. Your job as a speaker is to plan carefully, rehearse thoroughly and party later.

PATTERN

1. **Make a plan.** You need a three-part plan: introduction, body, and conclusion. The theme is the happiness of the bride and groom in their lives together, their adventures, their family. During a reception, you face competition from servers clearing dishes and a general hum of excitement. You need a strong plan to enable guests to follow your remarks easily.

2. **Frame your speech.** What sort of grabber will make a strong framework for your speech? Can you use the words of a favourite song, a special day the couple celebrates, a shared joke? If you start with such a reference, your conclusion is already set. Refer again to the song, the special day, the way they met, and your speech will have unity.

   One father proposed a toast by noting that the wedding day was also the anniversary of the birth of Martin Luther King Jr. He went on to wish his daughter and son-in-law the qualities that King embodied: courage, vision, and love.

3. **Research.** If you are a friend of the couple, you will have a good source of anecdotes. Otherwise you will have to research. Ask the couple for ideas; telephone family members, friends, business associates. Share the making of the speech and be sure to collect stories about both individuals. A good toast is well balanced.

4. **Consider the wishes of the bride and groom.** Talk to them about the speech, ask what they wish to have included, if there is anything to omit. Review the names of family members and make notes. If one or both of them have children, how will they be mentioned? In a recent toast, the speaker included the wishes of the children for their father and new mother.

   In the example of a toast to the parents of the bride, the speaker followed the wishes of the bride to toast all her parents. The speaker refers to the four people by their first names instead of outlining who is married to whom. A toast is no time for a flow chart.

5. **Use gentle humour.** Practise telling the stories to your own family. What is their response? Do they think the stories are kind?

6. **Practise.** Your friends deserve the best. Make notes, revise your speech, experiment. If you work hard on a presentation for work, work equally hard to honour and delight your friends. Weddings are busy times; give yourself at least a few days to concentrate on the toast before the prenuptial festivities begin. The countdown given below may help. And be prepared with an extra set of notes. I once lost my notes in the excitement of getting to the church on time.

7. **Refer to the bride and groom by their names.** Give them equal billing and refer to each person in his or her own right. Avoid references like "We wish Sebastian and his wife much happiness." They'll both be happier if you talk about "Sebastian and Megan." Make eye contact with the bride and groom and let them know that you are honoured to play this part in the ceremonies.

8. **Give the signal.** When you have given your friends the best gift possible—a good toast—give the verbal cues that everyone needs:

    Please join with me in a toast to the bride and groom.
    [raise your glass]:
    To the bride and groom—Megan and Sebastian.

9. **Enjoy yourself *after* you are finished.** Eat, rest, and drink after the job is done.

A TOAST TO THE PARENTS OF THE BRIDE
by Kimberly Mitchell

Change is inevitable and with change comes growth. Over the past 13 years I've watched Lisa go from a "I'll-try-anything-once" child to a serious, thoughtful woman. I don't think Lisa could have grown this much if it hadn't been for her family, especially her parents. They nurtured her as a child, watched her flourish with their love and care, and even helped her when she didn't know she needed help. Occasionally she was helped when she least wanted it. Like the time her father knew she had it for the boy behind the meat counter, and he decided to do his rendition of Quasimodo behind the shopping cart—just to get his attention. But, most of all they have given her their support. No matter what she has done, no matter what life has thrown her way, they have always been behind her, and she, in turn, has always been behind them.

Lisa really is one lucky person—she has an extended parent plan. She has four different people guiding her, four people sharing their love for her, and four different sets of ideas which have enabled Lisa to broaden her outlook on life. I'd like to make a toast to Lisa's parents and all the ways that they have helped her—to Marie-Ange, Raymond, Dawn and Patrick, Lisa's parents.

12-DAY COUNTDOWN FOR A GOOD WEDDING SPEECH

Day 1:	• Get the assignment. Ask the bride and groom if you will be speaking.	Days 6, 7, 8:	• Talk to bridal party for stories. Check family names.
Days 2&3:	• Brainstorm and plan. Get a theme. Talk to friends.	Days 9, 10, 11:	• Make notes. Practise.
Days 4&5:	• Talk to bride and groom. Design speech. Work on intro and main points.	Day 12:	• One last practice out loud. Good luck.

Themes That Work

Need help to get rolling? Here's a list of possible themes; they may trigger an idea for your toast. Most of them focus on everyday songs or objects. People relate to common items; while they may nod in agreement at classical quotations, they smile in surprise and delight when you mention something they recognize:

- The bride is like the flowers in the bouquet she carries: the enduring beauty of the rose; the loyalty of forget-me-nots, the mystery of the gardenia, and the luck of the shamrock.
- The couple are like classic cars: he's got the universal appeal of the Volkswagen Beetle, and she's got the joy of the rag-top convertible.
- Married life is like a fishing trip that they both enjoy: they have the equipment, the bait, and the boat. And like all good trips, the true fun does not lie in the catch but in the experience.
- Marriage is like the song "all my life's a circle"; as the moon rolls through the night sky, they will know the circles of joy, hard times, birth, romance, and age. And the circle always comes back to their love.
- In Lithuania, the couple is served a symbolic meal: wine for joy, salt for tears and bread for work. A good marriage has all three.
- This couple met while tree-planting, and wood is central to their lives—for heat and security; for happy campfires with friends; for magic and romance dreaming in the firelight.
- A gift to them of a set of keys: health, happiness, and humour. And if a key is ever lost, they can find it again. The "key point" is a wonderful time together.

The couple can reply to the toast. One bride returned the compliment and said that when she was a little girl, she used to look at the night sky and wish on a star. Then she thanked everyone who had come to her

wedding and said she was truly lucky because they were her stars—the
people who had helped make her dreams come true.

SAMPLE OUTLINE OF A TOAST TO THE BRIDE AND GROOM

Alex Cardinal was asked to give the toast to the bride and groom at the marriage of his friends
Farouk and Emily. These are the notes for his speech; he used the song "Amazing Grace" as
the base for his remarks.

A Toast to the Bride and Groom

Intro	• greetings to the bridal party, families and friends
	• bride's favourite song is "Amazing Grace"
	—one line is "I once was lost but now I'm found/was blind but now I see."
	—Emily and Farouk also have visions of what their love can bring them separately and together as a couple
Thesis	• *we wish them a vision of happiness*
	—in their careers
	—in the family they hope for
	—in shared adventures
Body	• careers: Emily is a child care and youth worker
	—caring, strong, perceptive woman
	—story of Brett and Duc
	Farouk is a technician in printing firm
	—artistic, competitive
	—remembers coming to Canada after escaping his own country by truck and boat
	• family: family means Love, Support, Freedom
	—Emily's life with her grandparents
	—Farouk's trouble at school and support at home
	—their plans for a new family with love for everyone
	• shared adventures: love of travel, auctions, commitment to each other and freedom to grow
Conclusion	• We wish them happiness and joy.
	We hope that the love they share will help them build a future of possibility and caring, and know the hard times they have had will make them kinder people.
	• I THINK OF AMAZING GRACE AS THE LOVE FAROUK AND EMILY HAVE FOR EACH OTHER.
	They are not lost—they have found themselves and each other.
	They are not blind—they see love and a future together.
	We wish them amazing grace, amazing love, and a life of health and joy.
Cue	Friends and family, I ask you to rise and join me in a toast to the bride and groom. —TO EMILY AND FAROUK, THE BRIDE AND GROOM.

Stand up, speak up, then clam up. The human mind can absorb only what the human seat can endure."

(Hugh Shantz,—B.C. Legislature, 1959-1963)

The After-Dinner Speech

After you have been initiated into the world of public speaking, someone will ask you to provide "the entertainment" at a luncheon meeting or banquet. Generally, you are expected to speak rather than tap-dance. The experience can be enjoyable: the ambience is good and the audience friendly.

An after-dinner speech provides the intellectual dessert to the meal. It may be informative or persuasive, but its distinguishing feature is your awareness of the audience, and your desire to please or stimulate them. Your audience analysis will help you choose a topic that is appropriate without being heavy. Wildlife biologists working for the National Park System do not need more data on rabies control. However, they may relate to your analysis of the most rabid species of all: the tourist.

Pattern

Many topics you are familiar with will make good after-dinner speeches if you follow these guidelines.

1. **Tailor your speech to your audience.** Although this may be the tenth time you've spoken on sailing around the world with your cat, you must tie it in to the interests of the present group or you'll sink. Nobody likes generic speeches; they sound the same in any city and they're disappointing. Repeat performances are also boring for speakers; you'll lose your edge.

    Research the group and work on an upbeat approach. What do solo sailors and your audience of nurses have in common? Too much work to do in too little time? Bedpans in the night? Life-or-death emergencies? Find good parallels and you've earned your chocolate mousse.

2. **After-dinner does not mean out-to-lunch.** Respect the intellectual skills of the audience. Include some thoughtfulness or challenge in your speech. Humour is welcome if it works for the topic and the occasion, but a string of unrelated jokes will fall flat.

3. **Have a challenging but not baffling topic.** Analogies and anecdotes are more suited to this occasion than complicated proofs. A clear plan will enable your listeners to follow you easily.

4. **Fit in with the occasion and enjoy yourself.** Commenting on the occasion, interacting with audience members, and referring favourably to other speakers' remarks are all appropriate. Be friendly and reward the group's taste in speakers (you) by giving your best.

5. **Prepare first—eat later.** As the other guests dig into their kiwi cheesecake, gather your thoughts, check your notes, and start your breathing and relaxation exercises. At the same time, talk to the people at your table to find out more about the audience. Tune in to the mood of the event.

◑ VOICE AND GESTURE EXERCISES

Before undertaking a major speech, you should develop some skills in controlling your voice and gestures. Speakers need clear, resonant voices and significant gestures.

This section deals with specific exercises and goes on to investigate how important the words themselves are to the impact of your speech.

What are these exercises supposed to do? They will help to develop

1. **resonance**: the richness or mellowness of the tone;
2. **volume**: controlled and suitable loudness;
3. **pitch**: the highness and lowness of your voice;
4. **pace**: the speed at which you speak;
5. **enunciation**: the correct formation of sounds and words;
6. **inflection**: the use of your voice to create mood and meaning.

You are not aiming for a constant pace or pitch; you are trying to control your voice; it is a very powerful instrument. By using a variety of pitch, pace, and inflection, you will be able to maintain audience interest and determine the sonic shape of your speech.

Breathing Exercises

Where does the air come from?

Have you ever seen someone yell until the tendons in his throat bulged and his temples pounded? The distended tendons, red face, and protruding eyes were all caused by lack of air. *Air* makes our voices work, and anyone who breathes only in the back of the throat ends up foolish and gasping as the air runs out. Try this: assume an angry frame of mind and a threatening posture. Take one big breath and then berate and threaten an imaginary foe. Do this without breathing again. Did you feel yourself losing control as your air ran out?

Try it again, but this time breathe from deep inside your chest, from your diaphragm. It's a muscle, like a wide elastic belt located just above your waist. You should feel it move if you encircle your middle with your hands. When you breathe, try to get the diaphragm to move. Is there an improvement when you breathe? (Do not prolong this exercise; it's too hard on your voice.)

Rhythmic Deep Breathing

This exercise is used by speakers, actors, and students of yoga to relax and control their air supply.

Sit cross-legged (or sit comfortably in a chair) and keep your back straight. Imagine a thread suspended from the ceiling and attached to the top of your head. That should bring your head perpendicular to the floor.

Your back is straight and you pull yourself up in your chest. (Imagine your sternum or breast bone is pointing the way.)

Now, shut your eyes and breathe as the instructor gives the count: *In-two-three-four, Out-two-three-four, In-two-three-four, Out-two-three-four.* Concentrate only on your breathing and the instructor's voice. The exercise should continue for three to five minutes and, as you breathe, your muscles and your mind are getting ready. Many people accompany this exercise with imagining themselves on a beach or other tranquil spot and concentrate on their breathing and the details of their surroundings.

Every good public speaker does this exercise (with eyes open) just before speaking. *Never* **speak without relaxing your larynx and setting a breathing rhythm. You can do the exercise in the classroom, at a conference or banquet table, or in your boss's office.**

Blowing Out the Candle

There is a candle in front of you. Take one breath and expel it slowly, very slowly and evenly, in order to make the candle flame flicker but not go out. See how long you can maintain an even stream of gentle air.

Neck Rolls

It's hard to breathe if you are too tense to move. Slowly rotate your head and neck to the right; hold it there. Then roll it slowly to centre, pause, to the left, and pause again. Back to centre and repeat. Then gently tilt the neck down, pause, to centre, pause, and up. Pause, repeat. (Do not rotate your neck and head in a circle; use this exercise instead.)

Million-Dollar Stretch

Stand comfortably with your feet spread. Stretch one arm out in front of you at shoulder height and *reach* for the million dollars someone is holding just beyond your fingertips. Reach as far as you can without bending your body. Do the same exercise to the side, and then switch hands.

Vocalization (or Grunting)

Sometimes your voice clogs and you need to exercise it. Take a breath, make a series of grunts—the kind they use in martial arts just before they clobber you. You can make several series of grunts, each at a different pitch.

Inflection and Pacing

"Where Canadians got the monotone that you're listening to now, I don't know—probably from the Canada Goose." Northrop Frye jokingly criticized his own voice on a CBC radio program, but his comments are valid.

Too often we use the same note for everything we say, and yet it is our voice that gives real meaning to our words. Do you want to express curiosity, determination, outrage? Your voice does it. To develop a vocal range, an exercise that involves a bit of exaggeration is useful.

Exercise: Reading to the Wall

Everyone in the group selects the same passage (from a newspaper, a pamphlet, or part of this book), and assumes her or his own place *facing* the wall. Try to leave an arm's length between each of you. Then, on a given signal, read the passage *at the same time, and at full volume.*

Read the passage four times, all simultaneously, but adopt a different persona each time, trying to make your voice express the character. As a judge, you will raise the grave implications of the subject; as a television evangelist, you will assure your audience (the wall) that they will go to hell, etc.

Reading #1: the television evangelist
Reading #2: the complainer
Reading #3: the drunk
Reading #4: the airhead—fast as you can, no pausing

(You can also choose to be someone who is spaced out, putting pauses where none should be or a person who prefaces all remarks with "like...you know, eh?")

Newspaper Headlines

Each person brings in a newspaper headline and reads it three different times, each with a different mood or meaning. You can try for various effects from the quizzical to the comical.

Be Firm

In English our voices go down at the conclusion of a statement, and up at the end of a question. Don't they? Some people tend to make statements sound like questions, which makes them sound very unsure of themselves and the situation. Their discussions sound like this: "Well, I think that first aid is really important? They should have it in all high school health classes? Definitely, I'd be more confident if I knew I could cope with a medical emergency?" Translate this series of uncertainties into assertions. "Digital clocks are far easier to understand than the old-fashioned kind? Everyone can say '8:15', even small children? However, I wonder if kids understand the concept of time any better, just because they can say the words? When I was younger, and had trouble telling the difference between a quarter *to* eight, and a quarter *after*, I was often late. Today, six-year-olds can say the words but they're still confused? Perhaps being late is an adult hang-up?"

Tongue Twisters Tamed: Exercises in Articulation

"Walking" and "talking" are hard words to pronounce. Familiar as they are to us, they often come out "walkin'," and "talkin'." To get used to enunciating your words correctly, look in the mirror and exaggerate your face and lips as you say vowel sounds: a—ee—i—o—u, and oo (as in "moon"). Watch the movement of your lips, teeth, and tongue. They, along with your palate, make the sounds; we need to practise articulation that is clear, but not affected.

Say the following words slowly and clearly, giving full sound value to them:

marsh-mallow	crank-case
reek	lolly-gag
tin-tin-nab-u-la-tion	tart
fuzz	Tor-on-to
moon	Iqal-u-it
ratchet	ex-post-u-late
per-am-bu-late	poop

In speaking, it is necessary to *slow down* when you are trying to pronounce a word of several syllables. "Practically" is a good example; in a rush to get it finished, people transform the word to "practickly." Slow down and give each syllable its due: "prac-tic-al-ly." The same goes for words like "megalomaniac," "dis-associate," "antediluvian," "recognize," and "Arctic." You must also watch that you do not insert syllables that do not belong: film, *rather than* fillum; athlete, *rather than* athalete.

Resonance, Pitch and Pacing: Exercises

Swallowing Honey. By making a conscious effort, you can improve the resonance of your voice. If you do the breathing exercises and your voice still seems brittle or hollow, pause, and imagine someone has fed you a large spoonful of liquid honey. Roll it back in your throat and swallow slowly. Speak again, and see if the golden richness has reached your vocal cords. If you experiment, you should be able to alter the mellowness of your voice several times.

The Stage Whisper. Have a partner go to the back of the room. Then, making eye contact, whisper a secret so that your partner hears and understands the message.

The Rich Relative. This time your partner is your rich uncle or aunt. Convince your munificent relative to give you the gift you want or need. Your reasons must be so convincing and the gift so wonderful that no one could resist.

Get Thee Hence: A Note on Gesture. If you have seen old movies, you know the melodramatic use of gesture favoured by so-called orators and thespians. Clasping their hands in anguish, covering their eyes in shame, averting their gaze in resolution were common. Gesture should be a *natural* use of your body to

illustrate,

clarify,

emphasize.

If you need to show your audience how to position your hands for the Heimlich manoeuvre, how big a drop the stock market took, or how positive you are that your advertising concept will work, use gestures. The only guidelines are to

make them simple,

make them big,

make them count.

In the following exercises, use gestures that seem natural. Avoid the extremes of constant, nervous, jabs and flutters, or the frozen posture of terror.

Opposite Sides. A and B take positions on opposite sides of the room. They have two to three minutes to engage in discussions in which they each have definite views. Concentrate on voice and gesture. Suggestions for discussion follow; augment them with your own.

- A wants to go out for the evening; B wants to say home.
- A thinks there are flying saucers; B does not.
- A thinks Yellowknife is an ideal place to live; B prefers Acapulco.
- A and B are two crooks planning a robbery. A wants to break in at night; B thinks a daytime plan is easier.
- A thinks B should unplug the boiling kettle; B is sure that it's A's turn.
- A thinks television is primarily entertainment; B thinks its function is education.
- A thinks the Beatles were the finest musicians of the twentieth century; B knows it was Elvis Presley.
- A thinks cooked vegetables should be served crunchy; B likes them mushy.
- A thinks spring break should be eliminated; B thinks it's essential.
- A thinks you should buy only new cars; B thinks that used cars give better value.
- A and B are going on holiday. A wants a quiet place to read; B lives to dance.

Charades. This standard party game is ideal for developing significant gestures. Play it in teams using the standard categories of song, book, or movie titles.

Reading Aloud: Poetry, Plays, and Children's Stories. Performing real material gives you the best practice and the most fun when it comes to voice and gesture development. When you read plays or tell children's stories, you use your whole being to convey the drama and the mood—the experience is in your performance. The following titles and excerpts are only suggestions. There are many more for you to find and work with; the skills you refine by reading this material aloud should spill over into your speeches.

Children's Stories to Read. These stories emphasize character, mood, and dialogue. They are available in most libraries and have been performed for college audiences with great success. Prepare for 15 minutes and then perform.

Free to Be…You and Me, a Ms. Foundation Project. "The Southpaw," "Ladies First," and "Boy Meets Girl" are hilarious.

The Paper Bag Princess, by Robert Munsch. All Munsch's stories are full of sound and character.

Plays to Perform in Class. A play by Ken Gass, *Hurray for Johnny Canuck.* This is an uproarious spoof of World War II super-hero comic strips, starring the all-Canadian, Johnny Canuck, Corporal Dixon and his dog Laddie, and the brave Derek Bras D'Or. The characters, sound effects, and humour make this a good play to use for a dramatic reading with only a little advance preparation.

Saint Joan, by George Bernard Shaw. Joan of Arc, a French peasant girl, was burned for heresy, witchcraft, and sorcery in 1431. Shaw's play shows her courage and youth. At one point, Joan agrees to recant and signs a paper that she believes will bring freedom. Instead, it promises a life of imprisonment. Joan tears up her confession and attacks her oppressors. The following passage can be read loudly and defiantly, quietly and bravely, or sadly and with resignation. Understand what is being said and find your own style.

You promised me my life; but you lied. You think that life is nothing but not being stone dead. It is not the bread and water I fear: I can live on bread: when have I asked for more? It has no sorrow for me, and water no affliction. But to shut me from the light of the sky and the sight of the fields and flowers; to chain my feet so that I can never again ride with the soldiers nor climb the hills; to make me breathe foul damp darkness, and keep from me everything that brings me back to the love of God when your wickedness and foolishness tempt me to hate Him: all this is worse than the furnace in the Bible that was heated seven times.

I could do without my warhorse; I could drag about in a skirt; I could let the banners and the trumpets and the knights and soldiers pass me and leave me behind as they leave the other women, if only I could hear the wind in the trees, the larks in the sunshine, the young lambs crying through the healthy frost, and the blessed church bells that send my angel voices floating to me on the wind. But without these things I cannot live; and by your wanting to take

*them away from me, or from any human creature, I know that your counsel is
of the devil, and that mine is of God.*
    (BERNARD SHAW, SAINT JOAN, SCENE VI)

Group Sound Poetry—"Salad Days". Each person selects a vegetable or fruit,
and repeats the name over and over, with the "conductor" indicating pitch,
volume, emotion, pace, etc.

    Barnyard Melody. The class is divided into three groups: cows, pigs, and
sheep. The cows sing "moo moo," pigs croon "oink, oink," and sheep bleat
"baa-baa." Using the tune usually known as "Good King Wenceslas," the
conductor points to each group. When a group is pointed at, it sings its animal sound to the melody, and must stop when the conductor moves to the
next. This is a hilarious exercise, and on paper the first two lines might
look like this:

◑ WORDS, WORDS, WORDS

As well as developing vocal skills, you need to examine the way you look
at the world and the words you employ to express your perceptions. Words
are like the tip of an iceberg: what you say reveals the values you adopted
as part of your upbringing. Some of those concepts may need examination and consequently your words may change.

Opening Your Mind as Well as Your Mouth: Changing Lifestyles

Is a boy living with his father considered a family? How do you differen-
tiate between the mother who gave you birth and the mother who raised
you? If you are arranging the menu for a national convention, is roast pork
a good choice? How do you introduce Danielle March, the wife of your
client, Keith March?

    These questions are asked to give one message: our lives and social
patterns are changing. You should be aware of lifestyles other than your
own and respect those who live them. Families don't depend on certain
numbers of players; birth mothers and adoptive mothers are both important in our lives; religious and dietary preferences should be considered at large gatherings, and Danielle and Keith March (alphabetical
listing) are at the head table. When you speak in public, a hasty, un-
thinking remark can hurt or alienate members of your audience. You
have a moral responsibility to avoid spreading narrow-mindedness and
prejudice, even unintentionally.

How can you become more aware of the way others live? THINK. Thoughtfulness, kindness, and *common sense* are what you need.

Exercise: Broadening Your Horizons

In groups, discuss one of the following scenarios. At the end of the time allotted, one member of each group should outline the situation to the rest of the class and present the group's response. (This is still public speaking: stand—breathe—make eye contact.)

Scenario #1
Anna and Robert Sanchez objected strongly to the person who said they came from a "broken home." Why?

Scenario #2
Liz Markovich, mother of Simon and Jeanette, spent a long time replying to Renata, an engineer, who remarked, "Oh, so you don't work."

Scenario #3
Your class decides to have a high school reunion for graduates and teachers. You want everyone to attend and to bring the people they live with. How do you phrase the invitation so that all those invited will know that their friends and partners are welcome?

Scenario #4
The chairperson of the fundraising campaign for a youth centre in a large city has used the terms "surname" and "christian" name four times in the last half hour. You are uncomfortable; what can you do?

Scenario #5
As part of a special campaign, a guest speaker comes to your class and starts his speech with several sexist remarks. When your friend objects, the speaker says he was "just joking." What can you say?

Scenario #6
Gina Cengarle and her husband, Mike Rochas, received an invitation addressed to Mr. and Mrs. Mike Rochas. What should they say to the person who issued the invitation? How do you find out how to address a couple?

Scenario #7
You work in a community recreation centre and need to talk to Mark Beesley's mother or father. Before you call the home, what information should you get from Mark? To whom will you ask to speak?

Scenario #8
Lin Wah left the meeting in a hurry. During the coffee break, one of the advisory committee asked him how he was adjusting to living in Canada. Lin Wah was born in North Battleford, Saskatchewan.

Scenario #9
My grandfather was in a rage because the host at a recent movie fundraiser had asked all the "people in their golden years" to raise their hands. There is more than a euphemism causing trouble. Why was he angry at being singled out by that or any other name?

Scenario #10
Kevin MacKenzie, a graphics design student, was told that the cover he created for a student paper looked "too faggy." What impressions do people have of speakers who believe that they can make homophobic remarks? How should a listener address the remark?

Eliminating Redundant Phrases

What prompts us to use redundant expressions? Have we become so used to repeating ourselves that we can't help saying "that shirt is fuchsia in colour" or "the crew was surrounded on all sides by the fire." We know the shirt isn't fuchsia in smell, and it's hard to be surrounded on some sides only, but our speech is replete with redundancies. What's wrong with the following expressions? What should you say instead?

circulate around
true fact
8 a.m. in the morning
proceed ahead
irregardless
repeat again
disappear from view
genuine leather
at this point in time

Do you know expressions that, although not redundant, have become so trivialized by overuse that they are almost meaningless? Here is a list of phrases that one group of students considered to be annoyingly overused. How many more can you add?

the long and short of it
I know where you're coming from
I personally think
really very unique
have a nice day
political promises
interfacing with others
in point of fact
world class
the bottom line
state of the art

When we consistently overuse words, our speech becomes bland. That is the danger of using clichés, words that once had significance now mean little. Although it is more difficult to search for expressions that accurately convey our meaning, the increase in clarity and impact is worth the effort.

SPEECH ASSIGNMENT: SOCIAL OCCASIONS

The following situations can be written on cards and placed in an envelope. Each speaker draws one of the assignments. If the speech is a reply to another person's remarks (as indicated), you should consult with each other to get details clear. Or, you may choose your topic.

Your assignment is graded for two things:

a) the speech itself: research, design, and delivery;

b) your feeling for the situation, and the degree of sensitivity and courtesy that you bring to the occasion.

Dressing for the occasion may inspire your delivery; some groups have held their classes in college restaurants or hospitality labs to create a social atmosphere.

Scenarios

Supply details appropriate to your field of study.

1. Vote of thanks to the chairperson of the United Way campaign of your company. He or she made the goal of $500 000.

2. Introduce a guest speaker—an expert on tropical diseases. Your audience may not be generally aware of how the topic affects their industry.

3. A toast to the founder of your company. The founder is now deceased, but his family is at the banquet.

4. Presentation of a gift to someone in your agency or business who has done the most to improve business in the last year.

5. Reply to the above speech.

6. Thank the representative of a major airline who has spoken to your group. (You choose an appropriate topic.)

7. A toast to your grandmother on her 80th birthday at a large party in her honour.

8 Thank your local Member of Parliament for coming to hear the complaints of your group. The government position is not popular.

9. Present a gift to your course coordinator in appreciation of his or her efforts during your time of study.

10. You have visited a class of grade eight students to speak on a career in your field. They present you with a gift. Thank them.

11. Introduce the head of the

French trade delegation who is going to speak to your group on a topic you devise.

12. Thank the head of the French trade delegation and present her or him with a Canadian souvenir.

13. The provincial Premier is a guest at a convention. Thank him or her for the government's work in promoting your field.

14. At the annual national conference, you are to make a speech and presentation to a colleague who has recently received the Order of Canada. He was honoured for his outstanding contribution to the cultural life of Jews in Canada. You are to congratulate him on behalf of your group, and to wish him well on his upcoming trip to Israel. (You have no way of knowing the religious and political backgrounds of the many people at the gathering.)

15. You are proposing a toast to the parents of the bride. You are her friend. Toast her original parents who are both present, although they are divorced and in the company of different spouses. The bride also wants her stepfather mentioned, with whom she has lived for eight years. The two couples are seated at separate tables and are pleasant to each other.

16. Reply—you are the mother.

17. Reply—you are the father.

18. You are a member of a sports team that has been together for eight years. You have all become close friends. The coach of the team is moving to New Brunswick and you have been chosen to present the gift to her or him at the farewell dinner. Your team members want you to combine humour and sincerity.

19. You are making a presentation to a member of your staff who is blind. She is an excellent worker, and you want to mention her disability but not overemphasize it.

20. You have been asked to make a few "brief remarks" at a banquet of volunteer workers (you can choose the volunteer agency). You are the president of the national organization and are a guest at this event. Make a brief speech that is warm, friendly, and inspiring.

DELIVERY TECHNIQUES TO REMEMBER

1. Practise your approach. Make your walk to the front of your room part of your presentation. It should help set the mood.

2. Get your voice to perform. Use tone, pace, volume, and pitch to create variety, emotion, enthusiasm.

3. Work your audience. Build audience rapport and involvement. Use their responses, verbal and nonverbal, to enhance your speech.

INTERVIEW

June Callwood
Journalist and Social Activist

June Callwood is a journalist, novelist, indefatigable speaker, and fundraiser. More than any other Canadian, she has the ability to perceive the needs of a community, and form co-operative working groups to fulfil those needs. She founded Nellie's, Jessie's, and Casey House in Toronto, and was an early advocate of palliative care. Her energy, her generosity, her joy make her a national hero—one who coined her own watchword: "Eventually you save the world. And if someone has to do it, it might as well be *you*."

Q
In the convocation address you urged the audience to do something outrageous every day. Do you?

A
I think my whole life is outrageous. I'm suffering somewhat from the fallout from a series of columns I've just done on women who have lost custody of their children. I think I live outside what is considered normal behaviour.

Q
Why do you speak? You must spend almost all of your personal time speaking.

A
Well, I turn down 15 to 20 speeches a week. I give them for two reasons: it's for a cause I support—like the opposition to the censorship bill—or for Nellie's, [a shelter for battered women] or Jessie's [a centre for single pregnant teenagers] or Casey's [a hospice for people with AIDS], or for palliative care, or better services for children, or the problems of poverty and homelessness. I frequently speak at fundraisers for battered women's shelters; soon I'm going to Ottawa and Bracebridge to speak for interval houses there.

Public speaking is also my pension fund. As a freelancer, without a company pension plan, I have to plan for my own retirement, and I am paid for a number of my speeches. As an older woman, it will be a good income for me.

Q
You speak well to audiences made up of people of very diverse backgrounds. How do you approach your audiences?

A
I make a lot of assumptions. I see it as a very personal relationship, and that a belligerent or scolding tone, hectoring, or a critical approach is going to mean you're not going to be heard. People aren't going to listen to you.

I also assume that no matter how people look (and I don't mean their physical appearance but the stoniness of their faces, or the fact that they don't look like an interesting group), there's going to be a lot of surprises. I never underestimate an audience.

I assume I'm speaking to highly intelligent, well-informed people. I also make the assumption that they share my views, as long as I stick to the ethical component, which is responsibility for one another. I urge them to open themselves to participating in their society more fully. It's a gentle message but it's very, very important.

Q
What public speakers do you admire?

A
Eddie Greenspan is probably the best in Canada. Alan Borovoy is dynamite; Julian Porter is a remarkably fine speaker. I once heard Ralph Nader, and understand why he is such an important consumer advocate. He's a great speaker. Rosalie Abbella is one of the best speakers anywhere. Pierre Berton is compelling; you pay attention. It's his size, the big voice, and big thoughts. He has a big view of the country that he communicates.

Q
How well do people do at introducing you?

A
I've had some awkward ones, including the ones where they get your name

wrong. One student at the University of Toronto, Scarborough College, introduced me as the founder of NATO. It was a bit much. I have also been thanked and introduced with wonderful elegance.

Q
How do you prepare for a speech?

A
I work only from notes. I'm getting five honorary degrees this spring, and four would like me to do the convocation address. They also want a print copy of the speech—but I don't have one. The second speech I gave was entirely written, and I nervously read every word. I found that I'd left the last page on the seat where I had been sitting. I had to leave my seat and come down the stairs to get the page, and I've never had a written speech since. I prepare by giving a lot of hard thought to the audience, what experience they've got, and where they're at. I don't want to patronize people with information they already have.

You don't tell social workers about the feminization of poverty—they knew that 10 years ago.

I think about what kind of expertise I'm addressing and where it is that I've got anything that's useful or helpful. Most of the time, you're there because someone on the planning committee thought you have information that is useful for the group. They don't always know exactly what it is, but you take their ideas, and add your own judgment of where that group is at, and what would be useful to them from your experience, for you to talk about. I write in note form, sometimes full sentences, on folded pieces of white paper. Never any longer than five sides of notes. Just one word will sometimes remind me of a story. I take care with the opening and with the end.

Q
Can you see the audience when you're speaking to them?

A
Yes, I watch carefully; I watch faces. Usually, I find several faces that are sympathetic. I couldn't talk to a hostile face; I'd stop looking at that person. It would discomfort me too much. I look at fairly sympathetic faces and I watch them carefully to see what's happening.

I check them over and over again.

Q

Do you still get nervous?

A

Some audiences. The convocations are nervewracking. I didn't finish high school, and was intimidated being at a convocation at all. I'm nervous of extremely well-dressed people; it always has bugged me. When I was a kid we were awfully poor, and clothes were a way you could tell we were poor. Teenagers with better clothes always made me feel vulnerable, and I envied them, so a room of extremely well-dressed people still makes me feel vulnerable.

I really sweated over a speech to the Canadian Bar Association, Ontario. It was a very prestigious group, and I worked all day trying to figure out what would be of interest to them. I spoke on altruism.

Q

What speech do you remember?

A

Psychiatrist John Rich, a friend of mine, once said there are two kinds of people: the ones who remember only their mistakes, and those who remember only their victories. Lamentably, I only remember the duds.

If I've misjudged things, or been picketed and gotten distraught, been attacked in question periods, I can't forget. I don't rise to that kind of challenge, I sink. I have a resilient ego, and I don't take it personally, and I believe they're wrong, *but* I can't take the anger in their looks, the bitterness. It's how they behave when they attack: the lack of compassion, humanity, generosity, and civility. The bad manners depress me terribly. It's much more complex than what they're attacking; I feel the same way when they attack someone else.

Q

What advice do you have for beginning speakers?

A

Be prepared! Know the content. The most nervewracking thing in the world is not being sure of what you're doing. It's awful to get up with notes half done, poorly phrased, not well thought out. It's terrible to get halfway through and have nothing more to say.

Get the material ready and be sure you know it. Whether you're using notes or a prepared speech, be absolutely comfortable with it. You're going to be uneasy anyhow the first few times, so concentrate on knowing your material.

You know your subject; you have a good reason to be there. Take heart from the fact that people asked you to speak because you do know your subject.

People don't want to see you fail; nobody enjoys a speaker's pain. The audience takes no pleasure at all when a speaker can't find a place, or the voice or paper shakes. The audience feels so uncomfortable. They don't want to watch you make a mess of it. They yearn for you to do well, they're totally on your side, and there's very positive energy going for you.

June Callwood

Speech: It Might As Well Be You

This is a convocation address given at a community college. June Callwood spoke from brief notes, and used humour to engage her audience and build rapport. You can hear the vigour and humour with which she touches her audience, and the incredible directness with which she leads them to action. Her style is at once homemade and eloquent.

I take my cue from our oldest child's graduation 21 years ago from McGill University. When I asked her about the convocation address (which I missed while taking our four-year-old to the washroom), she replied, "It was superb. It was ten minutes long!" So, that's what I'm aiming at—to give a superb address. You'll be comforted to know. You'll notice I don't wear anything that indicates I graduated from anywhere; I didn't get enough education to qualify for this school, let alone graduate from it.

I hasten to assure all the graduates that not a moment you have laboured to reach this achievement has been wasted because the world is vastly more complex and alarming than when I began to work on a newspaper when I was 16 years old (and that was 46 years ago.)

You've mastered technology, you're full of facts, and most important of all, you've learned how to learn. That's a process that begins with the awareness that there is something you need to know, then enough organizational skill to give that gap a heading so you know what it is you want to find out, some library skills to find a resource centre or a resource person, the nimbleness to assimilate and substitute....So you're all set. Also you must be terrified. I've heard nothing but how few jobs there are—it's a most encouraging way to start a convocation. There is the yawning unknown that begins tomorrow, and that really is not so much a question of a job, but what kind of life you'll have. I can't speak of jobs and opportunities—I've been a freelancer for 41 years. I know a good many of you, maybe all, will succeed despite the odds. You may find another career path. But nothing is lost in the universe; whatever you've learned now—nothing is lost.

However, I can speak with some authority about how devastating it is to be a young person, to feel injustice as acutely as young people do, to have ideals, to believe that there is honour and consideration, and compassion, and that's what you want for yourselves. Adolescence is very painful; it's filled with the high tides of infatuation and hope, and the twists of self-disgust and depression. But your eyes are still open. It's not beyond your imagination to sense that most people experience depression, and that most people have hope destroyed, and most people suffer agonies of remorse.

What I ask is you don't lose that empathy. No one, *no one* is really a stranger to you. The commonality between men and women—and I'm a feminist; this is what a feminist looks like: this is the profile of a feminist, this is full-face, this is a feminist!—but there is commonality between men and women, between the races, and between religions, and between your parents and yourself, and between workers and management. What we all share is our vulnerability and our mortality. In that sense, there is nothing between you and anyone else you know, or have ever hated, or have ever admired. You're made of the same substance. You can be warm and caring but you've got to trust that people are like you, that inside people are alike. They have the same fears as you have. We humans are a tribe, we're herd animals. And we need one another, we need to trust one another, and we need one another's kindness.

One thing more. Hannah Arendt said this; it is the thing that has meant the most to me. When she was analyzing the evil of Eichmann during the Holocaust, she looked to find the essence of evil. What is it? Six million people killed. What is the essence of that magnitude of evil? She came to the conclusion after a long time that the real evil is not so much what Eichmann was. The real evil was the apathy of people who did nothing, who were spectators.

That's what I want to leave with you. There is no innocence in the spectator. If you do not get involved in an accident, in a racist or sexist slur, or someone being even mildly humiliated, or someone in need. If you don't get involved, you are as much the cause of what is happening as the person who is actually doing it. If you're aware that something is unfair and plain wrong, you've got to act!

You have to be nonviolent, I think; you have to be calm, you have to be resourceful, but *don't just stand there*. Everyone longs to be the good person that is inside, and there is a splendid person inside. That's the person we want to come out, but it takes a little practice. Gloria Steinem said, "Do one outrageous thing every day." Say to the bank manager, "How come the bank managers in here are always all men? There are these lovely little old ladies who've been here for 45 years, and 27 of you young men have been coming in and out as managers?" Say that. Go to the president of Loblaws and say that you're very anxious to shop at a Loblaws that has a woman manager. Could he just tell you where the nearest one is.

It just takes practice. You start by helping a small child who is sobbing away about a broken crayon. Easy to do, eh? Then you politely tell someone it's not fair to cut in on a line-up for a movie. Then you protest in some visible way the pollution in the drinking water. And so on.

Eventually you save the world. And if someone has to do it, it might as well be *you*.

I salute you. I honour and I treasure you. May the wind ever be at your back and the sun on your face.

Centennial College
Scarborough

OUTLINE OF A SOCIAL SPEECH

Name: _____

Date of Speech: _____

Purpose Statement: _____

INTRODUCTION

Grabber:

Thesis:

Overview:

BODY

Supporting Argument #1

Supporting Argument #2

Supporting Argument #3

CONCLUSION

Reference to purpose (thesis):

Summary of main steps:

Zinger:

SELF-EVALUATION FORM

This form is to help you evaluate your own speech. It can be kept private or shared with your instructor or peers.

Type of Speech: _____

Name: _____

Title: _____

Date: _____

DELIVERY

Physical Presence

Did I make eye contact with others?

Was my posture natural and appropriate?

Was I aware of my facial expressions and hand gestures?

Were there any distracting mannerisms that I was aware of?

Did I feel good?

Could I feel an energy exchange with my audience?

VOCAL DELIVERY

Was my voice under control?

Did I sound confident?

Was I aware of breathing calmly?

How was my enunciation?

Did I manage to avoid um's and ah's?

Did I sound interested/excited/committed?

How did my voice sound to me?

DESIGN AND CONTENT

How well did the introduction and conclusion work?

Did the framework unify my speech?

Was there a natural progression from point to point?

Did my notes keep me on track? Did I use them?

Did the audience seem to understand the organization of my speech?

Was the information clear?

What was the energy level of the conclusion?

What would I change the next time?

What worked very well?

OVERALL EFFECTIVENESS

Did I connect with this audience?

Did I achieve my purpose?

What do I remember most about making the speech?

What unexpected or unforeseen things happened?

What am I most pleased about?

OTHER COMMENTS

Grade: _____

PEER EVALUATION FORM

Peer evaluation should be done in a constructive and supportive fashion. The speaker may choose people to do assessments or they may be assigned alphabetically. Some groups maintain the same speaker/assessor teams for the entire course; others change for each speech. The instructor may wish to see this evaluation before it goes to the speaker.

Type of Speech: _____

Speaker: _____

Title: _____

Assessor: _____

Date: _____

DELIVERY

Physical Presence

Did the speaker maintain eye contact?

Did she or he establish a rapport with the audience?

Were gestures natural and effective?

VOCAL DELIVERY

Did the speaker sound convincing/spontaneous/excited?

Was his or her voice clear and loud enough?

How did you respond to the speaker's mood?

DESIGN AND CONTENT

Did the introduction interest you?

Did the overview give you an indication of the main proofs?

Did the speech flow easily and logically from one point to another?

Was the conclusion strong and memorable?

Did the conclusion reinforce the thesis and main points?

What was the thesis of the speech?

OVERALL EFFECTIVENESS

Did you learn something new or worthwhile from the speech?

Were you moved by it?

What was the most outstanding part of the speech?

What changes do you recommend?

What parts should the speaker definitely keep?

OTHER COMMENTS

Grade: _____

EVALUATION FORM

Type of Speech: _____

Name: _____

Title: _____

Length of Speech: _____

Date: _____

Legend: S=Superior   E=Effective   NW=Needs Work

DELIVERY

Physical Presence

Eye Contact

Rapport with Audience

Posture

Gestures

Use of Notes

Appropriate Use of Audio-Visual

Support Material

VOCAL DELIVERY

Naturalness/Spontaneity/Enthusiasm

Clarity

Variety (Tone, Pitch, Pace)

Volume

Absence of Verbal Tics (um, ah, okay, like)

Sense of Control and Calm

DESIGN AND CONTENT

Use of Framework for Introduction and Conclusion

Clear Thesis and Overview

Coherence/Use of Transitions

New/Interesting Information

Strong Finish

Language

Word Choice

Impact on Audience

Grammar

OVERALL EFFECTIVENESS

Treatment of Topic

Intelligent Awareness of Audience

Achievement of Purpose

Impact on/Connection with Audience

OTHER COMMENTS

Grade: _____

6

Keeping Bored Out of the Boardroom: Presentations and Meetings

You have to connect with people at a personal level—forget about being abstract and talk about real people and real issues, real concepts they can relate to in terms of their own lives.

Svend Robinson

TIPS FOR SPEAKERS

1. Tailor your business presentation to each group.

2. Business does not mean boring—people are tired of dreary, low-energy lectures.

3. Balance logic and emotion. Add energy and wit.

4. Do NOT read to people; it insults them. Talk to them as directly as you would speak to a neighbour over your back fence.

5. Successful meetings do not happen by chance; they need active participants and skilled chairpersons.

W A R M - U P S

If I Had A Million Dollars: Persuasive Proposals

Design a better pet, breakfast cereal, wheelchair, television remote, bottle opener—or any device you choose. Prepare a presentation to market your invention to a potential investor.

In the last 15 years, business presentations have changed as radically as advertising and marketing techniques. Exciting, well-paced, thorough presentations have replaced the old-fashioned lecture format. People who never thought they would have to speak publicly are now required not only to speak but to persuade. The civil engineer finds herself outlining her project to a municipal council; the accountant discusses his strategies with senior management of a large corporation; and the representatives of a community bicycle network must convince a residents' group to fund better bicycle paths and facilities.

What makes a successful presentation? First, you must realize that compiling a report or proposal is *not enough*. You must now spend time organizing your speech—a separate entity complete with grabber, visuals, three-part plan, and dynamic delivery. That delivery depends on how well you have learned the lessons in previous chapters:

- analyse your audience and tailor your speech to them specifically
- do not read to your audience: make eye contact and connect with them
- know your material well and blend logic and emotion
- use audio-visual aids to add clarity, drama, and liveliness
- have a clear plan and move through it smoothly

This chapter features a variety of sample presentations with suggestions for organization and delivery. It also covers the essentials of community and business meetings and the secrets of effective participation. The chapter concludes with an interview with Svend Robinson, a person who presents challenging, often controversial ideas.

◑ CONNECTING WITH YOUR AUDIENCE

Each speech you make must be tailored to a specific group. Of course you can use segments of similar presentations as building blocks, but use references to shared interests, to specific people, to company goals or community events, to tailor your speech to the group. *Never assume that professional groups like boring speeches.*

What they yearn for are interesting talks by people who speak with lively persuasiveness. One vice-president of a large college commented that he had rejected the proposal of a management consulting firm because their presentation was so poor; if they couldn't present themselves well, how could he trust them to carry out an efficient performance evaluation? Use your knowledge of the group to include references that will trigger responses from them. If you don't know them well, interview someone who does.

As Svend Robinson says in the interview that concludes this chapter:

There is nothing *more devastating than speaking to people who just aren't with you. To bring them around you have to connect with them at a personal level....Forget about being abstract and talk about real people, real issues, real concepts they can relate to in terms of their own lives.*

◑ BUSINESS REPORTS AND PROPOSALS THAT SPARKLE

Here are three speaking situations—each presentation was successful. The speakers followed the outline for speaking to a business proposal that is described later in this chapter and worked hard to find a way to make their presentations come alive.

Remember, no matter how sound your ideas may be, people won't choose you if they can't remember what you said. And if you have to present at the end of a long day or evening, you will be dealing with tired, often bored individuals.

Drainage Systems—and Lively Visuals

A civil engineering student decided to enliven her proposal to a municipal council; they were hearing the plans of three companies bidding on a contract to replace a major section of the town's drainage ditches. She knew that if her proposal was as heavy as concrete blocks, no one would remember her speech. She used three briefcases to create interest. The first one, a traditional black attaché case, held the papers and overheads for the financial picture; the second, a bright green plastic case, held the environmental report, with all major findings summarized on the first page and printed on green paper; the third case was a brightly coloured knapsack containing overheads that highlighted the benefits to the community inherent in her company's proposal. It took effort to come up with the idea but the council members were alert during the presentation and told her later that they remembered the report with the bags.

Benefits of Bicycle Paths—Wheels Win the Day

Chris Rodriguez and Leslie Tran were asked to represent their community bicycle club at the ratepayers' meeting at which their request for funding for improved bike paths was being discussed. Their thesis was simple: bicycles are better for individuals and communities and their main supporting ideas were benefits to the environment, to one's health, and to one's wallet. But how could they enliven the presentation? They thought of overheads and posters and eventually decided to actually bring a bike to the meeting. They made small signs to attach to the bike to show how much various items cost on a bicycle—maintenance, repairs, fuel bills, etc.—and relied on the audience to supply comparable figures for cars.

The presentation was a success; individuals came up later to talk about bikes and costs involved. Chris and Leslie were also heartened by the fact that several people said that they were motivated to start cycling on a regular basis. A good concrete object or interesting visual can excite an audience.

Consumer Behaviour—Four-Letter Words

The success of the next speech rests on the fact that the speaker knew her audience well and anticipated their humourous reaction to the mention of four-letter words. As part of her Automotive Technicians course, Sheri Gardner spoke on consumer behaviour. She wanted to intrigue her classmates so she devised a superb grabber and great plan. Throughout her speech, she used a compression ring and diagrams to illustrate her points.
Consumer Behaviour

Introduction

I Introduction

Consumer behaviour is motivated by emotion. Let's play the game Mind Bender and guess which powerful emotion is a four-letter word that begins with the letter F.

The answer is FEAR. What do consumers have to be FEARFUL of:
- fear of being ripped off
- fear of being taken advantage of: what do they know about cars?
- fear of taking their car in for a $30 lube and oil and coming out with a bill for $400

Here are three techniques that can be used to help customers alleviate FEAR.

They are building trust, communication skills, and reflection.

1. Building Trust
   - something about people in your life that you trust
   - we have trust in friendships—why?
     - there is caring, someone to talk to, someone who listens, and shared interests
   - how can we transfer this trust to our customer relationships?
     - get to know the person, ask questions and build rapport, find something you have in common and build on it
   - we know from class that 85 per cent of the population learns through relational learning, which is the use of comparisons, analogies, and applications
2. Communication Skills
   - one of the ways to achieve this is by "show and tell":
     - yes, you need a $5 dollar compression ring (hold up ring) and it will cost $200 to have it installed and here is why (show diagram)
     - for a muffler, you can show them their car, their muffler, and the hole
   - talk to people in a language they can understand
3. Reflection
   - what do I mean by reflection?
   - looking at our past experiences and learning from them
   - we've all eaten in a restaurant—have you ever left the server a larger tip because that person was friendly or courteous?
   - the bottom line is that you had a good experience and you will go back again

II Body

III Conclusion

When we graduate, we will have the opportunity to use some of these techniques to alleviate customer fear. Until then continue
Building Trust, Improving Communication Skills and Practising Reflection and you and your customers will have nothing to FEAR.

Finishing the 80-page business plan or the 20-page audit is only half the battle; if you don't present it with energy and conviction, your stacks of paper will soon be in the wastebasket. From the simplest of retail sales pitches to the most sensitive boardroom presentation, your ability to speak determines the future of your proposal.

If you have to

- present a business plan and convince senior management to accept it,
- boil down a 100-page proposal and get approval for the project,
- present the results of a major audit in an interesting fashion,

you need the following strategy.

Presenting a Business Proposal or Formal Report

Let's assume you have just completed a major retention report that your firm did for your local college or a tourism survey for the business improvement association.

The report has been printed and distributed; now it's time to plan your presentation to the client. How do you prepare?

1. Review the report, familiarizing yourself with its content and its most interesting or problematic features.
2. Focus on the summary sheet and know the appropriate section of the report for each point mentioned.
3. If there is a page of recommendations, make sure you understand which are immediate concerns and which ones require a long-term plan.
4. Prepare a speech outline—with a three-part plan. This speech outline is based on your report but it is an entirely separate entity. Your grabber must be effective:
   Use a story about the way the report was done; an interview that you still remember; a news event that highlights the necessity of the project. The three-part plan can be as simple as summary, background, and recommendations. Whatever it is, you must have a practical way to handle mountains of material or you will ramble.
5. Your presentation will be thorough but not exhaustive: there is complete written back-up. You can also rely on your audience to ask questions that will lead to more discussion.
6. Believe in your proposal or report. Get fired up about it and use the enthusiasm or fire from within to convince others.

TAKE A LESSON FROM A PRO

For many years Dave Nichols was responsible for the success of President's Choice products; he and his dog appeared on television promoting a wide array of food products including key lime pie and "decadent" chocolate chip cookies. In the process, he put his company in an enviable financial position. When I interviewed him about the importance of speaking in business meetings, he was emphatic that a combination of logic and emotion was essential. Here are a few of his comments:

Q.
How do people convince you about a product or a concept?

A.
If it's a product, seeing the product. Having their arguments well marshalled. Being able to communicate on an emotional level.

Q.
Is it important to be able to speak in business on an emotional level?

A.
Absolutely! Everything is emotion. You need a good balance between logic and emotion.

Q.
Do you get scared?

A.
People should be nervous; if you're not scared to death before you give that speech, chances are it's going to be a bomb. Don't be afraid of the fear. Use it to your advantage.

Q
How do you speak to your employees and management teams?

A.
Same way. I try to get excited, and to get others excited. Most people are afraid of dying during their speech. And most people are afraid to let emotion enter into it. So they hang onto that script, they read it—I mean, they shouldn't have chairs, they should have beds for the audience.

Q.
If you had all the beginning speakers of the world assembled in your office, what would you tell them? What is the most important part of speaking well?

A.
Emotion—use it. Don't be afraid of it. If you're not nervous, your speech isn't going to be good.

◑ KEEPING BORED OUT OF THE BOARDROOM— SUCCESSFUL BUSINESS PRESENTATIONS

Business presentations are either informational or motivational—you either present information for its own sake or use that material to motivate others to take action.

Never underestimate the power of a well-prepared, well-rehearsed talk: the following pointers may help.

1. The basis of your presentation is the summary sheet and recommendations but the essential element is YOU—your energy, your conviction. Set up the room so that you can see each person AND—

2. Stand up! Use physical energy to reinforce your personal commitment. Look at your clients, use gestures effectively, point to your overheads. Find the difference between invigorating action and distracting busyness and aim for the former.

3. Find a story, a fact, a goal, or a concrete object on which to hang your grabber—then outline the parts of your talk: reasons for the report, significant findings, chief recommendations (or decisions to make).

4. Your presentation will look something like this:

Introduction:	Grabber: Object of your presentation: to highlight the report and focus on its implications or recommendations. Overview: three main sections: background; methodology, major findings. or skip the background and get right to the recommendations—select the most significant ones to discuss.
Body:	Obviously, your talk follows the plan and concludes with a fresh declaration of your estimation of the strengths of the report.
Conclusion:	Either a declaration that the information presented is sound and/or a strong recommendation that the group move to implement the recommendations.

Remember that as you move through the summary, you may have to outline in a condensed form the necessary background information, analysis of the problem or issue, limitations that may have been imposed on the project, and relevant history or details. You may also wish to discuss not only the recommendations you are making but also your reason for rejecting other possible courses of action.

As you refer to your summary sheet, you should direct your audience's attention to pertinent sections of your report. In this way, you ensure that everyone present is familiar with the material, even if they did not give it careful attention in advance.

Using Visuals

By using computer programs to prepare business graphics, you can quickly create effective materials to show with a computer or use as slides or overhead transparencies. You can incorporate photographs, graphs, line drawings, charts, etc. All materials should strengthen the presentation; do not use them because everyone does. And always be prepared to deliver a captivating proposal—even if the machinery malfunctions. *Always* carry extra copies of the A-V material in a simple printed format that can be photocopied or even held up if you encounter mechanical problems.

Exercise: Persuasive Proposals

1. Take a formal report that you have done for a business or marketing course and present it to the senior officers of the firm. Your aim is to cover the material smoothly and concisely and to outline the recommendations so convincingly that they will be adopted.

2. Prepare a proposal that requires a client to adopt the project or suggestion that you are recommending. This can range from purchasing a brand of office equipment, to a tourism strategy, to improving the public image of a corporation or government agency.

The mark of a good meeting is whether anything comes out of it. And that's usually a function of being organized in terms of knowing what you want to accomplish, and having a plan to get there.
   (DAVE NICHOL)

◑ GOOD MEETINGS

Good meetings are like sailing. If you take good material, assemble it carefully, get an experienced person at the helm, chart your course, enlist crew members who know their job, use the wind to your advantage, and react well, it's smooth sailing. But if your preparations are sloppy and the crew uncooperative, you will be either becalmed or exhausted from zigzagging your way nowhere.

The best preparation for participating in or chairing effective meetings is to attend other effective meetings. Observe the chairperson. How does she or he keep things on track? How does a good chair determine when brainstorming or discussion has gone on long enough and bring it to a conclusion? There is a fine line between hearing someone's ideas and allowing them to hijack the meeting. As a participant, your goal is to help the meeting achieve its goals in a reasonable length of time. As a chair, you should strive never to waste people's time or to let meetings become so tedious that people do not want to attend. Establish an agenda and move things along smoothly and courteously.

In order to discuss the components of good meetings, we will look at two examples. The first is a national meeting of Levi Strauss & Co. (Canada) Inc., known as the Special Integration Sales Meeting. This meeting was held to integrate the sales and marketing functions of Levi Strauss and GWG, both owned by the same parent company since the early 1960s.

The second example is a community meeting coordinated by the Ad Hoc Committee to Stop Sexual Assaults in Guildwood Community, part of Metro Toronto. Citizens, concerned about the number of rapes by strangers in their area, met several times to arrange a public meeting.

How did both groups start?

Aims and Objectives

Why are you meeting? What goal have you set? Too often, people hear the word meeting and start to spout jargon: quorum, rules of order, closure, point of order, minutes, seconders, limiting debate. These steps in the *process* should not obscure the *purpose*. When you plan the meeting, establish a philosophical base: it's your purpose or goal. You will also have objectives; these are tasks or actions.

If you cannot identify goals, the meeting may be unnecessary. *Never call a meeting that is not required.* Everyone's time is valuable; it is insulting to spend 35 minutes in transit when there is nothing to discuss. Small details can be handled by mail or by conference call.

John De Shano, President of Levi Strauss & Co. (Canada) Inc., stresses that, in order to work well, the company espouses three values: openness and honesty, mutual respect and trust, and teamwork. The purpose of a Special Integration Sales Meeting of Levi and GWG sales representatives was to build a team founded on those goals, and to exchange a vast amount of information. As De Shano says, "There was a lot of history to get rid of." The meeting sought to build one team composed of equals; thus, internal competition would be eliminated, and retail service increased.

The task was related to the goal—information exchanged. De Shano jokingly called the meeting, "Everything you always wanted to know about the other brand but nobody would ever tell you before."

Diverse community groups often require more time to establish a common purpose. The Guildwood group identified four goals:

1. to allow women to move freely at all times of the day and night;
2. to turn anger into future action;
3. to express sympathy to the victims and families;
4. to inform and educate people about sexual assault on the street, and how to maximize their own safety and that of others.

Their specific objectives were to have each person

1. take away a practical idea to increase his or her own safety, and that of others;
2. commit herself or himself to one action related to personal or community safety.

Once your aims and objectives have been clearly identified, the next steps follow logically.

Setting the Agenda

When setting the agenda—the terms of business to be considered—it is customary to call for input. Once the tentative agenda is set, you may wish to circulate it (by telephone, fax, or mail) for approval, and then make any necessary adjustments. It is important to distribute the agenda well before the meeting. Some items need brief descriptions, reasons for consideration, or supporting material. If you append background material, be sure to note the pertinent agenda item. Allow yourself enough time to get translations done, and remember to supply them whenever necessity or courtesy indicates.

At the beginning of the meeting, it is customary to restate the objectives of the meeting. You may ask if the agenda as presented is satisfactory; at this point others may add items.

Doing Your Homework

"I could hardly keep up. Everyone except me knew what was going on." This common cry of the novice means that he or she thought going to a meeting simply meant remembering the date and location. For meetings to accomplish anything, participants must be prepared. Have you read all the previous minutes? Have you thought about what you've read? If you have a suggestion regarding one of the agenda items, have you done preliminary research and prepared a brief summary, with copies to be distributed if necessary? Have you noted pertinent questions? Too often, I have attended meetings where the business discussed seemed to be a surprise to some people. Do your homework. You can't speak if you haven't thought.

If you are new to a group, if there are factions you need to deal with, if you want support for your ideas, spend time on the telephone. People need time to consider suggestions, and an informal call can prepare the groundwork for a productive meeting. Often, this preparation determines the outcome of the meeting; it is naive to neglect it.

Setting the Scene

Picture yourself at your first big meeting. You leave home early, shovel out the driveway, drive 25 minutes through rush-hour traffic, find a parking space, and crowd into an elevator. When you emerge on the ninth floor, what do you need to be greeted by? A friendly welcome, the smell of fresh coffee, introductions, and directions to the room. Good visuals, flowers, or a thematic display also create positive feelings.

Meetings start well before the chairperson calls for order. An atmosphere of courtesy and efficiency can help to get the meeting off to a good start. When you coordinate events, pay attention to details. There are entire marketing books that tell you how to *win* the client. They outline such "techniques" as gourmet snacks and table linen in the national colours of foreign clients. These are just good hospitality. Make people feel important as soon as they walk in the door; the feeling of goodwill that you create will extend to the meeting itself.

Parliamentary Procedure

Who chairs the meeting? The person who called the meeting (in business meetings—the boss) often does, but there are other possibilities. Any person can act as leader or chairperson. This allows the head of the organization to participate and speak more freely.

Parliamentary procedure and common rules of conduct are given in great detail in *Robert's Rules of Order*, the most widely used guide of this type in Canada. However, the following brief outline may help you to follow or conduct your first meeting. With luck, the meeting will start and finish on time, deal with matters intelligently and decisively, show respect for the rights and needs of all members, and accomplish something positive.

Sample Agenda

a) Opening
  — call to order, welcome, introductions by chairperson
  — check on quorum (a majority of members eligible to vote [50 per cent plus 1] unless otherwise stated in bylaws). This is necesssary for voting, making motions, etc.
  — presentation of agenda

b) Approval of minutes
  — approved as read, corrected, or written (is it a wise use of time to read minutes that were circulated?)

c) Reports of elected officers
  — corresponding secretary's report
  — financial statement given by treasurer
  — president's report if required

d) Reports of standing committees
  — standing committees report in logical order or in the order they are listed in the bylaws
  — motions arising from the reports of officers or standing committees are taken up immediately

e) Business arising from the minutes
  — any question arising from the minutes are shown as carried over from the last meeting

f) New business
  — correspondence that requires action
  — disbursements of funds
  — additional new business: members may introduce further items or can move to address any matter before the group

g) Program
  — program items in order: each should be introduced and outlined by one person. The chair will then open the discussion.
  — motions may be made by the person introducing the item or by any member. Amendments are made and the vote taken. This

should be an efficient procedure:

all in favour;

all contrary-minded (a reasonable alternative to "all opposed");

all abstentions;

the motion is carried (defeated, tied).

h) Further business
   — chair asks if there is further business before adjournment
   — date of next meeting is usually set

i) Adjournment
   — this is done by motion and vote or general consent.

Putting Ideas to the Meeting

1. **Obtain the floor.** Address the chairperson by his or her official title and wait to be recognized.
2. **Make a motion.** Begin by saying, "I move that...." Make your statement clear and concise. Write it out ahead of time if it is detailed. To ensure that it is recorded correctly, pass a written copy to the recording secretary. For example, "I move that the college consider observing Groundhog Day (February 2) with a one-day holiday."
3. **Seconding a motion.** An idea must be seconded before the floor is open to discussion.

Speaking in the Meeting

You will quickly learn the correct procedures for speaking in a meeting. Such things as addressing the chair, making succinct motions, and asking for clarification come with experience. However, you need good communication skills to listen to what is being said, *and* what isn't, to present your own ideas clearly with thesis (your suggestion) and overview, followed by brief supporting statements. Remember that although you are sitting, you are making a speech. Your presentation must be well-thought-out, and rehearsed if necessary. Meetings are groups in action and good members know and perform the functions of healthy groups.

Communication Patterns

Personality and purpose determine the communication patterns of meetings. Look at the following diagrams and discuss what is happening in each situation. How will the communication pattern affect the members of the group and the results of the meeting? How effective is each in the short term and in the long term? How do seating arrangements set the tone for the group, and influence discussion?

Communications Patterns

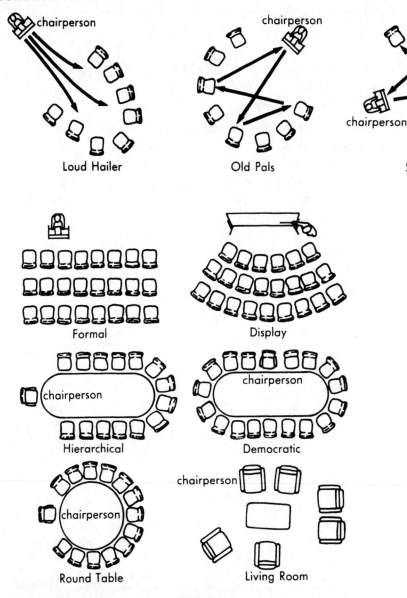

Loud Hailer

Old Pals

Spiderweb

Formal

Display

Hierarchical

Democratic

Round Table

Living Room

Business involves people; whether the product is processed steel or health care, people and ideas are most important. And business leaders are unanimous: good communication skills are essential. Dave Nichol says that people convince him about a concept by

Having their arguments well marshalled, being able to communicate on an emotional level.

Don't Read to Me!

There is nothing more futile or alienating than watching someone read a report. There are human beings in front of you—talk to them. As John De Shano says:

Don't read to people! Don't stand up in front of four people or 400 and read to them. It's insulting. Hand it to them. Let them read it. Then ask if they have any questions. Talk to them.

Have notes: don't get lost, but whatever you do, don't read to them. It's a personal insult for people to read to me. I know how to read. Tell me how you feel about it. Talk to me.

You may gather from De Shano's comments that people often read in meetings. They do. Perhaps they think it adds authority to their reports. It doesn't. It's boring. Save reading for times when you need to agree on the exact meaning of a sentence: then use your reading and reasoning skills appropriately.

Keeping on Track

It's easy to start off on topic and end up on a totally unrelated subject. We can plot a discussion of health costs like this:

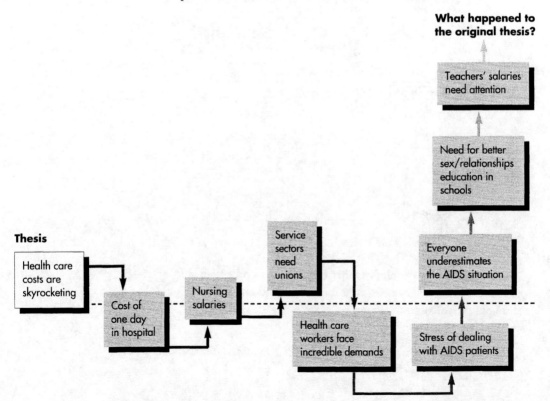

When do you bring people back to the matter at hand, and when should they be given time to explore? If you set goals for the meeting, you can assess if they are being met by the discussion. Avoid being too quick to rule people off-topic; sometimes you may be so task-oriented that you cannot perceive the potential value of the discussion. However, if neither the needs of the group nor the purpose of the meeting is being satisfied, you (as chair or as member) can steer the group back to the topic of discussion. Use a polite reminder such as, "That brings up possibilities I'd like to ask you about later. Could we finish with this item now?"

Remember, we all get off-topic; our own diversions only *seem* inspired.

Covering a Lot of Material

Some chairpersons, when faced with many reports or papers, establish that they will focus on three or four points from each. They can call for areas of concentration or establish them arbitrarily. Similarly, the meeting can divide into groups, spend some time on particular papers, and then highlight the significant parts to the committee as a whole.

Groups who, because of distance, meet infrequently often use these methods to make handling of routine material more efficient. Obviously, critical or contentious issues must be handled differently.

Convincing Others

Follow the rules for all good speeches.

- Analyse your audience.
- Research carefully.
- Establish your thesis and overview in a three-part plan.
- Marshal your supporting arguments.
- Use ethical, emotional, and logical appeals.
- Use eye contact and body language to communicate.
- Avoid rambling and unnecessary apologies or self-deprecation.
- Deal with the suspicions or criticisms of others *before* they do, and put things on your own terms.
- Make your point and *stop talking*. The hardest part of making impromptus is knowing when to stop.
- Use good group communication skills and get into the right frame of mind. Some people are sought after for committees because they make meetings productive events.

Exercise: Mock Meetings

a) Divide the class into groups; you may organize yourselves around vocational interests.

b) Form an imaginary company or organization, assign yourselves appropriate roles, and decide on a reason for meeting.

c) Draw up an agenda and include any supporting materials.

d) Wearing name tags to identify your role, participate in a mock meeting, showing good speaking and group skills. The chairperson will use a reasonable form of parliamentary procedure.

e) Groups can work simultaneously or present their meeting for the class. Evaluation should be done by each group of its own performance.

Exercise: Communication Patterns

a) Each group of five or six people is given a ball of wool and a topic of general interest (bulk-food stores, liquor at sports events, body-building, vegetarianism, how to get rich, etc.) The first person to speak takes the end of the wool and continues to hold it. She or he passes the ball of wool to the next speaker.

b) The discussion should last three to four minutes, during which the participants pass the wool from one person to another in the order in which they speak, the speaker always keeps hold of the wool as it comes to them, and passes the rest on (Jane talks; when Thanh follows her, he gets the ball of wool; as soon as Kim starts, the wool passes to her, etc.).

c) At the end of three minutes, observe the pattern created. Do some people have more strands of wool than others? Does the number of strands relate to their function or to an imbalance in speaking patterns?

◗ GOOD MEETINGS REQUIRE EFFECTIVE GROUP SKILLS

A successful meeting depends on how well the people in attendance work together to accomplish their goal. To do this they should realize that they are a working group and are not operating alone—the way they interact is as important as the job at hand. That is, the task and the method or process, are interrelated. If you concentrate only on getting the job done as fast as possible, the group will not be as efficient. Some members may later sabotage decisions or impede further progress.

Groups need to talk together honestly and with courtesy. If controversy and conflict occur in a meeting, then everyone needs to talk openly. Smoothing issues over for the sake of "getting the job done" will only hide the problem, not solve it. If you understand the roles you may assume in a group meeting and know that your role can vary from situation to situation or even within the meeting itself, you will be able to assess your own contribution to a good meeting—and talk with your colleagues about how the group is functioning.

Exercise: Matching Terms and Definitions

You are already familiar with many of the roles that you might assume in a group. See if you can match the terms and definitions given below. Some of the roles involve accomplishing the task and some concern maintaining a healthy group.

Group-Building Functions

1. Participation builder
2. Tension reliever
3. Problem solver
4. Supporter and praiser
5. Operations monitor
6. Comprehension monitor

a) asks for facts, opinions, background, feelings, ideas, and information.
b) makes sure that group members understand what each other says.
c) builds on previous comments.
d) tells jokes, increases fun.
e) mediates conflict and helps resolve it.
f) keeps track of topic and brings discussion back on course if necessary.
g) synthesizes or pulls together similar ideas.

Task or Goal Functions

7. Information and opinion giver
8. Information and opinion seeker
9. Summarizer
10. Energizer
11. Clarification checker
12. Elaborator
13. Direction and role giver
14. Gatekeeper

h) asks others to summarize or give feedback to make sure they understand.
i) expresses liking for group members and acceptance of all, especially new people.
j) offers facts, options, background, ideas, feelings, and information.
k) encourages others to keep working hard to achieve goal.
l) lets members know that their contribution is valued.
m) monitors tasks to be done and may ask for volunteers or assign responsibilities.
n) observes working of group and relays information to help group discuss ways to improve.

Answers: 1.l, 2.d, 3.e, 4.i, 5.m, 6.h, 7.j, 8.a, 9.g, 10.k, 11.b, 12.c, 13.n, 14.f.

Exercise: Scripts Please

Depending on your role, how would you speak? Imagine that you are a class meeting to discuss the problem of racism. There are eight black students, almost all were born or have roots in the West Indies, yet all of the material studied in your English course is written by and about white North Americans. (If it's more appropriate, the minority group could be native Canadians or French Canadians, or Vietnamese, or Chinese.)

Develop remarks suitable for each of the roles mentioned in the previous exercise, remembering that in a successful group

- each person is valued,
- the goal is achieved, and
- open communication of ideas and feelings is encouraged.

Evaluation:

Once you have finished this exercise, divide into groups of five to six people to check your answers and discuss the following:

1. Are all these roles necessary in every group?
2. How many of these roles have you played? How many have you played at one time?
3. List the various meeting situations in which these roles would be helpful.

What happens when they are neglected?

Open-Ended Questions and Open-door Voices

How can a group build openness and trust in its meetings? By communication and example. Good discussions can grow from questions like this one:

"How is this sales policy consistent with our values?"

This is an open-ended question. It provokes thought and discussion. Other examples of open-ended questions are

"What problems can you see getting in the way of our completion date?"
"What sort of things would make you more agreeable to the change in our original outline?"
"How can we make sure the client group buys into this proposal?"
"When you're living in a tent for six weeks, what sorts of things really distress you or please you?"
"When you went through the travel brochures, what places or activities caught your eye?"
"How should we go about getting feedback on the caterers we've shortlisted to supply the cafeteria?"

"Genuine speech is the expression of a genuine personality. Because it takes pains to make itself intelligible, it assumes that the hearer is a genuine personality too—in other words, wherever it is spoken it creates a community."

(Northrop Frye)

Break It To Them Gently: Using Your Voice to Help

In group situations, the tone of your voice is as expressive as the words you use. How many ways can you say, "I suppose you have a good reason." If a group is committed to its goal and to its members, group members should avoid sarcasm; people can hurt each other with a quick word or smart remark, and the open wound may fester. Unchecked, it can infect the group.

At school and at work, we've learned to bully with our voices. A loud voice, an aggressive or pushy approach is often mistaken for efficiency. Don't be fooled by such people and don't try to intimidate others. Loud voices in a group are like bidders at a country auction; the loudest and the quickest are rarely the serious buyers. Serious buyers wait patiently, and bid only when it counts.

Let's Get Physical

What is your body saying to other people? Have you turned to one side and pushed yourself back from the table—a position of dislike or alienation? Are your arms crossed in a "prove it" attitude? Are papers and books piled around you like a fortress to protect you from other people?

Groups often meet in rooms without tables so that their chairs are arranged in conversational clusters. Individuals learn forward and call each other by name to encourage exchange. Talkative individuals discipline themselves to give others a chance to speak, and use their natural conversational skills to draw out their shyer colleagues.

Is all this interpersonal stuff necessary? Ask yourself. If your job, your family celebration, your personal safety, your reputation, and your productivity depend on other people, is the time devoted to making the group a success worth it?

Exercise: Dividing Up the Money

This exercise allows you a chance to work in a group and to examine the roles you play. Working in groups of five to six people, complete the first drill and then identify which roles you assumed at various times. Were you able to use open-ended questions? Was your body language appropriate?

All groups may work simultaneously or you can use the fishbowl method: one group works and one group observes. (20-30 minutes)

Your group is responsible for dividing $3000 a month among the following services and organizations. You may divide the money any way you wish as long as the allocation is a group decision based on criteria you discuss with each other.

1. An HIV/AIDS education project for three local high schools. The project leaders would work with school staff, but their approach

would be informal and oriented to the students. Project workers have liaisons with provincial health workers and HIV/AIDS support groups.

2. Drop-in centres before and after school for elementary school children whose parents work outside the home. The drop-in centres would be located in the elementary schools, open during early-morning and late-afternoon periods, and staffed by both paid and volunteer workers. Snacks and milk are provided.

3. The local food bank needs money for rent, heat, special supplies, and salary for one full-time worker. It has been used regularly since it opened one year ago and demand for its help is growing.

4. Save the Stream Citizens' Group. The local stream, a scenic attraction of the area, is badly polluted and filled with garbage. The citizens' group needs money for a special assessment to determine which chemicals are in the water and at what level.

5. Transportation services for seniors. Many senior citizens live independently and can get out to shop and do business. However, they are unable to carry their groceries home and cannot walk far or take public transportation in the winter. A local group wants to start a free taxi service for seniors to help keep them in their own homes as long as possible.

6. The Rape Crisis Centre is in danger of closing. The Centre has maintained a 24-hour-a-day counselling and referral service for three years, but staff need help with rent and utilities or they will be forced to close. They have statistics to prove that they handle a significant number of calls each week.

7. Jobs for unemployed youth. The high school is trying to start a work project for people who have graduated from high school and are unemployed. They need seed money.

Discuss the following questions in your work groups and report back to the class.

a) Who assumed the leadership role? Was it a spontaneous action or did it have to be negotiated?

b) How well did participants assume group-building and task functions?

c) How important is the way you talk to and with people in group situations? How do your words, tone, and manner affect others?

d) Do people in business and industry (or nursing, teaching, etc.) have the time or the money to invest in making group experiences positive? What determines their ability to share leadership?

Exercise: Recognizing Your Changing Roles

How well did your group function as it divided up the money?

Some members focused on getting the task accomplished and some tried to keep a good working relationship within the group. This exercise will make you more aware of your ability to increase group effectiveness, and will help your group be more cognizant of its leadership patterns.

a) Keeping in mind the work you just did to divide the money, complete the following questionnaire.

b) Determine your score. You will find one score for actions that help get the job done (task actions), and another score for efforts that help maintain the group's working relationships (maintenance actions).

c) Scoring: In the space next to each item, write 5 if you always behave that way; 4 if you frequently behave that way; 3 if you occasionally behave that way; 2 if you seldom behave that way; and 1 if you never behave that way.

When I am a member of a group:

1. I offer facts and give my opinions, ideas, feelings, and information to help the group discussion.
2. I warmly encourage all group members to participate. I am open to their ideas. I let them know I value their contributions.
3. I ask for facts, information, opinions, ideas, and feelings from other group members to help the group discussion.
4. I help communication among group members by using good communication skills. I make sure that each group member understands what the others say.
5. I give direction to the group by planning how to go on with the group work and by calling attention to the tasks that need to be done. I assign responsibilities to different group members.
6. I tell jokes and suggest interesting ways of doing the work to reduce tension in the group and increase the fun we have working together.
7. I pull together related ideas or suggestions made by group members and restate and summarize the major points discussed by the group.
8. I observe the way the group is working and use my observations to help discuss how the group can work together better.
9. I give the group energy. I encourage group members to work hard to achieve our goals.
10. I promote the open discussion of conflicts among group members to resolve disagreements and increase group cohesiveness. I mediate conflicts among members when they seem unable to resolve them directly.

11. I ask others to summarize what the group has been discussing to ensure that they understand group discussions and comprehend the material being discussed by the group.
12. I express support, acceptance, and liking for other members of the group and give appropriate praise when another member has taken a constructive action in the group.

To obtain a total score for task actions and maintenance actions, write the score for each item in the appropriate column and then add the columns.

Task Actions
1. information and opinion giver
3. information and opinion seeker
5. direction and role definer
7. summarizer
9. energizer
11. comprehension checker

Total for Task Actions

Maintenance Actions
2. encourager of participation
4. communication facilitator
6. tension reliever
8. process observer
10. interpersonal problem solver
12. supporter and praiser

Total for Maintenance Actions

Description of Task-Maintenance Patterns
1-6 Task Score; 1-6 Maintenance Score

Only a minimum effort is given to getting the required work done. There is general non-involvement with other group members. The person with this score may well be saying, "To hell with it all." Or he or she may be so inactive in the group as to have no influence on other group members.

1-6 Task Score; 18-30 Maintenance Score

High value is placed on maintaining good relationships within the group. Thoughtful attention is given to the needs of other members. The person with this score helps create a comfortable, friendly atmosphere and work tempo. However, he or she may never help the group get any work accomplished.

18-30 Task Score; 1-6 Maintenance Score

Getting the job done is emphasized in a way that shows very little concern with group maintenance. Work is seen as important, and relationships among group members are ignored. The person with this score may take a drill-master approach to leadership.

18 Task Score; 18 Maintenance Score

The task and maintenance needs of the group are balanced. The person with this score continually makes compromises between task needs and maintenance needs. Though a great compromiser, this person does not look for or find ways to creatively integrate task and maintenance activities for optional productivity.

30 Task Score; 30 Maintenance Score

When everyone plans and makes decisions together, all members become committed to getting the task done as they build relationships of trust and respect. A high value is placed on sound, creative decisions that result in understanding and agreement. Ideas and opinions are sought and listened to, even when they differ from one's own. The group as a whole defines the task and works to achieve it. The creative combination of both task and maintenance needs is encouraged.

1. Together, discuss the pattern of group behaviour revealed by the scores. Are you satisfied? Could the pattern be improved?
2. What have you discovered about your group?

This exercise is adapted from David W. Johnson and Frank P. Johnson, *Joining Together: Group Theory and Group Skills*, 2nd ed. (Englewood Cliffs, NJ: Prentice-Hall 1982).

◑ THE GAME PLAN: MAKING DECISIONS

How do you make decisions? Do you rely on the way you've always done things? Take others' advice? Use research? Reflection and thought are necessary for good decisions. Furthermore, it's important to realize that there are different ways of making decisions; the situation determines the method. For example, you use one kind of decision-making when you go for the handhold that your climbing instructor tells you to use, and another kind of decision-making when you choose one job over another.

You're on a camping trip with friends and have just pitched your tent at the Tunnel Mountain Campsite, just outside Banff. Your friends are organizing the site and you are starting dinner. Suddenly it starts to rain—it's so heavy, you can hardly see. What should you do first? Arrange the following activities in the order you would do them. When you have finished, find a partner and compare answers, and the reasons for your decisions.

RAINSTORM: WHAT SHOULD YOU DO FIRST?

- Take clothes off the line
- Get rain gear on
- Close the car
- Put away food and supplies
- Cover firewood
- Finish cooking dinner
- Close up the tent
- Put away sleeping bags
- Take off your sunglasses
- Cover Coleman stove

The same choices exist for groups; the procedure matches the situation. However, for major decisions, group discussion is essential, and consensus should be sought. Involving all group members improves the effectiveness of the decision, reinforces the members' sense of belonging to the group, and increases their commitment to carry out a decision that everyone agrees to. Before you do the exercise on consensus, remember that in thinking and deciding, you have four rights.

1. **The right to pause.** You're working on a committee looking at halfway houses in the community. The chairperson calls to tell you an emergency meeting is planned for Tuesday night. You'll be there, right? **Pause.**

    Give yourself time to think. Do you already have other arrangements? If you go to the meeting, will you be ready for a big commitment at work later in the week? Why don't you ask the chairperson for time to think and promise to call back in an hour?

2. **The right to ask questions.** What's on the agenda for the meeting? Is it necessary that you attend the entire meeting? Is your attendance essential to the group? When is the next meeting scheduled? Do you have a specific contribution to make, or could you send your remarks with someone else? You may wish to attend the meeting; in that case,

there's no problem. However, if your days are already full, if you are robbing yourself of family or private time

ask questions.

3. **The right to say no.** You can be a good worker, friend, committee and group member, and still say no. You have to be able to make decisions that will help you function well in all areas of your life. You can decline the invitation to the meeting and offer alternatives: can you send along suggestions? can you call someone else and get caught up? is there another job that you could manage? Friends, co-workers, committees will always need you. Consider each situation carefully; you do have the right to

say no.

It may help the caller if you offer support and encouragement. Saying no to one thing is not a rejection of the activity or the people involved.

4. **The right to say yes.** The chairperson calls again, this time to say there's a meeting in Quebec City, all expenses paid, and your name was chosen in a draw. Do you want to go? The chairperson happens to know that Roberta has never had a chance to represent the group, and she's been overworking lately but if you really want to go.... Some people (and I include myself) find it hard to resist hints like this. It takes some time and determination to value yourself and

say yes.

Consensus Decisions: Feeling Together

Reaching a decision by consensus takes time and requires a skilful leader or leaders who can ensure that every member is heard. A decision arrived at by this method has the advantages of using the resources of all members—ensuring the commitment of each person to the decision. This in turn increases the future effectiveness of the group. It is likely to produce creative and high-quality decisions. Follow these guidelines when using the consensus method.

1. Avoid arguing blindly for your own opinions. Present your position as clearly and logically as possible, but listen to other members' reactions and consider them carefully before you press your point.

2. Avoid changing your mind only to reach agreement and avoid conflict. Only support solutions with which you are at least somewhat able to agree. Yield only to positions that have objective and logically sound foundations.

3. Manage conflict effectively. Think of conflict as energy that your group can harness. If you sense conflict, name it. Say, "I feel conflict around this issue—can we talk it out?" As a group, name conflict, explain the

issues as calmly as possible, discuss solutions and find a plan that everyone can accept. Techniques that supposedly save time such as majority voting, tossing a coin, and averaging only work for a short time—then you're on thin ice again.

4. Seek out differences of opinion. They are natural and expected. Try to involve everyone in the decision process. Disagreements can improve the group's decision because they present a wide range of information and opinions, thereby creating a better chance for the group to develop more adequate solutions.

5. Do not assume that someone must win and someone must lose when discussion reaches a stalemate. Instead, look for the next most acceptable alternative for all members.

6. Discuss underlying assumptions, listen carefully to one another, and encourage all members to participate.

Exercise: The 14 Worst Human Fears

In a survey of 3000 people included in the *Book of Lists*, a popular compendium of trivia, participants were asked, "What are you most afraid of?" The results may surprise you.

1. Listed below are the 14 greatest fears. Your job is to rank the fears in the same order as that given in the list. Some answers are tied for the third and fourth places. Prepare your first list working by yourself.

2. Working in groups of five or six people, prepare a group list. You must prepare your answer by consensus, and each person must sign the sheet indicating that she or he agrees with the ranking and can explain the group's rationale for the order.

Biggest Fears

Elevators

Darkness

Loneliness

Insects and bugs

Death

Dogs

Sickness

Financial Problems

Flying

Heights

Speaking before a group

Escalators

Deep water

Riding/driving in a car

Answers

Biggest Fear	% Naming
1. Speaking before a group	41
2. Heights	32
3. Insects and bugs	22
3. Financial problems	22
3. Deep water	22
6. Sickness	19
6. Death	19
8. Flying	18
9. Loneliness	14
10. Dogs	11
11. Driving/riding in a car	9
12. Darkness	8
13. Elevators	8
14. Escalators	5

As a class, discuss the following:

1. How hard did people work to make sure that each person was heard?
2. What remarks were most and least helpful in getting the group to arrive at a consensus?
3. How satisfied was the group with the consensus method?
4. How accurate were your personal and group lists? Is an answer reached by consensus any more accurate? If not, what's the sense of using it?
5. In what type of meeting situations is consensus valuable? When is it essential?

GREAT CANADIAN QUIZ III

Real Canucks will know the following expressions. Select the correct answer or definition for each of the following.

1. The Latin version of our national motto
   a. *semper ubi sub ubi*
   b. *a mari usque ad mare*
   c. *injuria non excusat injuriam*

   Translate it into one of our two official languages.

2. *Castor canadensis*
   a. a laxative popular in pioneer times
   b. a recent line of fishing gear made in Red Deer, Alberta
   c. the beaver, symbol of Canada

3. Sugaring off
   a. a new treatment for diabetes
   b. a process used in maple syrup making
   c. motto of a Calgary diet clinic

4. Arctic char
   a. a variety of salmon found in northern waters
   b. Baffin island slang for burned food
   c. a green leafy vegetable, popular in Yellowknife
5. Tidal bore
   a. a deep cleansing laundry detergent
   b. any Maritime politician
   c. the high tide that enters the Bay of Fundy
6. The Group of Seven
   a. a financial conglomerate that controls western oil
   b. an internationally famous lacrosse team from Montreal
   c. a group of modern painters, founded in 1920
7. Sourdough
   a. the devalued Canadian dollar
   b. a fermented bread dough used in rough baking
   c. a bad-tempered cook
8. Potlatch
   a. a West Coast Indian celebration
   b. a dime-bag
   c. Canadian for the lid of a saucepan
9. Fiddlehead
   a. the name of a literary magazine published in New Brunswick
   b. an edible fern
   c. a Yehudi Menuhin groupie
10. Avro Arrow
   a. a high-performance car manufactured in Tofino, B.C.
   b. a light crunchy chocolate bar
   c. an advanced supersonic interceptor jet aircraft

11. Chinook
   a. a warm wind in Western Canada
   b. an Inuit toast
   c. an undesirable person
12. Ceilidh (kay-lee)
   a. a traditional Gaelic gathering for song and story
   b. a type of spice used for the peanut sauce that accompanies satay
   c. a large stick used to frighten off aggressors

To test yourself further consult:

John Robert Colombo, *Colombo's Canadiana Quiz Book* (Western Producer Prairie Books, 1983).

John Fisher, *The Complete Cross-Canada Quiz and Game Book* (McClelland and Stewart, 1978).

Sandra Martin, *Quizzing Canada* (Dundurn Press, 1987).

Answers: Great Canadian Quiz III
1. b, "from sea to sea," "d'un océan à l'autre"
2. c
3. b
4. a
5. c
6. c
7. b
8. a
9. b
10. c, program cancelled in 1959
11. a
12. a

◖ JARGON AND BAFFLEGAB

Draw left while we do an upstream ferry; then do a crossdraw to pull us into the eddy.

> (CANOEING JARGON)

Insert the program disk into the drive, select Floppy Disk A with the mouse pointer and drag it on top of the Floppy Disk B icon.

> (COMPUTER JARGON)

Jargon is the language of insiders that is used almost as a short form to discuss common interests. Every industry uses it; movie theatres don't have commercials, they have "corporate trailers." When is jargon appropriate? If your objective is to present your ideas clearly and convincingly, *everyone* has to understand. Describing your company's computer software to school trustees as, "this multi-tasking software offered by ComputerWhiz, which allows both an XTRA-based zowie and a 903-based whatzit to execute concurrently," is inappropriate—nothing less than self-aggrandizement.

Professor Richard Coe of Simon Fraser University writes:

Properly used, jargon allows precise, efficient communication among specialists. But use becomes abuse when those specialists (or anyone else) directs jargon at people likely to be confused or intimidated rather than enlightened by the technical terms. Whether jargon…is an efficient use or a pernicious abuse of language depends on context and audience.

As a speaker, you should listen to yourself and others to make your words accurate, lively, and descriptive. If you find jargon interferes with real communication, get rid of it.

Bafflegab is worse; it is the piling up of words, especially long, impressive ones, to avoid actually saying anything. Bafflegab includes such devices as euphemism, the prissy substitution of less specific language for direct words. Thus, you are not fired, you are "dehired," "released," or "nonretained." A fence becomes a "nonecological boundary," toilets are "guest relations facilities," and site police are "security hosts."

If you listen closely, you'll notice that the phrase "at this point in time" is a warning light that bafflegab is being used. A public official, put on the spot for an explanation, attempts to bluff his or her way through with a line such as

Although it is important to interface with the media in a significant mode, it is imperative that I interact with my peers at this point in time prior to releasing meaningful information on this overload situation.

Translation: I'm not talking now.

Examples of bafflegab are found everywhere. Fred Doucet, a senior adviser to Prime Minister Brian Mulroney, denied that the Mulroneys had a nanny. Rather they employed a staff member who "interfaces with the children in a habitual way." Airline officials tell their customers, "we're in a flight overload situation." *Translation*: the airline has sold more tickets than the plane has seats.

Avoid bafflegab; it is a pompous, deceitful way of talking. If you have nothing to say, admit it.

Exercises: Bafflegab and Jargon Decoded

1. Decode the following; the first five are proverbs, the last is a book title.

    a) "Individuals resident in crystal edifices should refrain from the promiscuous catapulting of geological specimens."

    b) "The ingestion of the edible product of the Pyrus malus vegetation at least once during the earth's cyclical rotational movement upon its axis will restrain the taker of the Hippocratic oath who is the medicinal prescriber."

    c) "Antithetical elements always seem to evidence an enticement effect upon one another."

    d) "The trek and expedition that consists of a multitude of distance units always commences with the act of completing the initial foot movement that will propel one forward."

    e) "The lack of that which is urgently required or desirable is the gestating principle of all experimental processes and fabrications."

    f) *The Covert Intelligence Gatherer Who Sought Shelter From the Intemperate Atmospheric Environment.*

    Answers:

    a) "People who live in glass houses shouldn't throw stones."

    b) "An apple a day keeps the doctor away."

    c) "Opposites attract."

    d) "The longest journey starts with the first step."

    e) "Necessity is the mother of invention."

    f) *The Spy Who Came in from the Cold*

2. How often do you use series of initials in your speech? When you speak to others use both the letters and the full form for the initial reference. How many of the following do you know?

CBC	NHL	RCA	TLC	MD	MS	CNE/PNE
CPR	CNR	TTC	MSE	JFK	NBA	NAACP
ANC	HIV	MVP	VIP	RRSP	RSVP	TGIF
FBI	RCMP	CIA	UFO	VCR	NATO	EEC
GNP	MBA	BMW	HBC	PMO	MP	MPP/MLA
CEO	BLT	NDP	NFL	PMS	PC	CRTC

◑ PANELS

Panels are a lively and effective way of examining an issue from different perspectives. The information given and the interaction among the panelists vary according to the occasion and the philosophy of the participants. Let's start with a straightforward panel on youth services in your community. When you are asked to participate on a panel, it's important to determine your role. Is your job to

- give background on the topic?
- rev up the audience for other speakers?
- present one particular aspect?
- ease tension?
- put the topic in a perspective that is acceptable to the audience?
- present a different or opposing point of view?

In other words, if I'm part of a panel discussion of opening an emergency shelter for street youth in my neighbourhood, my function may be to assess the role that such a facility would play in our community. Other panelists will outline the need for the shelter, the way it operates, the benefits, community involvement, etc.

Identify your function by discussing the program with the coordinator, telephoning other participants to discuss their viewpoints, and using your common sense. As Svend Robinson says:

Sometimes people forget that public speaking involves an interaction between the audience and the speaker. That's one of the most important things to consider: who are these people? what are their concerns? what will resonate with them?

As part of your preparation, you should also find out how questions will be handled. Will the moderator assign the questions? Will panelists volunteer to answer? Will the audience direct questions to one or more panelists?

Let's now examine the politics of the situation. Is the moderator unbiased? You can find this out by contacting the moderator in advance and assessing her or his position. This is a very important step. You should ensure that different points of view are allotted equal amounts of time and have equally good slots on the agenda. This is also the time when you discuss physical arrangements: floor microphones locked on the periphery of the audience so that speakers can look at the community as well as the panelists; adequate lighting so that everyone is visible; and a fair way of handling remarks.

No matter how many assurances you are given about the sound system, check it yourself. I learned this lesson early; I was a panelist for an anti-rape discussion and there was considerable media coverage of the event. When the moderator went to speak, he discovered that the television crews had tapped the main power source and that the "perfect" sound system was in trouble.

Experienced panelists arrive early enough to meet the organizers and other participants, and to gauge the mood of the audience. During the discussion, be attentive to other speakers and to audience reaction. Your personal credibility is often judged by how you treat others.

All this assumes you've been asked to be on the panel. What happens if no one representing your point of view has been asked? This happened in our community: as part of the referendum debate on whether the Constitution of Canada should be changed, a town-hall panel debate was arranged. Anglophones, francophones, the native community, the "yes" side and the "no" side all had representatives. When a women's group asked if women's interests were being presented, the answer was one of puzzlement; of course, women's concerns were being addressed—all these men would do it.

It is naive to believe that all groups concerned will be given a chance to talk; in the old way of speaking, only power groups were considered likely sources of speakers; it's time to work to be more inclusive. Members of minority groups must request time, insist on representation and be prepared for the old excuse— "No one (women, natives, people of colour) is willing to do it."

One response is to find the speaker yourself.

◑ DEBATES

Debates are the most exciting and often the most heated type of group presentation.

Generally, you will debate as part of a team and you can expect plenty of opposition from the opposing group. For this reason, most debates are regulated by a moderator who may also be the person who judges which team has the most effective argument.

Debating is supposed to be done in a fair manner with arguments presented logically and methodically. However, judges are also swayed by wit, style, and quick thinking; the debater who can play to the audience and refute the opponent with passion and humour generally wins. Thorough planning, solid proofs, and the ability to think on your feet will help you in this contest.

Exercise: Formal Team Debates

Organize the class in teams, two teams to a topic. One team will speak for the resolution, and one against it. Designate one person to chair the proceedings. That same person may judge the debate, or you may wish to appoint a panel. The debate is judged on the basis of the arguments presented and the effectiveness with which they are advanced.

Follow these guidelines:

a) Establish a set time for preparation, which is equal for everyone. You may wish to combine time in class and opportunity for outside research. Remember that timing is critical both in preparation and in the delivery itself. Debates are strictly timed so plan your strategy carefully.

b) Each person on a team must speak once.

c) No person can speak longer than 90 seconds at one time.

d) The team speaking for the resolution may have 90 seconds rebuttal time.

e) Each speaker addresses the chair. The team speaking for the resolution starts the debate, and the first speaker formally presents the resolution.

f) Judging: the chair or the panel announces a winner based on form and content. The class may then wish to have an open vote on the resolution itself.

Suggested Topics

1. Resolved that euthanasia should be a medical option available to those who are in great distress.
2. Resolved that the state of marriage is a necessary condition for a sexual relationship.
3. Resolved that censorship has no place in a democratic society.
4. Resolved that drug testing of employees in any industry violates human rights.
5. Resolved that all discrimination against people with AIDS and high-risk groups be made illegal.
7. Resolved that capital punishment is a deterrent to murder.
8. Resolved that city dwellers be limited to a maximum of two pets.

Exercise: Open Debate

This format allows more class participation. Each motion has a proposer and a seconder, and an opponent and a seconder. The order of speakers is as follows: proposer, opponent, seconder to the proposer, seconder to the opponent. The debate is then open to the floor. The chair maintains order, enforces the 90-second time limit, and ensures fair treatment for both sides.

In this type of debate, an outside judge or panel is useful.

Suggested Topics

1. Resolved that the business of journalism is to sell papers by whatever means necessary.

2. Resolved that the criminal justice system is biased against poor, non-white defendants.
3. Resolved that better education would be possible if grades were eliminated.
4. Resolved that television stations be required to have at least 50 per cent Canadian content in their programming.
5. Resolved that service technicians (auto mechanics, electronic and small-engine repair persons, etc.) have a right to charge as much as the market will bear.

SPEECH ASSIGNMENT: PRESENTATIONS AND MEETINGS

Your job is to create a situation that offers challenge and a chance to develop new skills.

1. In consultation with your instructor, choose one of the many examples of meetings, presentations, or proposals outlined in the chapter and create your own situation. You should prepare an outline of what the environment is, who is involved, your purpose, your methods. You may work individually or in groups.
2. Prepare the necessary background material (handouts, agendas, résumés, overheads).
3. Set the stage, and present your material speaking with energy and conviction.

DELIVERY TECHNIQUES TO REMEMBER

1. Concentrate on being interesting—as well as thorough.
2. Use a clear three-part plan to cover the material.
3. Focus on making connection with others—use your voice, eye contact, and body language to reach them.
4. Enjoy yourself. Be proud of your proposal.

INTERVIEW

SVEND ROBINSON

Environmentalist, Social Activist, Member of Parliament

Svend Robinson is a Member of Parliament and an outspoken advocate for many groups: he supported the Haida nation in their struggle for land claims; brought national attention to the Dying with Dignity movement; has long supported environmental causes; and is the first openly gay Member of Parliament. His speeches combine passion, integrity, and wit.

Q

You speak so often and so personally to each group. How much of your speech is prepared ahead of time?

A

I never, ever have a prepared text. If people ask for copy of my speech, I tell them that if they can read my chicken scroll, they're welcome to it. The way I prepare for a speech is to have some sense of what it is I want to say. What are the key points, key themes, key ideas that I want to communicate. I have a dialogue with myself.

The second thing I think about is who are the people I'll be speaking to? Sometimes people forget that public speaking involves an interaction between the audience and the speaker. That's one of the most important things to consider: who are these people? what are their concerns? what will resonate with them? why are they there? I do a hard-nosed assessment of the folks who will be listening. Do they want to be there because they're interested or do they have to be there?

Finally, what is it that I want to leave them with? When they walk out of the hall— what are the two or three key points that I want them to remember? That's what I start with in trying to figure out what I am going to say. Then I build around that to reinforce those themes in a variety of different ways.

Q

Do you make notes?

A

Yes. I scratch out a few notes about what I want to include and then do a rough outline of how I will approach the issue but that's all. My staff despair over all the snippets of paper that I use to refer to articles and quotes.

Q

No matter how you do it— you have a great speaking style. How did that style develop? Did you use other speakers as models?

A

Absolutely not. I've always loved speaking. I debated in high school and enjoyed public speaking. I think some of the debating skills I learned in school have been useful.

Q

How do you deal with difficult audiences, people you know may ridicule you or object to your position on lesbian/gay issues or the right to die with dignity?

A

It depends. There are some people with whom you can't reason. Particularly around tough issues like abortion or capital punishment, often people's minds are firmly made up and no amount of reason is going to persuade them to change their mind. The objective in that case is to be very clear about where you stand and why you stand there. Show some respect for the fact that while you have differences of opinion, you are not trying to impose your values on them.

Q

What about hecklers?

A

Sometimes a good vigorous heckler can bring out the best in a speaker. The other night I was speaking in Victoria, and a person from the extreme left interjected—I took the remark and rode that wave and bounced the energy back to the audience. It helped bring the audience along

with me. So much of your strength as a speaker depends on the responsiveness of the audience.

Q

How important is the audience?

A

There is *nothing* more devastating than speaking to people who just aren't with you. To bring them around, you have to connect with them at a personal level. It is sometimes most effective to forget about being abstract and talk about real people, real issues—real concepts they can relate to in terms of their own lives.

Q

When people target you for ridicule, what do you do?

A

It depends. If they are particularly outrageous, you just let them hang themselves.
During 1988, Brian Mulroney snickered about me being Minister of National Defence and that remark generated tremendous anger from the public. My response was to stay above the fray. Lashing out in anger is ultimately counterproductive. In most instances, that kind of hateful

thing backfires. Sometimes humour works—it can be the most disarming of all weapons.

Q

Who is your toughest audience?

A

The people who don't want to be there. If a teacher brings you in to speak to a class who are only there because they have to be, that's the toughest audience. It's a real challenge to bring them around and I relish that challenge sometimes. Kids are my favourite audience—they ask you questions that adults would never ask and they are honest and open. Also, they can distil difficult concepts and make solid examples. A grade five student recently told me that multiculturalism is like a patchwork quilt—the differences make for interest and depth. It was a wonderful parallel.

Q

How do you deal with the responsibility and pressure of speaking for thousands of people who invest their hopes and needs in you?

A

It's not just speaking—it's living. How do I live? Because I am seen as a representative of a community, I feel a real sense of responsibility. As an openly gay man, that's one of the lenses through which people view me. Ultimately, it affects how I live my life and I am very conscious of that. I want to be the best that I can be—a person that my community and communities in general can have a sense of pride in.

Q
What's your best advice for beginning speakers?
A
Understand clearly what you're trying to communicate. Focus on the message you want to get out. Be honest with your audience. Respect them, look at them—connect with them. Remember that wit and wisdom are often closely linked.

OUTLINE OF A REPORT, PROPOSAL, OR PRESENTATION

Name: _____

Date of Speech: _____

Purpose Statement: _____

INTRODUCTION

    Grabber:

    Thesis:

    Overview:

BODY

    Supporting Argument #1

    Supporting Argument #2

    Supporting Argument #3

CONCLUSION

    Reference to purpose (thesis):

    Summary of main steps:

    Zinger:

SELF-EVALUATION FORM

This form is to help you evaluate your own speech. It can be kept private or shared with your instructor or peers.

Type of Speech: _____

Name: _____

Title: _____

Date: _____

DELIVERY

Physical Presence

Did I make eye contact with others?

Was my posture natural and appropriate?

Was I aware of my facial expressions and hand gestures?

Were there any distracting mannerisms that I was aware of?

Did I feel good?

Could I feel an energy exchange with my audience?

VOCAL DELIVERY

Was my voice under control?

Did I sound confident?

Was I aware of breathing calmly?

How was my enunciation?

Did I manage to avoid um's and ah's?

Did I sound interested/excited/committed?

How did my voice sound to me?

DESIGN AND CONTENT

How well did the introduction and conclusion work?

Did the framework unify my speech?

Was there a natural progression from point to point?

Did my notes keep me on track? Did I use them?

Did the audience seem to understand the organization of my speech?

Was the information clear?

What was the energy level of the conclusion?

What would I change the next time?

What worked very well?

OVERALL EFFECTIVENESS

Did I connect with this audience?

Did I achieve my purpose?

What do I remember most about making the speech?

What unexpected or unforeseen things happened?

What am I most pleased about?

OTHER COMMENTS

Grade: _____

PEER EVALUATION FORM

Peer evaluation should be done in a constructive and supportive fashion. The speaker may choose people to do assessments or they may be assigned alphabetically. Some groups maintain the same speaker/assessor teams for the entire course; others change for each speech. The instructor may wish to see this evaluation before it goes to the speaker.

Type of Speech: _____

Speaker: _____

Title: _____

Assessor: _____

Date: _____

DELIVERY

Physical Presence

Did the speaker maintain eye contact?

Did she or he establish a rapport with the audience?

Were gestures natural and effective?

VOCAL DELIVERY

Did the speaker sound convincing/spontaneous/excited?

Was his or her voice clear and loud enough?

How did you respond to the speaker's mood?

DESIGN AND CONTENT

Did the introduction interest you?

Did the overview give you an indication of the main proofs?

Did the speech flow easily and logically from one point to another?

Was the conclusion strong and memorable?

Did the conclusion reinforce the thesis and main points?

What was the thesis of the speech?

OVERALL EFFECTIVENESS

Did you learn something new or worthwhile from the speech?

Were you moved by it?

What was the most outstanding part of the speech?

What changes do you recommend?

What parts should the speaker definitely keep?

OTHER COMMENTS

Grade: _____

EVALUATION FORM

Type of Speech: _____

Name: _____

Title: _____

Length of Speech: _____

Date: _____

Legend: S=Superior   E=Effective   NW=Needs Work

DELIVERY

Physical Presence

Eye Contact

Rapport with Audience

Posture

Gestures

Use of Notes

Appropriate Use of Audio-Visual

Support Material

VOCAL DELIVERY

Naturalness/Spontaneity/Enthusiasm

Clarity

Variety (Tone, Pitch, Pace)

Volume

Absence of Verbal Tics (um, ah, okay, like)

Sense of Control and Calm

DESIGN AND CONTENT

Use of Framework for Introduction and Conclusion

Clear Thesis and Overview

Coherence/Use of Transitions

New/Interesting Information

Strong Finish

Language

Word Choice

Impact on Audience

Grammar

OVERALL EFFECTIVENESS

Treatment of Topic

Intelligent Awareness of Audience

Achievement of Purpose

Impact on/Connection with Audience

OTHER COMMENTS

Grade: _____

There Comes A Time: The Persuasive Speech

CHAPTER 7

TIPS FOR SPEAKERS

1. Is your commitment to the topic sufficient to move your audience?

2. Your concern and attitude help establish your credibility.

3. Balance ethical, logical, and emotional proofs.

4. Hostile reaction? Remember that ideas are at odds, not people. Ask for a fair hearing.

5. Ethical speakers avoid logical errors such as Name-Calling, Poor Analogies, and Flag-Waving.

6. Convince your listeners; don't coerce them.

7. Good plans enable you to wing it.

I say what I mean and I say it with force.... I am a warrior and a woman.

(Waneek Horn-Miller)

WARM-UPS

Impromptu Persuasives: Survival Speeches

You are a passenger on a plane that has crashed in the Andes Mountains and are one of a handful of survivors. You have waited several days for rescue but to no avail. A map on board indicates that a village is located just over the mountains—about a two-day hike. Your group decides to choose one person to take the remaining food and water to travel over the mountains and seek help. It is highly likely that those who remain behind will die from dehydration and exposure. It is essential that the person chosen is capable of making the journey and is highly motivated to do so.

In groups of two or three, choose a character and work together to prepare an emphatic argument to support that person's bid to be chosen to walk. Find emotional, logical, and psychological appeals for your audience. After all appeals are heard, the class (or a panel of judges) votes on the best person to seek help.

Here is a list of some of the survivors; add your own characters.

1. Female. 23-year-old nurse. Marathon runner. Engaged.

2. Male. 55-year-old army captain with combat duty in Operation Desert Storm. Fit. Married with grown children.

3. Female English teacher. 35 years old. Fit. Widowed with two children, one of whom is handicapped. Former Girl Guide leader and camper.

4. Male. Medical researcher. 60 years old. On the verge of discovering a cure for cancer but has not shared his research with others. Single. No children. Former substance abuser.

5. Female. Medical missionary. 40 years old. Has been living in a small village in Peru for the last five years. Fit but not muscular. No children.

6. Male. 17 years old. High school drop-out. Strong and athletic. Girlfriend at home.

7. Female. Native. Elementary school teacher. 32 years old. Has lived outdoors much of her life and hunted with her family.

8. Male. Former Olympic runner. 28 years old. Athletic. Recently diagnosed with HIV but still healthy and fit. Family and partner at home. Calm, competent.

(Thanks to Wendy Struthers, Centennial College)

Whatever form you use, subtle or blunt, humourous or not, it's all to persuade.
  (EDDIE GREENSPAN)
When you're doing something that's right, you may have some setbacks but it's still right. You never quit.
  (KAHN-TINETA HORN)

All speeches involve persuasion. If you urge others to spend money on a major advertising campaign, to adopt slo-pitch for their ball league, or to speak out on sexual harassment, you are persuading them.

This chapter deals with types of persuasive speeches, appeals that you may use, adapting to your audience, and informal logic to help you. It then gets into **advanced technique**: how to adapt to the moment, how to ride the wave of audience reaction and enjoy it.

◗ WHY ARE YOU SPEAKING?

The first rule of persuasive speaking is *having something to say*. Avoid the temptation to talk just to hear your own voice. Think hard about the topic and hammer out a precise statement of your position. If you aren't sure what you think or what action should be taken, you have work to do.

Most important, *be sure your commitment to the topic is sufficient to move your audience*. Remember that not everyone can speak on all topics, even good ones. Acid rain is a major threat to our environment but it may not be sufficiently immediate to give you the power to convince others. On the other hand, the need for organ donors may be a subject that you can really get a handle on.

If you have a clear, specific purpose in mind, a purpose that you believe in, your enthusiasm will give your speech credibility and strength.

Types of Persuasive Speeches

A persuasive speech urges an audience to think or act in a certain way. Generally, your purpose is to move the audience

*   to adopt or change an idea;
*   to confirm or reinforce a concept or belief;
*   to adopt a course of action.

Speeches to Adopt or Change an Idea

Convincing your audience that airbags should be standard features in all cars, or that exotic animals should not be kept as pets, are examples of this type of speech. Obviously, some people will already share your opinions, and others will have to be persuaded. Once the idea is accepted, action may follow, but the focus of the speech is on the logical support of your thesis.

"You need good spokespersons, and you get organized and you raise hell. The social agenda is *so* crowded today that if you're not able to get your voice heard, nobody will pay attention to you."

(Jean Chrétien)

Speeches to Reinforce a Belief

Strengthening your audience's commitment against apartheid or for the protection of our wilderness areas confirms widely held ethical and social principles. Does this type of speech always have to be so serious? Not necessarily. Convincing others that real Christmas trees are better than artificial ones, or that a rural life is superior to an urban one, are also effective themes.

Motivating Your Audience to Act

One student made a powerful speech on behalf of Amnesty International, a civil rights group concerned with the release of political prisoners. He concluded by distributing stickers and buttons obtained from the organization, and gave each person a form for donations and an envelope. Another asked group members to take out their drivers' licences and check the section provided for consent to organ donation. She asked everyone to give the matter deep thought and sign the forms within 48 hours. In each case the speakers gave good arguments, and provided specific tasks for the audience to do. The time frame provided even firmer direction.

◑ HOW DO YOU PERSUADE OTHERS?

Use yourself as a test case to determine which kinds of information are persuasive. When the question of extra-terrestrial visitors arises, for example, are you more convinced by the opinion of a scientist from NASA, statistics documenting the number of UFOs reported last year, or a first-hand report of one such encounter? Most people lean toward one type of proof or another, and good speakers know that in order to touch all facets of each listener, and all segments of each audience, they must use a variety of appeals. The most common proofs are ethical, logical, and emotional.

Look at your audience as a group of people who have come to eat at your restaurant. Some anticipate a good meal because they know the chef's reputation and appreciate the atmosphere of your restaurant. Others are more concerned with selecting food that will give them the balance of nutrients they require without unnecessary additives and fat. The remaining diners are won by the meal itself: the presentation, the aroma, the *taste*.

In your speech, you require the same balance of credibility, solid information, and emotional or gut appeal.

Use Real Examples to Make Your Proofs Convincing

There is no better way to nail down each point than to give an example. References to real people, places, news events, or job experiences familiar to your audience will help them understand your arguments. Let's look at some examples.

You belong to a group lobbying the federal government to approve the sale of a particular pain-relieving drug. To prepare for your speech before a committee, you have collected many statistics and read many scientific studies. Just a little more research will give you specific stories of individuals whose present pain is intolerable, examples of the drug's success in other countries, estimates of the financial benefit to local companies, and the actual statements of doctors who wish to use the drug.

If you're discussing the benefits of pet ownership, you can quickly find examples of children, seniors, and people with medical problems, whose lives are enhanced by the love and companionship of animals. Your local humane society will supply pictures and histories of pets waiting for adoption. Intellectually, your audience will be convinced by your brilliant proofs; emotionally, they will be touched by your anecdote of Ben and Kodiak, a little boy and his adopted cat. The combination makes for a *memorable* speech.

Remember, whatever your proof, make your point, back it up with specific examples, and repeat it.

Establishing Credibility

When you set out to move others to action, to reinforce a belief, or to change an idea, you must establish your ethical base, your credibility. Your verbal and nonverbal messages affect your audience and their willingness to accept your ideas. For what reasons do you people believe you? Here are some of the more important ones.

1. **Your competence or experience**. Your knowledge of the field and your qualifications go a long way in establishing your competence in the minds of the audience. If you want to argue that all food and beverages should bear a full list of ingredients, which would cut down on the number of allergy-related deaths, what details will convince your audience that you know the topic? A background in nutrition, medicine, or food preparation will help. Experience in the restaurant business would provide insight, as would personal experience with allergies, or membership in an organization concerned with the problem. Tell your audience of the research you have done, such as interviews with victims of allergy-related illnesses.

    If you're trying to persuade a hotel chain to increase their wheelchair accessibility, your case will be strengthened if you demonstrate first-hand knowledge of the needs of wheelchair users, *and* familiarity with the hotels themselves.

Sometimes you have to establish a link with your audience. A young travel counsellor with *very* short hair, dyed a vivid red, made a presentation to a seniors' club regarding a group tour of the Rhine Valley, which would include visits to vineyards and castles.

In order to assure the group that she knew both the area and her clients' needs, she started by describing the trips she had taken with her grandmother and friends, and the physical demands of the Rhine trip. This established rapport with the group and added to their confidence in her judgment.

Make sure that the program notes and the remarks of the person introducing you include any background information (degrees or diplomas, work or volunteer experience, personal interests) that will establish your credentials.

2. **Your respect for the audience**. Speakers who arrive on time, who are well prepared, and who have practised their speeches demonstrate respect for their listeners. A speaking engagement is serious: you wouldn't go to a business presentation with notes half-done, and admit you threw a few ideas together in the car; don't do it for a speech. Take Gloria Steinem's advice:

I never use the same set of notes twice. I make them over again every time. I do repeat some of the same building blocks in each speech, but each situation is different …I interview the people in that place or from that group to find examples from that particular community.

Follow Steinem's example and show respect for the intelligence and sincerity of your audience. Work hard on each speech; find a way to connect with your audience and speak directly and from the heart.

3. **Your intentions**. The representative of an association of banking institutions recently announced the banks' intention to go into the auto-leasing business. When the interviewer asked how much money the banks would make, the spokesperson replied that it didn't really matter how much profit was involved, the banks were only interested in providing their customers with better services. Snickers were heard all the way to Moose Jaw.

Remember, your audience will wonder why you are so concerned. If you have a personal motive that is justified, state it. If you are presenting a plan that is in the best interests of your listeners, make sure they know it. The more positively others perceive your motives, the more likely they are to listen to you.

4. **Your character**. What sort of impression do your words, your warmth, and your concern make on your audience? Do you cite reasonable ex-

amples and select your words judiciously? Are you fair in your treatment of opposing sides? Do your words include your entire audience, without making disparaging assumptions based on education, income, gender, sexual orientation, or race? Are you interested in presenting your ideas intelligently or in belittling opposing views? Are you committed to your own suggestions?

When you talk to people, you can affect their lives. You may not think you're doing it, but your remarks can give others the courage to go on, a new idea, advice they need that very day. When you realize how important speaking is, it adds conviction and energy to your presentation.

Exercise: Coast-to-Coast Debates

From Prince Rupert to Corner Brook, Canadians have favourite topics for friendly debate. Divide into small groups and decide what your thesis would be in each of the following cases. Then, outline several ways to establish your credibility for each.

a) Is it worthwhile rustproofing your car?
b) Should you lie flat if a bear attacks you or face it in an upright position?
c) Is there such a thing as a Canadian identity?
d) What repellent is guaranteed protection against mosquitoes?

Facts and How to Find Them

Finding facts—verifiable information to support your arguments—is not hard, but you must have the *energy* to dig for it. First, you must formulate specific questions. Then, telephone calls, personal interviews, and library materials will provide the backup you need. Sometimes, just one statement from the *right* source will clinch your argument.

Most researchers know the value of telephone calls. If you're doing a speech on the success of franchises and need to know how much of every consumer dollar is spent in a franchise operation, go to the library. If the data given are not recent, use a telephone book to find the name and phone number of a national franchise organization. Call that organization and research the corporate structure—in other words, find out the best source of reliable information. This source may be the president, vice-president in charge of membership, or the public relations director. Be sure to get both names and the title right. Then, telephone that person directly, give your name, and your request, and make it clear that your interview will be brief—three to five minutes. What if it is a long distance call? Is the information worth the expense? You may wish to make a person-to-person call to ensure that the person is there and will speak to you, and then call back directly at a cheaper rate. If your source is out, you will have saved money and can leave your name and number for a return call. Telephone research is surprisingly successful; you get accurate, up-to-date information and inside leads. However, be prepared to work to get the call, ask specific questions prepared in advance, and record the details correctly.

Once you have the data, be sure that the proofs you present are reasonable. The section on informal logic that follows later in this chapter should help sharpen your sense of analysis.

What Facts Do You Need?

Consider your audience. Are you speaking to people who focus on dollars and cents? Will expert opinions convince them? Do some listeners have fears or biases that need resolving?

Once again, consider the example of the student who spoke on the need for organ donations. Her long-term goal was to make her audience more aware and supportive of organ donation; her immediate objective was to get them to sign their donor cards. She had done a thorough audience analysis:

I knew Milene could only be reached with facts and statistics. Gabriel responds well to humour, and you [the instructor] would be looking to see if I had covered all the angles.

She supplied statistics outlining the actual and potential numbers of lives saved and the reduction in health-care costs if donors are found quickly. A combination of humour, scientific fact, and expert opinion helped her address the unspoken distaste that some people have for losing parts of their bodies, even after death, and the fear of premature removal. By calmly presenting the information, she convinced many class members. Her conclusion was the clincher. In it she referred to the drama of a small child who had waited for a transplant. Everyone knew the story.

Follow Your Heart: Using Emotional Appeals

Our newspaper recently carried the story of a toddler whose life depended on finding a kidney donor. The story highlighted the need for a transplant; the story emphasized the need for organ donors. Eventually, when the child received new kidneys, her skin lost its sickly, greenish hue, and she became an active, vigorous three-year-old.

By using an actual example, the student made the issue of organ donation real and immediate. People who could not identify with an impersonal organ bank were able to make a personal connection with a suffering child. Her need and her recovery inspired and *convinced* them.

Stories of real people, with names, ages, and personal details, touch the emotional level of your audience. If you use the story as a *framework*, you can start by presenting a situation and the dilemma it involves, work through the solution—the main part of your speech—and conclude by finishing the story. Good storytellers include details to make their tales as real as possible—without violating the privacy of the individuals concerned.

Which Emotional Appeals Work?

The best advertising campaigns feature nostalgia, animals, love of family, a sense of adventure, and wacky humour. It takes great skill to assess which tactics work and which turn people off. You cannot manipulate your audience or take unfair advantage of their vulnerability. You can, however, make effective appeals to a wide variety of emotions. These are just a few:

- empathy with and sympathy for individuals and groups;
- pride in a neighbourhood, school, firm, or in the audience's potential or achievements;
- determination to preserve or attain a goal;
- pleasure;
- pride in having one's worth or work acknowledged;
- protective instincts for children or environment;
- anger at insult or injustice;
- competitiveness.

You can design your speech to include an emotional appeal in the introduction and conclusion; your listeners will pay attention quickly, and remember your comments clearly if they are emotionally engaged.

Exercise: Emotional Appeal

The last speech in this book is by Rose Anne Hart. It is one of the finest speeches I have ever heard and it uses an emotional appeal, in the form of a story, to make the main point. Read the speech and see how many different emotional reactions you have to it.

What Part Does Humour Play?

A computer specialist was speaking on the financial losses caused by the pirating or unlawful copying of computer software. His presentation was good, but inevitably his audience began to drift. The line, "Speaking of access, I have probably spoken to excess," brought them back with smiles and renewed interest.

For humour to be effective, it has to be natural for you. If you force jokes or inject them inappropriately, you will look silly. On the other hand, humour has great advantages. It relieves fatigue, and it can break the sombreness of a dry or heavy presentation. Outlining the problems of Canadian publishing, one speaker summarized a lengthy presentation of statistics with the pungent observation that "Canadians spend less money on new books by Canadian writers each year than Americans do on cat litter." The comparison was alluded to often in the ensuing discussions. If emotions are running high, a light touch may relieve a tense atmosphere. Humour, in the form of irony, can allow you to tackle a subject far more pointedly than is otherwise possible.

Humour can be used for serious purposes, to relieve the listing of impersonal data, or to create a bond among audience members. Experiment with it, using your friends for your rehearsals, and develop an approach that is natural for you.

◑ BALANCING YOUR ACT

Reason, emotion, or credibility alone won't win your audience. You need to balance your arguments in order to connect with the different levels of awareness in each person. Dave Nichol was asked if emotion was necessary in business. He erupted:

Absolutely! … You need a good balance between logic and emotion.

Speakers often feel as though they are doing a high-wire balancing act. The audience is there as a safety net and they're ready to respond to your appeal; design your act carefully and *practise.*

Exercise: Mini-Persuasives: Understanding the Strategy

To persuade means to induce or lead others to your way of thinking. This exercise is a trial run in formulating a clear thesis, and selecting supporting arguments that are balanced. Your proofs must also be geared specifically to your audience, taking into account the logical, emotional, and psychological approaches possible.

Decide whether the entire class will all do the *same* assignment, or choose among the four possibilities.

You have 24 hours to prepare your speech, and it should only be two minutes long. Strive for good audience rapport—CONVINCE THEM.

a)   What person or group has done the most, in the last month, to make the world a better/worse place?

b)   Your classmates have financial resources that they wish to invest. Persuade them to invest in a particular project that you have a personal interest in. It may be
   •   an invention,
   •   a movie idea,

- • a game,
- • a community group.
c) What is the best *new* thing in the business world? (Consider personnel policies, opportunities, machinery, concepts, markets, government support, etc.)
d) Give details of a court case that is being covered by the media. Outline which side appears more prepared, or more likely to win, *or* more justified in its claim.

Exercise: There is a Difference

There is a difference between a speech that sells a product and one that advances an idea. In one case, the focus is on getting the best deal; in the other, on adopting an idea or course of action. This exercise demonstrates the difference in approach and emphasis.

You may choose to make either Speech (a) or Speech (b). The presentations should only be one and a half to two minutes long.

Situation 1: Traffic Lights

a) Sell a traffic light— the fixture itself—to a town council that is about to instal several new lights.
b) Convince the council that a traffic light is necessary for safety at a busy intersection in your neighbourhood.

Situation 2: Safer Sex

a) Persuade your friend to talk to his/her girlfriend/boyfriend about safer sex.
Provide the information that would get your friend to act.

b) Convince your college senior executive that a Safer Sex Awareness Week is necessary to reduce the risk of transmission of STDs and guarantee that students will live long enough to graduate.

Situation 3: Automobile Insurance

a) Sell automobile insurance to a group of college/university students.
b) Convince an investigating committee that automobile insurance rates are unfair and outrageously overpriced.

Exercise: The Taped Interview

This exercise allows you to experiment with your voice as you project a character you invent. The interview should be taped and last approximately three to five minutes. The emphasis is on vocal quality and the interest level generated. Students have adopted such diverse identities as the math teacher whom students love to hate; a representative of Street Haven, which is a youth drop-in centre; the president of the society for the preservation and encouragement of respect for mothers-in-law; an Oreo cookie; an exchange student; and Garfield.

Instructions:

a) Keep your own identity or adopt another character or persona. Make sure you know exactly who you are and what you wish to say in your interview.

b) Prepare questions for a partner; they should lead into the responses you have designed.

c) Have a short rehearsal with your partner. She or he will introduce you and conduct the interview, using the questions you provide.

d) When you have finished, you may exchange roles.

e) Submit the tape to the instructor; listening to the tapes in class is a good lesson in character projection and voice control. The interviews may be graded by the instructor or by a panel of class members.

Evaluation Outline for the Taped Interview
Character Chosen:

Voice
   Enunciation:
   Emphasis:
   Clarity:
   Tone:
   Emotional content:
   Projection of warmth:
Pacing
   Use of pauses:
   Variation of tempo:
   Emphasis:
Overall Effect
   Projection of character:
   Awareness of audience:
   Special effects:

General Comment
                                        Grade:

◑ ETHICAL RESPONSIBILITY IN PERSUASIVE SPEAKING

Every time you speak, you have a responsibility to examine the ethical base of your remarks. When others give you time on their program, they accord you a special status. You should attempt to maintain an ethical principle; that is, a standard of beliefs and behaviour that you follow and that you expect from others. Our society has a general code of ethics; you may have your own as well. As a speaker, you hold a position of privilege and must consider which arguments are justifiable to prove your point. In an attempt to determine your own ethical standards, consider the following guidelines.

1. **Advocating dangerous or illegal behaviour is unethical**. Arguing for the legalization of marijuana is one thing; suggesting that teenagers use the drug is unacceptable. It is unethical for you to try to convince others to do something that may be harmful or unlawful.

2. **Lying or suppressing information is unethical**. Lying is universally unacceptable. During the Watergate crisis, Richard Nixon remarked, "I misspoke myself." His attempt to double-talk his way out of a lie made the situation worse.

   If you know of major drawbacks to your plans, you must mention them, and use the opportunity to present solutions or alternatives. This does not mean you have to include every single drawback or difficulty; common sense will help you make the distinction between a significant disadvantage and a minor problem.

3. **Name-calling is unethical**. Attacking another person or group by calling them names is unacceptable. A speaker who thinks that he or she is in the company of a sympathetic crowd may attempt such inflammatory references as "welfare bums" or "slime buckets," but such attempts usually backfire.

4. **Citing "technical ignorance" or "expert authority" as an excuse is unethical**. If you are discussing reducing costs in your business and a colleague recommends using someone who can crack computer codes and sell you software programs at reduced rates, what is your response? If your money-saving friend says that this person is a "computer expert" and knows what's legal or not, does that absolve you of the responsibility of verifying the legality of the action? Does your personal lack of computer knowledge make you any less innocent of wrongdoing?

What about a local politician who is speaking on behalf of a chemical company in danger of being shut down? The company is accused of emitting PCBs, cancer-causing agents, into the atmosphere. However, they have several "expert opinions" that the emissions are within the "safe" level. What is safe? Can the politician base her personal support on the experts' reports?

It does not follow...that the more facts you know or the more of the subject you have studied, the more morally relevant facts you know. Even in highly technical matters it is possible for the non-expert to obtain at least as good an understanding of the morally relevant facts as the expert. And, the non-expert may have a far superior understanding of the relevant moral considerations. Technical experts can be moral morons just as ethics experts can be technical morons.

(CONRAD G. BRUNK, "PROFESSIONALISM AND RESPONSIBILITY IN THE TECHNOLOGICAL SOCIETY," IN DEBORAH POFF AND WILFRID WALUCHOW, EDS., BUSINESS ETHICS IN CANADA. SCARBOROUGH: PRENTICE-HALL CANADA INC., 1987, P. 66).

◑ DEALING WITH A NEGATIVE OR HOSTILE AUDIENCE

How do you define a hostile audience? They are generally people who oppose an idea as vigorously as you support it. That's the key: ideas are in conflict, not human beings. By remembering that, you should stay clear of personal attacks and unpleasantness. Just because people do not agree with you, they may not disagree; they may be uncommitted. You can view the commitment of the audience to ideas on a sliding scale. If you believe in your proposal (and you should not be speaking if you don't), your aim is to bring the audience along the scale. A 100 per cent change of mind may not be possible *the first time* but you can attempt a process of gradual persuasion.

As Svend Robinson said in the interview in Chapter Six:

Often people's minds are firmly made up and no amount of reason is going to persuade them to change their mind. The objective in that case is to be very clear about where you stand and why you stand there. Show some respect for the fact that while you have differences of opinion, you are not trying to impose your values on them.

Remember these specific steps in dealing with an audience opposed to your ideas.

1. **Get yourself ready**. What is your purpose? Do you want to add to the conflict or defuse the situation? If you go into the group in a combative state of mind, your body language will communicate your antagonism immediately. If you concentrate on a rational presentation of ideas, if you admit that your audience may have justification for their outlook, you're in a better position to convince rather than clobber them. Is your voice under control? In Chapter 6, we discussed the way the voice can either adopt the tone of the situation or establish a new one. Concentrate on achieving an atmosphere of courteous exchange; use words that acknowledge the intelligence of your listeners. Breathing exercises can help you achieve a sense of calm that extends to your voice; that evenness will gradually affect others.

"It was not ideas I was giving them exactly, but rather ferments—something which I hoped would work like yeast in their minds."

(Nellie McClung)

2. **Acknowledge your audience's position**. Students who suddenly learn that their fees will increase 25 per cent, vacationers forced to move to a smaller, less convenient hotel, homeowners facing expropriation, all have a right to be upset. Admit that their distress is justified and do not trivialize their situation by citing other, more dramatic crises.

3. **Request a fair hearing**. Agreeing with your audience that they have valid complaints is a good way to start. You may be able to find one or two other points of agreement. It is psychologically important to concur on some points: the necessity of immediate action, the distress for everyone, the need for clarification. This puts you all on the same side. Then you must firmly request their time for a hearing. The mark of an intelligent person is his or her ability to give a fair chance to a speaker presenting an unpopular position.

   Explain that you have an ethical responsibility to present alternative ideas or plans. If you can, compliment your listeners on their fairmindedness, and remind them again that ideas, not individuals, are in conflict. After all, the search for truth or for a solution, not the passion of confrontation, should be the main object.

REQUEST A FAIR HEARING

4. **Predict objections and take care of yourself**. It's naive to assume that everyone will support such obviously good schemes as a national holiday in mid-winter or medicare for pets. If you realize that some people will be unsupportive, you'll be ready for those cold looks. Don't be put off by negative eye contact or people holding signs that state "You Door-knob." Somewhere, you will find someone who will offer support. As Waneek Horn-Miller says in the interview at the conclusion of this chapter:

If you want them to hear you, speak in a calm voice, look the other person in the eye and say, "I respect what you have to say, but this is what I want to say." You have to respect each other's point of view.

◑ LIBBERS AND BUBBLEHEADS: DEALING WITH PUTDOWNS

You've all seen the cartoon—one woman says to another, "Whenever *I* think I'm assertive, *they* think I've got my period [PMS or menopause]." It is fair to say that there is resentment towards women who speak their minds: they are rocking the status quo, which makes people uneasy, often angry.

Name-calling is common. Instead of arguing with the content of a woman's speech, her opponents will call her "bubblehead" or "hysterical." When that happens to you, don't think that you are the only one; it happens often.

Negative body language such as eye-rolling or shrugging the shoulders indicates the listener's hostility. And of course, use of the word "feminist" as an accusation is common. Want equal pay for work of equal value, harsher sentences for sexual abuse of children, access to birth control *information*? FEMINIST. How can such a reasonable word cause such outbursts?

More to the point, what can you do about them? Hold the line. When someone says, "Two women were promoted in one week. That's too much female power for one office," stand your ground, firmly. Say, "It's fair as far as I'm concerned." You might step forward if you can, but don't step back. Hold the line.

You can also refuse to be drawn in—"That's uncalled for, Ed" or use humour for a sharp retort. Some of us mistakenly still believe that answering back is unladylike, but we're learning. A teachers' aid with fifteen years' experience was rebuked by a young teacher. "You should have referred that question to me," he said, "I have a degree in education." "Oh," said the woman, "Didn't I tell you? I have an M.A. in common sense."

The list of top-ten putdowns would not be complete without mentioning accusations of brainwashing, exaggerating, or reverse discrimination. Last year, I spoke with a group of recent women graduates from Queen's University. Many of them had faced forms of sexual harassment in their careers—they wanted to know how they should respond.

The worst example came from a young woman who was called to the office of her top client; when she entered, he offered to demonstrate his new computer program— complete with sound. He proceeded to play her the excerpt that featured the sound of a woman obviously experiencing sexual ecstasy. What did she do? "I shut the door, told him that what he had just done was sexual harassment, and if he ever tried anything like that again, I'd tell the presidents of my company and his." No one has the right to intimidate you or harass you on the grounds of gender, race, sexual orientation, class, or language spoken. Speak up for yourself as well as your career.

AFFIRMATION FROM THE BEST: GLORIA STEINEM ON PUBLIC SPEAKING

For more than three decades Gloria Steinem has been a spokesperson and organizer for the feminist movement in North America. She was a founding editor of *Ms.* magazine, and has written three bestselling books. She discussed public speaking with me in a personal interview in 1993.

Q. You wrote a lot about your early "obsessive" fear of speaking. Do you like it now?

GS. Speaking wasn't something I came to naturally or early in my life. It was late and difficult. If I had to choose a form of communication, I would always choose writing. But I have learned that there is something that happens in a room together, physically, that could never happen from a printed page.

Q. Do you use notes?

GS: To write it out word for word, you might as well send a letter. There are things you think of or ways you express yourself while you're standing there. The atmosphere and the circumstances change what you say.

Q. What advice do you have for women who are afraid of being put down?

GS: Understand that you'll be put down for **not** speaking. When you approach a prejudice you can easily recognize it because nothing you do is right. So if nothing you do is going to be right anyway, you might as well do what you need to do. For instance, "if you're feminine you can't do the job—if you can do the job, you aren't feminine." Any double bind like that means that there's real prejudice at work.

Q: Does speaking out have a lot to do with the achieving of self-esteem?

GS: Yes, if you fail to use any part of yourself out of shame or fear, then the theft of self-esteem has begun. You have suffered the suppression of part of yourself. So, if you don't speak your thoughts, if you don't use your voice, your self-esteem is affected.

Q: Why has speaking become a pleasure after the terror of the early attempts?

GS: Not only is speaking different from reading because you are doing it in a group and communally (unlike reading a page when you're by yourself), but you also get a sense of intent and character from the speaker, from everyone.

Q: What is your advice to people, women and men, who want to speak, to be really good at it?

GS: I think first of all, each of us has a way of saying things, and things to say, that are unique: no one else can say them. That's our motivation for getting up there. I also think that there isn't a perfect model of what this speech should be like; there's our individual way of doing it. Once you take away the idea that there's a paragon we're supposed to meet, whether it's an ideal of physical beauty or the way a speech should be given, then I think we put the power in ourselves instead of in external judgment.

This is part of a large and endless and rich human conversation. Some of that conversation will take place now in the very room that you are in, and some of it will take place 50 years from now because you spoke. It's the butterfly theory—even hard-nosed physicists acknowledge that the flap of a butterfly's wing here can change the weather hundreds of miles away. So your speech will have an impact through the people you speak to, in many other ways for who knows how long—forever.

◑ "IT AIN'T NECESSARILY SO": A BRIEF GUIDE TO INFORMAL LOGIC

One thing that will have your audience fidgeting in their seats is a lack of a sense of logic. An understanding of logical reasoning will add strength to a foundation of research and good design. The most important step is simply to ask yourself, "Does this make sense?" Do your thesis, supporting arguments, examples, and statistics make sense to you?

Your audience will be asking, "Do I agree with this statement? Is it supported by believable facts? Is it a reasonable consequence of facts I know?" If you have done your preparation logically and well, they'll be on your side.

Logical Reasoning

There are three categories of formal logical reasoning behind most arguments: deductive, inductive, and syllogistic reasoning.

Deductive Reasoning

In deductive reasoning, a conclusion about a specific idea is arrived at after considering a number of general examples. In arguing against her city's bid to be an Olympic site, an alderwoman might quote examples from several past Olympic Games, "Every city that has hosted the Olympics in the past has exceeded the budget. We will exceed our budget too, and we cannot afford to do this."

In a way, deductive reasoning is used to predict the future from past events. This works well, provided that the past events are truly comparable to the event in question. Olympic events *are* perhaps fated to go over budget. If the general facts are not true, however, or if the situation is different, the conclusion could be invalid. The city might already have sufficient facilities available so that the budget could in fact be met. The alderwoman may have ignored some examples of Olympic Games that stayed within their budgets.

Is it reasonable to argue, "There has never been a woman prime minister. Therefore Ms. Tremblay will not succeed in her bid for election"?

Inductive Reasoning

With inductive reasoning, the thought moves in the opposite way, from specific examples to a general conclusion. The number of specific examples studied must be quite large to arrive at a valid conclusion. Statistics are often used in this type of argument. For example, census reports for two separate periods indicate a drop of 40 per cent in the number of people reporting any religious affiliation. These figures represent statements made by millions of Canadians. From these figures you may reach the general conclusion that religion currently has little effect on Canadian life.

This type of reasoning can be dangerous if the sample used to supply the data is too small. In the media, we often hear of one or two immigrants to Canada who have been terrorists or who are criminals. From these examples, many people conclude that all immigrants are threatening and immigration should be curtailed. Is this a logical conclusion?

Syllogistic Reasoning

A syllogism produces a conclusion from two or more pieces of information. These first two ideas are called the premises. For example:

All large cities have garbage problems.
Windsor is a large city.
Therefore, Windsor has a garbage problem.

If the first two premises are true, and if they are related, then the conclusion, as above, is valid.

There is a danger with syllogistic reasoning, however, if the first premises are based only on opinion, or on incorrect or incomplete facts:

Francophones and Anglophones can't get along.
Students from Laval are Francophones; students from Ryerson are Anglophones.
Therefore, students from Laval and Ryerson can't get along.

Is this valid?

Often, one or more of the premises is implied rather than stated. For example, "Many of Canada's top businesspersons dine at Splendido. Therefore, Splendido is an excellent restaurant." Unstated is the second premise that top businesspersons only dine at fine restaurants. Be sure that premises, spoken or unspoken, are valid.

These three types of reasoning form the basis of most conclusions or arguments that you will try to present, although they are not usually so clearly put as in the examples. In calling for restraint in the use of nuclear power, a speaker may say, "Look at what happened at Chernobyl and Three Mile Island." The thought moves from specific examples to the general conclusion: inductive reasoning. A plea to keep alcohol out of a local sports stadium based on experiences in other stadiums makes use of deductive reasoning. Knowledge of these three forms, will help you build strong, reasonable speeches, and can be used to test your arguments.

Errors in Logic

There are pitfalls to be wary of. Be sure to avoid the following errors that weaken the force of your arguments.

Name-Calling

Attacking a person rather than an idea is not a valid reasoning technique. Traditionally, this is called an *ad hominem* ("against the person") attack. The character of a person proposing an idea is usually irrelevant to the quality of his or her ideas, and using words like "wimp" or "pinko" does not advance your case. If you have proof that a person supporting a gambling setup is a known criminal, that is a serious allegation and a second attack of the proposal. However, most name-calling is not relevant. Referring to people who advocate stricter drinking-and-driving controls as a bunch of temperance nuts does not lead to audience confidence. Even when you challenge a concept, your words cannot be gratuitously inflammatory; you must back up your remarks with fact and logic. A speaker who claimed that withdrawal from NATO was a "dangerous and naive policy" may have had some reasons for such an opinion. But simply using these words with no backup would not convince anyone who already did not have those beliefs.

Generalities

Speaking about something in broad general terms suggests you don't have specific facts. Comments such as "Everyone knows that all our best doctors are going to the U.S." or "All the studies show that children need two parents" are signals that generalities are being paraded as truth. Have specific studies to back your points. Too general a statement leaves you open to contradiction.

Cardstacking

It's not fair to present your argument as if it's the only one. You don't have to argue the other side of the case, but you can't leave the impression that it doesn't exist. For example, in arguing for the retention of a wilderness area near your city, you must face the claims of developers and show how they could be met elsewhere. Then present the ecological and recreational benefits of the land. A balanced approach has more weight than one that stacks all the cards in your favour.

Can you outline balanced arguments for

- banning garbage dumps in agricultural areas?
- French-language schools?

Jumping on the Bandwagon

"*Everyone* is doing it!" Despite what you told your mother when you were 13, the fact that *everyone* is piercing their tongues and shaving one half of their heads is *not* sufficient reason to do so as well. It is deductive reasoning gone wrong: all too often everyone *isn't* doing it. The group sampled may be too small to give reliable data; the research methods may be insufficient; the circumstances in which the audience find themselves may be very different from "everyone" else. Do the following statements, heard in the cafeteria of a large university, convince you?

"Many athletes take steroids. Obviously it's necessary if they want to compete internationally."

"Everyone's investing in real estate. The profits are incredible, and you can double your money in a year."

"Joint custody of children by parents who have divorced is spreading like wildfire. It's obviously a good idea."

Reliance on tradition is another form of jumping on the bandwagon. The lament, "we've always done it this way" is not a convincing argument. There may indeed be valid reasons for actions confirmed by tradition to be continued; the practice of one vote for each citizen is an electoral process worth preserving. Other examples may be more questionable. The declaration that "we've always been a monarchy and always will be" is not a strong proof. The pros and cons behind the tradition must be explored.

Ridiculing

"We don't kill people who talk about self-esteem by beating them to death...we kill them with ridicule."

(GLORIA STEINEM)

Sometimes it is fun to make your opponent's ideas look ridiculous, and this can be part of a good argument. If it's your *only* tactic, however, think again. If in highlighting one facet of a position, you ignore other valid parts, your criticism of your opponent's position is weakened. An environmental group is trying to protect a marsh. An opponent jeers, "Who needs to save a bunch of bugs?" A thoughtful listener will realize more than bugs are at stake, and dismiss such a comment. William Lyon Mackenzie King, prime minister from 1921 to 1930 and from 1935 to 1948, often consulted the spirit world, communing with his mother and his little dog, Pat. A historian who dismisses King's achievements for this reason ignores, at the peril of his argument, the actual content of King's policies.

Experts

It's good to have experts to support your ideas, to have big names on your side. However, use experts with care. Be sure they *are* experts, recognized in an appropriate field, and well known to your audience. Be sure their comments are up-to-date and appear free from bias. A gay community leader speaking in support of the ordination of gay and lesbian ministers may *appear* biased to an audience. They may think, "What else would you expect him to say?" Balance your experts to include those who do not have such a strong identification *only* with the idea you are advancing. Ask another person in favour of gay and lesbian ordination to speak, as well as a representative of the gay community. Remember also that experts often conflict; your opponent may have an equally forceful expert to counteract your point. Thus, use experts only if they will really build your case.

If you are using an endorsement, that is, supporting your case with the statements of known authorities, avoid the appearance of bias. Do you remember those advertisements for "Shiney Bright," the toothpaste that nine out of 10 dentists recommend? Did you ever wonder *how* the sponsors conducted their survey?

Be sure that the endorser has some relevance to your cause and does not have an automatic obligation to support you. In the following examples, discuss the relative merits of the endorsers:

1. For your presentation on the need for wheelchair access to a new sports complex: wheelchair athlete Rick Hansen and/or Olympic rower Silken Laumann.
2. For the lobby for financial compensation for Japanese Canadians uprooted during World War II, David Suzuki and/or the leaders of the federal opposition parties.
3. For your fight against the use of animals for laboratory experiments in cosmetic firms, the head of ARK II, an animal rights group, and/or a fashion and beauty commentator.

Circular Reasoning

Beware of circular argument, which doesn't really prove anything, and only brings you back where you began. If A is true because B is true, but the proof of B is A, watch out. A statement such as "Canadian singers will never be internationally successful because they're too Canadian" only takes you back to your original premise that Canadian singers can't succeed outside Canada. You don't prove a point by stating it twice.

"Native peoples should stay on reservations because they can't integrate in our society" is also a circular argument. The reason native peoples can't integrate is their isolation on reserves. The circle of this argument needs to be broken by a broader definition of terms, and a wider exploration of the facts on which the opinion is based. Do native peoples wish to integrate?

Irrelevant Conclusions

A conclusion should not appear from thin air. It must follow reasonably from the speaker's previous remarks. In the following example, the speaker begins by detailing the problems of implementing the Official Languages Act, and how the implementation differs from the purpose of the legislation. Abruptly, he concludes that the act is discriminatory, although he has not raised the question of discrimination at all in his argument. The conclusion does not make sense:

The intent of the Official Languages Act is to guarantee a person's right to be served by federal agencies in either of Canada's official languages. But the implementation of the Act often serves a different purpose. That's the trouble with the Act, it's discriminatory.

Is the following conclusion logical?

The sale of cigarettes is not illegal. Therefore, a law that bans smoking in the workplace cannot be valid.

Misuse of Anecdotal Proofs

Stories of how your aunt's divorce cost her the business she'd helped build, or how the lack of basics in your child's primary education ruined his chance at college add force to your speech. But personal stories or anecdotes should not stand alone; additional reasons are needed. Businessman Bud McDougall said his only regret at leaving school at age 14 was that he hadn't left earlier. Does this prove that schooling does nothing for your career?

Confusing Opinion with Fact

Be careful to distinguish between facts and opinions, and acknowledge the latter for what they are. Do not pretend that they are facts. Facts can be verified; opinions must stand the test of time to be found true or false. For example, Maritime fishing crews wear copper bracelets to protect them from arthritis and rheumatism. Is the effectiveness of these bracelets a matter of fact or opinion?

False Facts

The most logical, well-reasoned argument will crumble if it is based on false facts. Be sure your research unearths the most recent and reliable information to support your case, and evaluate your sources carefully. (This is discussed in detail in Chapter 3.)

Is it a fact that sex education in the schools leads to promiscuity?
Is it a fact that it is illegal to pick trilliums in Ontario?
Is it a fact that one person in 10 is lesbian or gay?
Is it a fact that a balanced diet requires 170 grams of meat per day?
Is it a fact that ice worms exist only in folklore?

Flag-Waving

Although Canadians are not prone to this type of fallacious reasoning, they are sometimes sucked into a larger political machine. Statements such as "we must allow the testing of missiles with nuclear capabilities in order to protect the safety of the North American people," or "an armed presence in Central America is essential to guard our way of life," attempt to convince audiences with an exaggerated appeal to patriotism. Good citizens support governments that use reason, not hype, to justify their actions.

Faulty Cause and Effect

If you are citing causes and effects, be sure that the cause indeed produces the effect you claim. Have you considered all the variables that may lead to a particular result? Is it true that

If you eat less, you will lose weight?
If everyone in Canada spoke French and English, there would be equal opportunity for all?

Poor Analogies

Comparing your idea to something that the audience understands can be helpful. However, be sure the examples and analogies you use do not detract from the credibility of your argument. For instance, is it auspicious to compare planning a wedding ceremony to mapping out a military campaign? Is marriage really war?

Mayor Jean Drapeau of Montreal predicted that the Montreal Olympics could no more have a deficit than a man could have a baby. This analogy caught headlines (perhaps its purpose), but it was so far-fetched as to make the point laughable.

Be sure the analogy works.

Overly Emotional Appeals

Emotional appeals have a place in a speech, but not as the sole factor in a reasoned argument. A speech opposing nuclear arms that consists only of the spectres of nuclear winter, blasted landscapes, and the end of the human race will offend, repel, and alarm your audience. However, they may not be convinced. Avoid, as well, a maudlin approach, a sickeningly sentimental play for support. No one will fall for the description of overworked bankers, besieged by critics, as they work unstintingly for the good of their clients.

Using Isolated Abuses to Attack the Whole Policy

There are always individuals and groups who will abuse their rights. This is true of every aspect of life. However, the fact that something can be abused is no justification for its being prohibited to all. What's wrong with the following?

1. Eight people in one college filed false information on student loan applications and used the money for a trip to Florida in study week. Student loans should be abolished.
2. Some women do not take proper birth-control measures. Then they seek abortions to get rid of unwanted pregnancies. Abortion clinics should be banned.
3. Last year federal authorities denied entry to 38 people who claimed to be, but weren't, political refugees. If we don't tighten up our laws, the country will be swamped with illegal immigrants posing as refugees.

Exercise: Logic

The following activities provide an opportunity to test your understanding of what is logical and what is not.

Logical Pursuits: How Many Errors Can You Find?

Do you remember that game on the children's page in the newspaper? An apparently normal picture is loaded with illogical details: planes flying upside down, bicycles missing a wheel, children wearing only one shoe, batters swinging at footballs. The object is to find and identify as many mistakes as possible.

Tune into an interesting radio or television current events show and relax. While eating popcorn, tape an excerpt of a speech that contains some errors in logic. Political announcements or interviews are excellent sources. Play the excerpt in class, and present your list of logical bloopers, using the categories already outlined.

HOW MANY ERRORS CAN YOU FIND ?

Impersonation: The Great Pretender

Divide into teams of five or six people and plan brief speeches on the topic "Bald is Beautiful." Pack it with as many errors in logic as you can, at the same time *attempting* to sound reasonable. One person from each team delivers the speech while the other group tries to spot and identify as many thinning arguments as possible. (If, for obvious reasons, this assignment would be insensitive, alter the title to "Left-Handed People are Brilliant.")

◑ RIDING THE WAVE

Cast aside your practical down-filled jacket and duofold underwear. Beneath the sensible surface of every Canadian speaker is the derring-do of a surfing wizard. If you've followed the advice of the preceding chapters, you are ready for the thrill of catching the currents of audience reaction and riding the wave of oratorical brilliance. Even more, you should be ready to *enjoy it.*

The secret lies in your presentation: the plan and the practice. By the time you're ready for a major speech, you know how to organize. Your notes are clear, colour-coded, and precise, but there's more. *Advanced* note-card technique requires that you list your thesis, main proofs, and supporting ideas the usual way, *and* list alternative or additional material on the side, in case it's needed.

Imagine you have prepared a speech on eating disorders for an audience of teenagers. However, as you circulate in the foyer, you notice a fair sprinkling of parents and teachers. Have you any information about parent support groups, or anecdotes about families who were baffled for

months by someone's odd eating habits? Get out your pen and jot down reminders of that information and ****_asterisk_**** them so you'll notice the
addition. It's even better to predict this at home, but perfection comes
next year.

What happens when inspiration hits? As Dave Nichol, former President
of Loblaw International Merchants, says:

> _I like the security blanket of those little cards. But when you get off to a good
> start, when you're enthusiastic, you can forget about the notes, and let the good
> times roll. When the spirit hits you, when you've spent a lot of time planning
> and you're totally prepared, then you don't need the notes._

He's right. You don't need them—for a while.

Two examples illustrate the _brilliant_ improvisation of students. A hospitality student was speaking on shy rights, the need to protect the dignity of the reticent and scared-to-death. As he walked to the lectern, a
full-front, three-sided structure, he suddenly ducked behind and into the
lectern, and started with the words, "I'd much rather make my speech this
way than face you. Whenever I have to look at people to talk, I get so shy
I can't say a word." He won his audience immediately.

Another student, in a book and magazine publishing course, made a
speech on the legalization of prostitution. As she spoke on the financial
reasons for some people turning to prostitution, she noticed that most of
the class was with her, except for two obviously unconvinced men. Looking
directly at them, she said, "Look around you. Can you be sure everyone here
has enough money to pay the rent and buy food?"

Then, looking at each section of the audience individually, and speaking right to them, she said, "I'm not so sure what I may have to do in my
lifetime to care for myself and my children, and I'm not going to knock anyone for what she or he may have to do to survive." She cared a great deal
for her subject and her audience, and the rapport she established was moving. The feeling in the room caused the dissenters to listen carefully to her
point of view; agreement was not necessary, but open-mindedness was.

How do you ride the wave without wiping out? Here are a few pointers. I can tell you from experience that you sometimes surprise yourself
with how _good_ you are. Afterwards, you may shake and wonder how you
did it. That's the fun of public speaking: the skills you learn and the hours
of practice make winging it possible.

Watch Your Audience Closely

The way your audience sits, nods, nudges each other, and talks to you
with their eyes, gives you clues to their reaction to you. If you touch an unexpected nerve, there will be visible signs of agreement. Laughter is a sure

indicator. Unconvinced audiences may respond to a plea for a fair hearing, and once you have them listening you can explain your honest intentions. Choose faces and eyes that will support you and give you a fair indication of how you are doing.

Prepare Extra Material

Speakers also list additional examples of proofs that may come in handy. Pretend you're a musician working in a club. You know the musical taste of the usual clientele but still have a list of "extras" and "standbys" taped to your guitar.

When you practise at home, ask your friend or partner which anecdote works better, which example has more impact.

Have Faith in Yourself

You are good. Students in our universities and colleges make some of the finest speeches there are: they are accurate, moving, committed, convincing, *superb*. When you decide to tell a story that just came to you, or you remember yet another and better proof, go for it.

Use Your Plan

You knew it! First you're told to "go for it"; next is "use the plan." The plan is there to make sure that you come back to the topic, back to the thesis, back to the *reasons you are speaking*. You may get carried away by your unexpected remarks and get confused. "What was I talking about?" The notes tell you. They also help you to—

Finish Strong and Finish on Time

Running five minutes overtime is normal; running 25 minutes overtime can be *boring*. Help the organizers keep their schedules by keeping to yours. That's the purpose of your notes. After you have spoken off-topic, check your cards to make sure you are still on track.

Good speakers leave the audience wanting more. End on a high note. You can build your conclusion with alliteration, a series of parallel questions, or repetition. Jesse Jackson promised different segments of his party to "compete without conflict and differ without division." Eddie Greenspan concluded his speech on the futility of the death penalty by deferring to Donald Marshall, a New Brunswick native person convicted of a crime he did not commit. Greenspan asked:

Which of you, sitting her today, could have pulled the bag over his head? Which of you could have fastened the rope around his neck? Which of you could have sprung the trap door which sent Donald Marshall to his death?

Rose Anne Hart, in the speech that concludes this book, urges her audience to pause:

When you meet someone who is different from you because of nationality, or colour, or religion, obesity, handicap, or sexual orientation, before executing that clever imitation, before making that witty remark, before issuing that curt dismissal—think.

When you practise your speech, listen to your final words. Do you sound clear and strong? Have you put your whole heart into the finish?

By now you know that the secret of winging it is to prepare for anything. That way, if you want to improvise, you have the knowledge that you can do it. Your confidence will impress your audience and your reason, wit, and logic will convince them.

SPEECH ASSIGNMENT: THE PERSUASIVE

You must care about the topic you choose for this speech; your commitment will make it easier for you to persuade others.

Allow two to three weeks for this assignment so that you can prepare well.

1. Choose a topic (some suggestions are listed below).
2. After preliminary research, write down the purpose of your speech, the *thesis*, and main supporting points. Discuss these with your instructor.
3. Prepare a persuasive speech that is five to eight minutes long. Your presentation will show how much you have learned about designing and delivering an effective speech.

Possible Topics
- Music in the workplace
- Diet centres: rip-offs or help?
- The causes of math anxiety
- Hair styles: fashion or social comment
- Travelling by yourself
- Ethics in the workplace
- Body piercing
- Franchising is the way to go
- Advertising in the fashion industry
- Medical advancements based on human and animal experimentation
- Medical dilemmas: euthanasia, surrogate mothers, organs for sale on the underground market
- Should Canada be one country or two?
- Unsung Canadian heroes: Jack McClelland, Jane Rule, Norman Bethune, Rosemary Brown
- Sale of alcohol in local stores
- Marriage vs. living together
- Muscles for women

- Mandatory age for suspending drivers' licences
- 35-mm cameras vs. insta-matics
- Swimming in the ocean
- The key to finding a job
- Costume jewellery vs. real jewellery
- Square meals vs. gourmet
- Streetproofing children
- Bob Marley's popularity is due as much to his philosophy as to his music
- Price of long-distance telephone calls discriminates against students (or seniors or people in love)
- Minorities in the police and armed forces
- Stop biting your nails
- Become a block parent
- Car seats for babies
- Legalizing prostitution
- Strikes for teachers or doctors: necessity or crime?
- Danger in sports
- The relative safety of different products

- Changes to be made in an institution, or government agency or ministry
- **Group brainstorm for more**

DELIVERY TECHNIQUES TO REMEMBER

1. Use your voice to persuade: pause, vary volume, excite, ask questions.
2. Make connection as you speak. Feel the current of understanding between you and your audience.
3. Polish your introduction and conclusion. Give your all to a strong finish.
4. Build ethics into your delivery as well as your content. Move others but don't exploit them.
5. Take time to feel the experience and enjoy it.

Kahn-Tineta Horn

Kahn-Tineta Horn is a 55-year-old Mohawk woman. She first came to public attention 30 years ago when she spoke out for native rights. In 1990, she went behind the barricades at Oka with a handful of Mohawk women, men, and children where they were held under siege by the Canadian Armed Forces. At the centre of the dispute was a grove of sacred pines and a burial ground that the local towns-people wanted to destroy to make a golf course. Her actions at Oka have cost Kahn-Tineta Horn dearly and she would do it again—without hesitation.

Her gift of speech has been passed to her daughters. One of them, 19-year-old Waneek Horn-Miller, was with her mother behind the razor wire and still carries a scar on her chest as a result of a soldier's bayonet. Both mother and daughter speak calmly, with a sense of immense power. Often they smile. This is the gift of speaking. Across the stages of one's life, across the generations. They will never quit until the aboriginal people are free.

Q
After 20 years, what brought you back to speaking?
A
I got involved with the Oka crisis and the media asked me to explain the issue. I was able to provide background because I've worked with those issues. After that I was interviewed and spoke publicly. That's what happened.

Q
Were you behind the barricades with your family?
A
Yes, about half the people in there were members of my family. Two of my daughters were also there. Waneek was 14 and Kanieti was four.

Q
What happened as a result of your being at Oka?
A
I got fired from my job with the government and lost custody of my younger daughter. I had to fight to get her back. I had criminal charges laid against me. I defended myself and was acquitted. I even sued the government and won my job back.

Q
You said that you thought you were going to die. Did you mean that literally?
A
Yes. I was glad to get out alive. All of us, my family and my kids, thought about dying. It's taken me about three years to get over it, to rest up for the next stage of my life.

Q
Would you do it again?
A
I will always do what's right, always, without hesi-tation.

Q
Even with severe consequences?

A
Probably.

Q
In your speeches to non-natives, you don't mince words. What is it like to tell your whole audience that they stole your land?

A
I guess that's what has gotten me into trouble. I've always been very blunt. The reason is that the Mohawk language is very direct and when I express myself in English, I speak the same way—very bluntly. I think at first people were upset with the way I expressed myself. But they have gotten used to it and they can take it better now.

Q
Do you like speaking?

A
I feel it is my duty and I have a gift, so I do it. Some experiences I enjoy more than others. Some academic audiences are apprehensive. They expect to see a terrorist with an AK-47 and instead they see a middle-aged woman who smiles a lot and makes jokes at serious things. After that they start listening.

Q
The humour helps?

A
The jokes have to be relevant and you have to be fast on your feet. You have to size up the audience and decide ahead of time what you want to leave them with. I want them to feel better toward Indian people; I want them to see our side. And I want them to be so confused they'll go out afterwards and learn things on their own—especially our true history.

Q
Do you think they take it better or worse from a woman?

A
The men don't know how to take me. I show no fear—of anything or anybody—because of what I have been through in my life. So somebody with my cockiness and assurance—many men can't relate to that. The women love it.

Q
How much do you prepare your speech ahead?

A
I prepare every single word ahead of time. I like to think through everything. I always think of new things. I like to grow as I go along, research new issues in the places where I'm speaking. I'm super-thorough. If it's a formal speech, I will carefully write it and deliver it but often I work from jot notes. I can do it both ways.

Q
I saw conference organizers do a sweet grass ceremony before you spoke. Does it make a difference?

A
It makes it much better for me. It sets the tone, relaxes people, and makes them more open to what I have to say. And they take me more seriously.

Q
When you were a fashion model 30 years ago, did you speak out?

A
Yes I did. The same as now. I really hated being stereotyped as a "princess." I didn't consider myself radical. I was born into it. For maybe 10 or 12 generations, we have spoken out. I'm just doing what I'm supposed to do. The Great Law tells us we have to carry out our work until we win. We can't lose; when you're doing something right, you may have some setbacks but it's still right. You never quit.

Q

What advice do you give people who want to speak out?

A

I tell them not to go into anything like this unless they are prepared for the hardships and the suffering because they're fighting a system.

After that I tell them what I tell my daughters. Be very knowledgeable. Keep your ears open. Speak directly from the pit of your stomach because that's where you get your wisdom and guidance. It goes to your head, then it comes out through your mouth. When you do that, it will come out right.

Waneek Horn-Miller

Q

How do you feel when you talk to people about the blockade at Oka?

A

I talk about what it meant to me. I was only 14 and I made the choice to be part of it. I got tired of not taking a stand and not doing anything about it. I try to tell others about the history and politics behind it, not just what happened. People are afraid of using force but they don't understand that we've used diplomatic ways for hundreds of years. Now they'll take a second look at Mohawks and at all native peoples. We are prepared to back up our traditions and our love for the land.

Q

Does speaking make you nervous?

A

It makes me excited when I speak about things I know. I like informing people. I don't want them to go away not knowing. When people come up to me afterwards and say they are sorry, I say that I don't hate them if they try to correct what their forefathers did. But if they continue racist practices, I don't like them.

Q

Are people afraid of you when you speak?

A

Some of them are. I've been told I speak with a quiet anger. I speak very calmly; I don't yell, scream, or swear. I say what I mean and say it with force. I guess that scares people because it is the truth and it's right out there in front of their face. I am a warrior and a woman.

Q

What advice would you give people who want to speak about political issues?

A

You can be angry but don't let others in a debate make you yell or scream. If you want them to hear you, speak in a calm voice, look the other person in the eye and say, "I respect what you have to say but this is what I want to say." You have to respect each other's point of view.

Q
Do you think this kind of speaking will change the world?

A
Yes, but first you have to back it with action. I was 14 when I first spoke out; it was right after Oka and I spoke at Carleton University. The experience was fresh in my memory. If you put feeling into your words, people feel closer to you.

When I speak on native issues and rights I look around and see kids and my little sister. I want my kids to live the life my mother tried to create for me. I don't want them to have to grow up fighting and angry like I am. There's a lot of feeling inside me: politics tie in with the threads of my life. I live politics and I act politics and I speak politics. I get very emotional about it.

OUTLINE OF A PERSUASIVE SPEECH

Name: _____

Date of Speech: _____

Purpose Statement: _____

INTRODUCTION

Grabber:

Thesis:

Overview:

BODY

Supporting Argument #1

Supporting Argument #2

Supporting Argument #3

CONCLUSION

Reference to purpose (thesis):

Summary of main steps:

Zinger:

SELF-EVALUATION FORM

This form is to help you evaluate your own speech. It can be kept private or shared with your instructor or peers.

Type of Speech: _____

Name: _____

Title: _____

Date: _____

DELIVERY

Physical Presence

Did I make eye contact with others?

Was my posture natural and appropriate?

Was I aware of my facial expressions and hand gestures?

Were there any distracting mannerisms that I was aware of?

Did I feel good?

Could I feel an energy exchange with my audience?

VOCAL DELIVERY

Was my voice under control?

Did I sound confident?

Was I aware of breathing calmly?

How was my enunciation?

Did I manage to avoid um's and ah's?

Did I sound interested/excited/committed?

How did my voice sound to me?

DESIGN AND CONTENT

How well did the introduction and conclusion work?

Did the framework unify my speech?

Was there a natural progression from point to point?

Did my notes keep me on track? Did I use them?

Did the audience seem to understand the organization of my speech?

Was the information clear?

What was the energy level of the conclusion?

What would I change the next time?

What worked very well?

OVERALL EFFECTIVENESS

Did I connect with this audience?

Did I achieve my purpose?

What do I remember most about making the speech?

What unexpected or unforeseen things happened?

What am I most pleased about?

OTHER COMMENTS

Grade: _____

PEER EVALUATION FORM

Peer evaluation should be done in a constructive and supportive fashion. The speaker may choose people to do assessments or they may be assigned alphabetically. Some groups maintain the same speaker/assessor teams for the entire course; others change for each speech. The instructor may wish to see this evaluation before it goes to the speaker.

Type of Speech: _____

Speaker: _____

Title: _____

Assessor: _____

Date: _____

DELIVERY

Physical Presence

Did the speaker maintain eye contact?

Did she or he establish a rapport with the audience?

Were gestures natural and effective?

VOCAL DELIVERY

Did the speaker sound convincing/spontaneous/excited?

Was his or her voice clear and loud enough?

How did you respond to the speaker's mood?

DESIGN AND CONTENT

Did the introduction interest you?

Did the overview give you an indication of the main proofs?

Did the speech flow easily and logically from one point to another?

Was the conclusion strong and memorable?

Did the conclusion reinforce the thesis and main points?

What was the thesis of the speech?

OVERALL EFFECTIVENESS

Did you learn something new or worthwhile from the speech?

Were you moved by it?

What was the most outstanding part of the speech?

What changes do you recommend?

What parts should the speaker definitely keep?

OTHER COMMENTS

Grade: _____

EVALUATION FORM

Type of Speech: _____

Name: _____

Title: _____

Length of Speech: _____

Date: _____

Legend: S=Superior   E=Effective   NW=Needs Work

DELIVERY

Physical Presence

Eye Contact

Rapport with Audience

Posture

Gestures

Use of Notes

Appropriate Use of Audio-Visual

Support Material

VOCAL DELIVERY

Naturalness/Spontaneity/Enthusiasm

Clarity

Variety (Tone, Pitch, Pace)

Volume

Absence of Verbal Tics (um, ah, okay, like)

Sense of Control and Calm

DESIGN AND CONTENT

Use of Framework for Introduction and Conclusion

Clear Thesis and Overview

Coherence/Use of Transitions

New/Interesting Information

Strong Finish

Language

Word Choice

Impact on Audience

Grammar

OVERALL EFFECTIVENESS

Treatment of Topic

Intelligent Awareness of Audience

Achievement of Purpose

Impact on/Connection with Audience

OTHER COMMENTS

Grade: _____

8 Flying On Your Own: Last Words of Advice

> *You reach out and you fly, there isn't anything that you can't do.*
>
> *(Rita MacNeil)*

TIPS FOR SPEAKERS

1. Build speeches to be proud of.
2. Speak from the heart — connect with your listeners.
3. The checklists will help *if* you remember to use them.
4. Breathe deeply and —
5. GO FOR IT!

As a teacher and a speaker, I hope that you will use the skills outlined in this book and speak your mind with courage and conviction. This chapter is short: it is my last chance to share with you the insider secrets that professonal speakers know and use. There are 10 tips, a series of checklists, and a final example, a speech that had the greatest impact on a class that I've ever experienced.

◑ 1. KEEP THIS BOOK

What happens three days before a speech and you don't know how to get into the topic and you can't find a grabber? Reach for this book. It is a valuable resource for your professional, personal, and community activities. It has helped you learn to make good speeches, and it will be there, with outlines and reminders, for future assignments.

The next time you just can't get to planning or making notes, and you feel anxiety building, turn to the Seven-Day Countdown and follow it. I use the steps myself to keep on track. This is a book that will help you many times in the future. Keep it handy.

◑ 2. USE YOUR NERVOUSNESS WELL

Have you ever had nightmares in which you are on a stage and can't remember your speech? I have. Several days before an important speech, I'll wake up in a panic from a nightmare in which I can't see my notes and can't think of anything to say. That's my good-luck sign; it terrifies me into checking my speech again. You can bribe friends, your family, your cats, your canned goods, to sit there and look interested as you practise. Hear how you sound.

Your anxiety is used well if it prompts you to review and revise your presentation. Go over it on the way to work, polish phrases in spare moments, redo your note cards.

◑ 3. SOUND LIKE YOURSELF

Practise! People often tell me their wooden delivery is due to fear—and that's the end of it. I don't deny the severity of nervousness—I've had to lie down before a speech to ease the knots in my stomach. But nervousness is a symptom, not a terminal condition. Practise! Get a good coach. Speaking well is partly a gift and partly a skill that can be developed. Listen to yourself—do you sound believable? Build a speech to be proud of.

◑ 4. POLISH YOUR INTROS AND CONCLUSIONS

You may want to write your intros and conclusions out in dramatic fashion, with pauses and emphasis noted. Now, remember, *you don't read the intro and conclusion.* Before you start, pause, make eye contact, glance at your intro, and address your audience with full eye contact. To conclude, pause in a dramatic fashion while you check the conclusion, and then *give it to them.* If you can grab your listeners with an interesting remark spoken in an intelligent and confident fashion, and leave them with a strong, memorable statement, they'll remember you *and* your speech.

◑ 5. DO NOT *READ* TO YOUR AUDIENCE

Nothing turns people off more than having someone read to them. Remember this—speaking is not reading and speaking to people is not reading to them. Several years ago, I wrote out a speech for a government hearing. My own classroom warnings came true: *the more you have to read in front of you, the more you will read.* Like magic, my eyes were drawn to the page, and away from the audience. If I dared look up, I immediately lost my place and had to fumble my way back. I looked like a bumbler, and worse: the presentation was *boring.* As a written statement it was fine, but it was a poor speech.

Don't tempt yourself. Prepare cards, use them wisely, and you'll be able to forge a bond with your listeners. Even better, they'll think that you did it without notes.

◑ 6. CONNECT

Do you feel isolated when you stand up in front of others to speak? Wrap yourself with reassurance. Look at people who show interest in their eyes. Sometimes I stand on the same level as the audience and position myself close to the people in the first rows. If there is a centre aisle, I stand in it with people on either side. It makes me feel protected, less isolated, and more a part of the group. Look forward to speaking to those people. Stand and breathe and look as if you can do it—you'll feel more confident.

◑ 7. BE PREPARED: SPARE NOTES AND INSTANT SPEECH PLANS

Spare Notes

On my way to the wedding of my best friend, my purse, containing the groom's ring and my speech, was stolen. Of course I had rough notes but

FORGET YOUR NOTES ?

they were at home, and I had not yet taught my cat to answer the phone. Take an extra set of notes with you.

Instant Speech Plans

If you have to make a speech tomorrow and can't think of a way to intrigue your listeners, the following list may help. Audiences enjoy relating plans and theories to everyday objects. Even better, they remember what you say.

- Seed catalogues: The spring ritual of choosing, dreaming, selecting leads to planting, hard work, and crops.
- Spicing your work: Using techniques that combine sweetness and hot pepper to get a good product.
- Loons: This bird is like many of us: it has an eerie call, knows when to duck, and manages to survive.
- Fishing: Successful people are like good anglers: they are patient, know what bait to use, have the right equipment, and keep a good tension on the line. They know when to reel in and when to let go. On top of that, they share the catch.
- Parades: The view is different depending on your position—on the float or on the sidelines.
- Inukshuks: Lifelike figures of rock erected by the Inuit in the Arctic. They serve as directional markers on treeless horizons to guide those who follow. They remind us of our dependence on one another. Which Inukshuks do we erect in our daily business and personal lives?
- Packing the "knapsack of success": As you hike through life, you need a compass or values to keep on track; a first-aid kit for emergencies; an apple for health; wool socks for when you get cold feet; and a lucky sweater to remind you of friends. What do you need to pack for your own personal or professional journey?

◑ 8. PRIVATE MOMENTS

This is really called "Adjust Your Clothes in Private" but I wanted to be tactful. Many beginners are so intent on their speech that they get swept away on a wave of greetings and seating arrangements. Then, in front of 50 or 500 people, they are seized by an urge to pat their hair, check to see if their buttons are fastened and their pants done up.

Schedule a private moment.

A professional media consultant who coaches corporate executives confesses that the most common advice required is, "Don't adjust your underwear in public." Make sure you have time to check your appearance before you start.

◑ 9. COACH YOURSELF: BREATHING EXERCISES

What are you doing during the speech preceding yours? Of course you are listening, *but* you are also doing your deep breathing exercises, "In-2-3-4, Out 2-3-4, In-2-3-4, Out-2-3-4."

If you need further coaching on your way to the podium, try

Relax	Breathe	Pause
Eye Contact	Relax	Breathe
Pause	Eye Contact	Smile!!

Some people write their coaching on their notes:

Pause Here/   Look At Map/   Breathe/   Wait For Laughter

◑ 10. GO FOR IT!

The very act of speaking is empowering—speak up and speak out for your community, your work, your beliefs. You can do it.

Rose Anne Hart
Speech: The Golden Rule

Rose Anne Hart is a graduate of a Traveller Counsellor program, the mother of eight children, a community worker, and a person now pursuing her third "22-year plan." During her public-speaking course, she discovered that real examples worked best for her; through anecdotes, she could get involved in her material. In her introduction, she heads off a "ho-hum" reaction, and goes on to outline a clear three-part plan. In the last part of her speech, she anticipates being charged with over-simplification, and provides a rebuttal.

I want to speak to you today about a very old-fashioned idea—one you've heard a thousand times. In fact, you've probably heard it so often, that it's become meaningless to you. I want to talk about the golden rule, "Do unto others, as you would have others do unto you." I'm going to tell you a story to illustrate some of the errors we make in dealing with people, the consequence of these errors, and I'm going to tell you how to avoid ever making these errors yourself.

I had a friend named James; he was in his forties, had his own business, and was a loving and caring member of his community. I met James when we were both volunteers for a care-giving organization here in Toronto. I was a counsellor and he was in fundraising. In his spare time, James crocheted blankets for the people we helped; I remember one time he brought me a small red one and asked me to save it for a Chinese baby, because he had heard that to the Chinese red is a symbol of good fortune.

My friend was gay. He had many of the mannerisms we see parodied on TV, and in nightclub comedy routines. He had a longstanding relationship with another man; they owned a home in the community; and they attended church regularly where they helped out with all the functions. At one point James's friend became very ill. In fact, the doctors told him that they didn't expect him to live very long. James phoned the church and asked the clergyman to make a housecall. The clergyman agreed, but a little while later, he phoned back and told James that he had thought it over, and he felt it would be giving scandal to the community if he was seen entering their home.

James's friend recovered, but James never did.

He fell into a depression which caused the breakup of his relationship, and eventually caused him to take a bottle of sleeping pills. And as if that weren't enough, he wrapped a garbage bag around his head, and secured it at the neck with tape. He was determined to die and he was successful.

Now, we all know that not every slight is going to have such tragic results, and we know too that James's death was not caused by a single incident but rather by a lifetime of small hurts piled on top of another to form one unbearable burden. I don't expect my speech today will heroically save lives, but I would be delighted if it would save one of us from adding one more measure of pain to someone else's growing burden.

Being aware of the consequences of our actions is one sure way of guarding against ever having to use the saddest of all phrases, "I just didn't know." As the Roman philosopher Plutarch put it, "Boys throw stones at frogs in sport, but the frogs do not die in sport. They die in earnest."

I didn't tell you this story to make you feel sorry for James. I told you this story to make you think. When we meet someone who is different from you because of nationality, or colour, or religion, obesity, handicap, or sexual orientation, *before* executing that clever imitation, *before* making that witty remark, *before* issuing that curt dismissal—think. Think about how you would want to be treated if your roles were reversed. If we follow this one simple rule, "Do unto others as you would have others do unto you," we can *never* go wrong.

BE PREPARED: USING THE CHECKLISTS

When you sign up for a wilderness adventure—hiking in Costa Rican rainforests or paddling the Nahanni River—you receive a package of trip information. Most valuable are the checklists. By referring to these lists, you can quickly determine if you have done sufficient preparation and have all the equipment necessary for each facet of the trip: personal belongings, first-aid and repair kits, nature books and charts, kitchen gear.

Use these checklists in the same way. Start with the main menu and then consult the ones you need. A quick glance will remind you of essential items. The trick is to remember the lists!

CHECKLISTS: MAIN MENU

Use these lists to remind you of various aspects of your preparation. Then consult the ones most appropriate to your situation.

1. Equipment to Take With You
2. What to Ask Your Contact Person
3. Questions to Ask About Your Audience
4. Matching the Format to the Audience and Occasion
5. Purpose of Your Speech
6. Is Your Speech in Shape?
7. What to Check for in a Rehearsal
8. On Arrival
9. Are You Prepared?
10. Taking Care of Speakers
11. When You are Part of a Panel
12. Using Audio-Visual Back-Up
13. Using Tapes
14. Using Visual Back-Up
15. Saving Face When You Make Mistakes
16. Speech Breakdowns
17. Unexpected Media Requests
18. Working with Translators
19. Inclusive Language
20. Evaluation

1. EQUIPMENT TO TAKE WITH YOU

Keep all Material for Your Speech in Carry-On Luggage

1. speech notes
2. extra set of notes
3. pen and paper
4. music or book for relaxation
5. tapes/slides/film
6. handouts: reports, outlines, booklets
7. watch
8. short biography for person introducing you and/or media
9. extra glasses/lens-cleaning solution
10. identification and health care numbers
11. medication
12. props

13. A-V equipment and spare parts, extension cord
14. clothes pegs or spring clips to fasten notes to lectern in breezy conditions
15. timetable
16. address of meeting and map
17. name and telephone number of speaking location
18. name and number of contact person and back-up contact
19. business cards
20. press release
21. umbrella
22. tissues or handkerchief
23. comfortable shoes
24. change of clothes in case of accident or spill
25. cash for personal expenses

2. WHAT TO ASK YOUR CONTACT PERSON

1. TIME   DATE   PLACE
2. What is the purpose of the meeting/conference?
3. Exact directions to the meeting place, even if you are being met.
4. Name and phone number of local contact and back-up contact.
5. Telephone number of hotel to leave at home.
6. Time limit.
7. Names and topics of other speakers.
8. The occasion.
9. Dress guidelines.
10. Will the proceedings be taped? Does it matter?
11. Questions about your audience: see Checklist 3.
12. What kind of room will you speak in? What kind of sound system is there?
13. Who takes care of your equipment needs?
14. Have you told the contact person your time of arrival, special dietary needs, and how to recognize you?
15. How will your expenses be covered? When will you be paid?
16. Where is the most convenient place to park?

3. QUESTIONS TO ASK ABOUT YOUR AUDIENCE

1. Why did they choose you as a speaker?
2. What is the group or organization?
3. What is the occasion?
4. What does the audience know about the subject?
5. Are they interested/uncertain/hostile?
6. Has anybody ever talked to them about the subject before?
7. How much background is necessary?
8. Are there internal or community politics to be aware of?
9. Will there be a question period?
10. Do they know the level of expertise you bring to the subject?
11. What sort of local information would be useful?
12. Is there a possibility of a negative response to prepare for?
13. Is there anything special about the date, place, or group?
14. Basic Information: size of group/ age range/ gender/ occupational background/racial composition/ traditional or alternative family groups/ level of education/ disposable income/ concerns/interests and hobbies/ languages spoken.

4. MATCHING THE FORMAT TO THE AUDIENCE AND OCCASION

1. How much time have you been given?
2. Are you the only speaker?
3. How much does the audience already know about your subject?
4. What is their attention span?
5. What time of day and where in the program are you speaking?
6. Would a speech followed by a question-and-answer period be better for a knowledgeable group?
7. How long a question period does the group need?
8. Are you prepared to be put on the spot?
9. Would your speech be strengthened by A-V back-up or by a joint presentation?

5. PURPOSE OF YOUR SPEECH

agitation?
demonstration?
education?
entertainment?
evaluation?
information?
inspiration?
interrogation?
persuasion?

1. Is it to advocate a position?
2. Is it to change your listeners' minds?
3. Is it to be liked?
4. Is it to reinforce a belief?
5. Is it to explain or demonstrate?
6. Is it to advance your own position? (pass the interview, get elected, etc.)
7. Is it to speak your mind on something you consider important?

6. IS YOUR SPEECH IN SHAPE?

1. Does your speech sound like you?
2. Do you believe in what you are saying?
3. Is there a thesis and three main points?
4. Do you stick to the topic?
5. Is the grabber effective?
6. Is there a strong finish?
7. Are you having a conversation with the audience?
8. Do you need all of the speech?
9. Do you need to supply a title for the program? Is there a good line or example to appeal to the audience?
10. Are there ethical, logical, and emotional appeals?
10. Are the transitions from one point to another smooth?
11. Is the speech suitable for
    - the audience?
    - the time allotted?
    - the occasion?
12. Is your language inclusive? Have you avoided words that are racist, sexist, or homophobic?
13. Have you practised with your notes?
14. Are your notecards numbered and in order?
15. Does your test audience like and understand your examples?
16. Have you timed your speech? Don't be a speaker who says, "I know I'm running overtime, but I just have six more points."
17. Can you state your thesis in one sentence?
18. Ask a friend to check your speech for phrases that slip out unthinkingly:
    - Have you avoided racist/ sexist stereotying?
    - Do you use non-sexist words for occupations?
    - Check the obvious landmines, using words like black, white, queer, retarded, in derogatory ways.
    - Racism is often a result of omitting anyone who is not of the dominant race. Does your speech mirror the experience of a cross-section of our society?
    - Do you honour a person's origin? Do you make an effort to pronounce names correctly?
    - Do your words acknowledge and value a diversity of lifestyles and families?

7.WHAT TO CHECK FOR IN A REHEARSAL

1. How do you **sound**? Reading over your notes is not the same as a rehearsal; set up a lectern and practise out loud.
2. Practise with the notes you will use.
3. Listen to yourself:
   - do you sound confident?
   - are you rambling?
   - is your material interesting?
   - are you having a conversation with the audience?
4. Do your words sound natural?
5. Is your eye contact effective?
6. Recruit a practice audience. Which of your main points or examples do they enjoy and/or remember?
7. Do they find your speech logical and complete?
8. Do you handle props and visuals easily?
9. Get rid of clunkers—overly complicated examples, awkward or affected language, boring and unnecessary statistics.
10. Time yourself. Good speakers contribute to the event by speaking well and keeping to the time frame.

8. ON ARRIVAL

1. Check in with the organizers; they'll be relieved you've arrived.
2. Put belongings in a secure place.
3. **Private time:** before things speed up, take time to check notes, adjust clothes, attend to personal details.
4. Check the room with one of the coordinators:
   - Is the seating and placement of chairs appropriate?
   - Is the lighting adequate?
   - Is there a watch or clock to monitor time?
   - Is there a lectern that facilitates full communication?
   - Is there water handy?
   - Is the microphone working? **Test it.** Locate the on/off switch.

   Is the technician present? Explain your needs and test equipment ("Mayl see the first three slides please.")

   - Are paper and pen handy if you expect written questions from the floor?
   - Do the floor mikes promote a feeling of community and discussion?
5. Mingle with other speakers and panelists; compare notes.
6. Talk to audience members and get a feeling for the group.
7. Introduce yourself to the moderator and the person introducing you.

   Do they have your name right? Ask about details of the intro.
8. Make sure your notes are ready.
9. Psych yourself up. These people want to hear what you have to say.
10. Breathe...Relax...Connect.

9. ARE YOU PREPARED?

What if...

1. the electricity goes off?
2. a fire bell rings while you are speaking?
3. the room is set up in a different way than you requested?
4. double the number of people show up?
5. you lose your notes?
6. the translator or signer is late?
7. you can't find the room?
8. the speaker ahead of you rambles on and on?
9. there's a storm and you're an hour late starting?
10. you can't go at the last minute?
11. other panel members don't show up?
12. the microphone doesn't work?
13. your speech isn't geared to the audience?
14. someone heckles you?
15. you spill food on your clothing?
16. the media show up unexpectedly to cover the event and do an interview?

10. TAKING CARE OF SPEAKERS

If you are co-ordinating arrangements for a speaker, focus on making the event rewarding for both the audience and the speaker:

1. Provide full information about the audience and the occasion. Send the speaker a reminder two weeks before the event.
2. Determine the speaker's needs (room set-up, A-V) in advance. Check accommodation requirements.
3. Ask for a biography in advance and make sure the person introducing the speaker sees it ahead of time.
4. Set a fair and realistic agenda. Don't let the business meeting ramble and then ask a speaker to cut short his presentation.
5. Offer to meet the speaker. If she gets to the hotel on her own, make sure she is pre-registered and leave the number of her liaison person.
6. Assign a liaison person to show the speaker around and introduce him to others. Don't drop your guest after he has spoken; the liaison person stays with the speaker for the whole event and makes sure he is included.
7. Show the speaker the room where she will be speaking and introduce her to the A-V technician. Help her test the microphone and check acoustics. If there are visual aids, assist her in displaying them.
8. Pay all expenses such as hotel room and meals and provide a form for travel costs. Have the fee ready.
9. Send the speaker copies of any press reports of the event.

11. WHEN YOU ARE PART OF A PANEL

Before You Leave

1. What is the purpose of the panel presentation?
2. Why have you been asked to participate?
3. What position have you been asked to represent:
   - supplier of background information?
   - proponent/opponent of a particular stand?
   - representative of an interest or professional group?
   - community member?
4. Talk to the moderator. Is she or he unbiased? The moderator's attitude may be reflected in the treatment of each speaker, the assigning of questions, and the limiting of discussion.
5. Are different points of view allocated fair amounts of time?
6. Do they have equally good slots on the agenda?
7. What is the format:
   - individual presentations followed by questions?
   - one speaker followed by questions to or from a panel?
   - presentations only?
   - questions only?

8. How will questions be handled:
   - moderator assigns questions?
   - questioner directs remarks to panelist/s?
   - panelists volunteer responses?

When You Arrive

1. Talk to other panelists. Is there adequate variation in presentations?
2. Do you have enough information and experience to change your approach if there is too much overlap?
3. Listen carefully to other presenters. You may be able to make direct links with their remarks or find significant points of difference.
4. Give direct eye contact to each speaker: the audience will notice if you read, look around, or appear bored.
5. Your body language is important during the *entire* program. You are speaking, verbally or non-verbally, all the time you are present.

12. USING AUDIO-VISUAL BACK-UP

Before You Leave

1. Does your A-V material support your speech?
2. Is it big enough, simple enough, colourful enough?
3. Do maps and charts show enough detail?
4. Do the graphs have a minimum of lines?
5. Does the material speak to the mind and/or the emotions?
6. Have you rehearsed with it?
7. Does your test audience understand the A-V immediately?
8. If you are using slides, have you edited them? Use only as many as you need to make your point.
9. Are visuals in order and numbered? Is your name on them?
10. Do you have all support material in your hand when you leave home?
    If you are flying, make sure it is in your carry-on luggage.
11. If you are supplying equipment, take spare bulbs and extension cords.

When You Arrive

1. Is there a technician? Introduce yourself—this person is important to you.
2. Explain your needs clearly; can you supply a script with cues?
3. Test the microphone and other equipment *with* the technician.
4. If you are doing your own work, find the electrical outlets.
5. Position the screen.
6. Test the controls.
7. Do you need someone to dim the lights? Do they know the cues?
8. If you are using videofilm, test the machine. If you are using more than one segment of the video, be sure you can move from clip to clip smoothly.
9. Are there plenty of markers for flipcharts and whiteboards?
10. Is the overhead projector positioned and focused? Are your transparencies in order and easy to handle?
    Always make time for sound and equipment checks.

13. USING TAPES

1. Does the sound fill the room comfortably?
2. Do you have all the tapes on hand?
3. Test the tapes with the equipment you will be using.
4. Is the tape ready to go without any fiddling?
5. Do you or your assistant know how to work the controls?
6. If you have to fast-forward, have you noted the exact numbers on the tape counter?
7. Have you rehearsed?
8. Is there back-up equipment on site?

14. USING VISUAL BACK-UP

1. Have you rehearsed with the visuals and the equipment?
2. If you are using an illuminated pointer, can you handle it well and evenly?
3. **Test** the equipment well in advance. It's your speech—insure it.
4. Have you got the right tape? Are slides in order? Make sure they're not reversed.
5. Adjust focus and volume level in advance.
6. Know how to remove a slide that sticks.
7. Rehearse with your assistant; he or she should know cues (significant phrases) and approximate time for A-V. Note if lights have to be turned on and off.
8. Locate light switches in advance. If electrical panels have banks of switches, find the ones you need and label them.
9. Extension cords should be taped down so people don't trip on them.
10. Check sight lines by sitting in the audience and looking at the screen and speaker's position.
11. Turn off the projector at the end so that people aren't blinded by a dazzling white screen.
12. After using the equipment, leave it alone until the presentation is complete.
13. Thank the technician before you leave.
14. Always be prepared to do your speech without the back-up material. If a mechanical breakdown occurs, don't tinker with the machinery until your audience is frustrated. Apologize and go ahead without it.

15. SAVING FACE WHEN YOU MAKE MISTAKES

1. Admit the mistake.
   "You are right. I made a mistake; I'll check this point and get back to you."
2. Don't over-apologize.
   People can accept a mistake; they become impatient when you refer to it frequently.
3. Move on.
   "Aside from this error, the point is still valid," or "Now, we'll look at the major focus of my presentation."

16. SPEECH BREAKDOWNS

Questions You Can't Answer

1. Repeat the question into the mike so the audience can hear it. Use your discretion regarding which questions to repeat.
2. Admit you don't know the answer.
3. Promise to get back with the information.

Hecklers

1. If the comment is valid, pause, repeat it to the audience and deal with it.
2. If the remark is rude or inappropriate, ignore it.
3. If the speaker is too disruptive to ignore, offer to speak to him or her later.
4. Do not play platform chicken and invite the heckler up to speak.
5. Remain cool. "Look, why not allow me to finish. I was asked to speak here."
6. If you anticipate hecklers, think of a few responses in advance. "You're my very first heckler, could you come back when I've got more experience?" (Thanks to Rita Rudner.)
7. Don't be heavy-handed. If you are ruder or more sarcastic than the heckler, you'll seem frightened. You may even lose audience support. Remain patient.

Crying

1. Crying is one of many emotional reactions to situations that move you. It's normal.
2. Know where in your speech you will cry—find this out in rehearsal—and anticipate it.
3. If you know you will cry, try to estimate how long it will last; you have the reassurance that you will stop.
4. If the tears come unexpectedly, pause and give yourself time. Then continue.
5. When you start to cry, make a gesture to let the audience know you're all right, and when you are finished, carry on. Do not apologize.
6. You may have to fend off kindly attempts to remove you from the stage. Use the phrase, "These are tears of concern, not weakness."

7. Never sniff into an open mike.

Running Late
1. *You* won't run overtime because you will have practised your speech.
2. If problems arise because the speakers before you are running late, what can you do?
   a. Assess the situation: Are you presenting an opposing point of view and need all the time you were originally allotted? Or are you presenting a complementary position? Can you allow a colleague to elaborate?
   b. Pass a note to the moderator outlining how long your speech is. Suggest that she or he make the decision to go overtime or give the present speaker a time signal.
3. If the moderator does not take action, and if the previous speakers go overtime, you may still need to give your full presentation. Explain to the audience that the schedule is running late, but you trust they want to have the full story and you need their feedback. Assume you are dealing with reasonable people.

17. HANDLING UNEXPECTED MEDIA COVERAGE OR INTERVIEW REQUESTS

1. Be courteous. The reporter is doing a job and will get news of your speech to a wider audience.
2. Do not be unnerved (or overly flattered) by an insistent reporter.
3. Keep to the checklist "On Arrival."
4. Ask how long the interview will take. Take care of your business first.
5. Be sure to leave yourself five minutes between the interview and your speech. If you will be too rushed, offer to do it afterwards.
6. Be prepared. Have a brief biography to give to the reporter and a few good stories to illustrate your main point. Stories are the heart of media reports.
7. If the proceedings have attracted a lot of media coverage, don't be anxious. Concentrate on your speech and the audience.

18. WORKING WITH TRANSLATORS/SIGNERS

The translation referred to in this checklist is direct translation; one person sits with the person or small group for whom translation is necessary.

1. Ask organizers if translation or signing for the deaf is being offered to anyone in the audience.
2. If possible, talk to the translator or signer beforehand and outline your presentation. Ask for their suggestions.
3. Supply a copy of your notes if requested.
4. In general, try to keep your language direct; don't clutter it with excessively complicated or technical terms or strange English phrases like, "it's no skin off my nose" or "in a pig's eye."
5. Work with the translator/signer. Watch him or her to see if the pace is natural and workable.
6. As you speak, look for frenzied signing or conversation—you may be going too fast, or using too many technical terms or acronyms to translate/sign easily.
7. Thank the signer/translator publicly in your remarks and personally afterwards.

19. INCLUSIVE LANGUAGE: AVOIDING SEX/RACE/CLASS BIAS

No one intends to be offensive and speakers can't afford to be. Check your language for inherent bias.

1. Is your language inclusive? Have you avoided words that are racist, sexist, or homophobic?
2. Is your speech free of sexist/racist stereotyping? Do you avoid suggesting that all members of a gender, race, ethnic group, or class are the same?
3. Do you use non-sexist words for occupations, professions, and other general terms?

Avoid:	**Use:**
anchorman	anchor, anchorperson
businessman	businessperson, manager, executive
cameraman	cameraperson, technician
cleaning lady	cleaner, housecleaner
chairman	chairperson, chair, convenor, coordinator, facilitator
female doctor	doctor
fireman	firefighter
forefathers	ancestors
freshman	first-year student
girls (for adult females)	women, colleagues, manager, office staff
heroine	hero
ladies	women
mailman	letter carrier
manned observatory	staffed observatory
history of mankind	history, our heritage
policeman/policewoman	police officer
saleslady/salesman	sales person, sales representative
spokesman	spokesperson, speaker, representative
stewardess	flight attendant
waiter/waitress	server
weatherman	weather forecaster
workman	worker, employee, staff member
workmens' compensation	workers' compensation

4. Do you avoid statements that promote stereotyping?

   Rather than:

   "Ask a doctor about allergies. He has the facts."

   "Adequate manpower is essential for the project."

   "Six strong men are needed for this job."

   Use:

   "Ask a doctor about allergies. She or he has the facts."

   "An adequate workforce is essential for the project."

   "Six strong people are needed for this job."

5. Do you avoid using adjectives that, in certain contexts, have racist or homophobic overtones? Words such as primitive, black, yellow, perverted, and savage, fall in this category.

6. Do you avoid using the adjective white as a symbol for goodness?

7. Racism is often a result of omitting anyone who is not of the dominant race or culture. Does your speech mirror the experience of a cross-section of our society?
8. Do you honour a person's origin? Do you make an effort to pronounce names correctly?
9. Raise your level of awareness! Attend workshops. You'll be a much more effective speaker when you understand the issues.

20. EVALUATION

1. Did you say what you wanted to?
2. Did you like your speech and the way you sounded?
3. How did you feel at the end of your presentation?
4. Was there a good feeling in the room?
5. What was the feedback from others—audience members and organizers?
6. What did the audience response or questions tell you?
7. What will you change next time?
8. What will you keep next time?

CREDITS